english
grammar
DeMYSTiFieD

Demystified Series

Accounting Demystified
Advanced Calculus Demystified
Advanced Physics Demystified
Advanced Statistics Demystified
Algebra Demystified
Alternative Energy Demystified
Anatomy Demystified
Astronomy Demystified
Audio Demystified
Biochemistry Demystified
Biology Demystified
Biotechnology Demystified
Business Calculus Demystified
Business Math Demystified
Business Statistics Demystified
C++ Demystified
Calculus Demystified
Chemistry Demystified
Circuit Analysis Demystified
College Algebra Demystified
Corporate Finance Demystified
Databases Demystified
Diabetes Demystified
Differential Equations Demystified
Digital Electronics Demystified
Earth Science Demystified
Electricity Demystified
Electronics Demystified
Engineering Statistics Demystified
Environmental Science Demystified
Everyday Math Demystified
Fertility Demystified
Financial Planning Demystified
Forensics Demystified
French Demystified
Genetics Demystified
Geometry Demystified
German Demystified
*Global Warming and Climate Change
    Demystified*
Hedge Funds Demystified
Investing Demystified
Italian Demystified
Japanese Demystified
Java Demystified

JavaScript Demystified
Latin Demystified
Lean Six Sigma Demystified
Linear Algebra Demystified
Macroeconomics Demystified
Management Accounting Demystified
Math Proofs Demystified
Math Word Problems Demystified
MATLAB ® Demystified
Medical Billing and Coding Demystified
Medical-Surgical Nursing Demystified
Medical Terminology Demystified
Meteorology Demystified
Microbiology Demystified
Microeconomics Demystified
Nanotechnology Demystified
Nurse Management Demystified
OOP Demystified
Options Demystified
Organic Chemistry Demystified
Pharmacology Demystified
Physics Demystified
Physiology Demystified
Pre-Algebra Demystified
Precalculus Demystified
Probability Demystified
Project Management Demystified
Psychology Demystified
Quantum Field Theory Demystified
Quantum Mechanics Demystified
Real Estate Math Demystified
Relativity Demystified
Robotics Demystified
Sales Management Demystified
Signals and Systems Demystified
Six Sigma Demystified
Spanish Demystified
sql Demystified
Statics and Dynamics Demystified
Statistics Demystified
Technical Analysis Demystified
Technical Math Demystified
Trigonometry Demystified
Vitamins and Minerals Demystified

english grammar

DeMYSTiFieD

Phyllis Dutwin

New York   Chicago   San Francisco   Lisbon   London   Madrid   Mexico City
Milan   New Delhi   San Juan   Seoul   Singapore   Sydney   Toronto

2 3 4 5 6 7 8 9 10 11 12 13 14 15 16   WFR/WFR   1 9 8 7 6 5 4 3 2 1 0

ISBN 978-0-07-160080-4
MHID   0-07-160080-9
Library of Congress Control Number: 2009925526

McGraw-Hill books are available at special quantity discounts to use as premiums and sales promotions or for use in corporate training programs. To contact a representative, please e-mail us at bulksales@mcgraw-hill.com.

CONTENTS

v

INTRODUCTION

Why should you study English? Do you speak and write English? That's reason enough. When you speak or write, you present yourself to others, and if you care at all about how you're perceived—and who doesn't?—you care about how your use of language represents you. Certainly, not all jobs depend exclusively upon writing and speaking skills, but most do to some significant extent. If you are in school, your teachers have probably set a standard for written and spoken English.

As you begin *English Grammar Demystified*, get ready for a different learning experience. *English Grammar Demystified* will help you better understand and use the English language, but you will find that this book takes a different approach from the usual English improvement text. In the first two parts of this book, you will learn the basics of English grammar with a thorough overview of the parts of speech and punctuation and capitalization rules. The third part of the book builds on these skills, giving you sound advice on mastering proper sentence structure and refining your writing. The fourth part covers important spelling and word usage skills.

In support of all of these concepts, you will also find great emphasis on finding common errors. In other words, this is not simply a grammar book. Rather, this book identifies where errors are most commonly made—so you can avoid them. You may, for example, know the definition of a pronoun (i.e., a word that takes the place of a noun), but you may not recognize one of the most common pronoun errors. Read the following sentence:

Incorrect: Me and Tom work in the same office.

You know that *me* is a pronoun. It takes the place of someone's name, so you conclude that it should be used as half of the subject of the sentence. Why is it incorrect in this context? In Chapters 2 and 3, you will learn why it is incorrect, but beyond that, you will read many examples of this common error and have an opportunity to correct them.

Correct: Tom and I work in the same office.

How to Use This Book

Each chapter is filled with Written Practice exercises that help reinforce the new grammar concepts you learn. You are strongly encouraged to complete each exercise to help identify your strengths and weaknesses as you use this book. Check the Answer Key to find out where any errors exist in your use of English.

Each chapter ends with an open-book quiz with ten questions that review the concepts introduced in the chapter. You should try to achieve a score of eight out of ten on a quiz before moving on to the next chapter. Each of the four parts ends with a test of fifty multiple-choice questions that review the content of that part. These are closed-book tests, and you should try to get a score of 75 percent before moving on to the next part. The book concludes with a final exam with one hundred multiple-choice questions that test your knowledge of all the grammar and usage content of the book. A good score on this exam is 75 percent.

The *English Grammar Demystified* chapters are meant to be studied consecutively. From the first chapter on, you will build your English language skills, one upon the other. Don't skip anything! The only chapters that may (and probably should) be studied on a different schedule are Chapters 10 and 11. Spelling and word usage are almost never-ending challenges for some people; consequently, an organized, segmented approach works better. You simply can't absorb all that these chapters teach in one sitting. So make studying those chapters an ongoing activity.

PART ONE

ALL ABOUT THE ENGLISH SENTENCE

CHAPTER 1

The Essential Elements of the English Sentence

In this chapter you will learn:

Subject and Verb

Sentence Fragments and Run-Ons

Time and Number: Agreement Between Subject and Verb

Perfect Verb Tenses

Irregular Verbs

Subject and Verb

Although it would not be very interesting, the simplest English sentence might be composed of two words and still be correct:

I voted.

Tom drove.

Trees fell.

The point, of course, is that a complete English sentence is composed of a subject (*I*, *Tom*, *Trees*) and a verb, or action (*voted*, *drove*, *fell*).

See if you can identify the subjects (person or thing) and verbs (actions) in the following sentences:

1. The senator won.
2. Tom crashed the car.
3. His wife screamed.
4. Arctic air froze New England.
5. We huddled together.

You probably chose the following: *senator/won*, *Tom/crashed*, *wife/screamed*, *air/ froze*, *We/huddled*. In each case, someone or something performed an action.

Now read the following examples, and as you do, ask yourself what's missing: what else do you need to know to get real meaning from the incomplete sentence?

1. A wandering child.
2. Driving too slowly and stopping frequently.
3. Stormy, then clear.

Undoubtedly, in the first example, you wanted to know what happened to the child. What did he or she do? In the second example, who was driving and stopping? In the third example, what was stormy, then clear? Clearly, something is missing in each example. You weren't satisfied when you read the examples because they are all incomplete thoughts missing essential elements: subject (i.e., person, place, or thing) or a verb (i.e., the action). Because of the missing pieces, this kind of incomplete sentence is called a *fragment*—a piece of a thought.

The following examples include possible completions for the previous fragments. Notice that either a subject or verb was added to each one:

1. A wandering child ran into the street. (The verb *ran* answers the question, "What did the child do?")

2. The new driver was driving too slowly and stopping too frequently. (The subject, *driver*, answers the question, "Who was driving?")

3. The skies changed from stormy to clear. (The subject, *skies*, answers the question, "What changed from stormy to clear?)

Sentence Fragments and Run-Ons

You just read examples of incomplete sentences (e.g., A wandering child). Because the examples represent only parts of complete thoughts, they're called *fragments*. If, on the other hand, you were to string together sentence after sentence—with no periods or semicolons in sight—you would be committing another type of error called a *run-on* sentence. You'll learn about both fragments and run-on sentences in the following sections.

SENTENCE FRAGMENTS

Fragments sometimes result when writers start sentences with words such as *when*, *after*, *because*, *since*, *before*, and *as soon as*. For example, does the following group of words have a subject and a verb? Is it a complete sentence?

When the new product arrives.

The example has a subjectlike word, *product*, and a verblike word, *arrives*, and it is still not a complete sentence. If you say it out loud, you will hear that it is unfinished:

When the new product arrives . . .

Then what will happen? Possible completions include the following:

When the new product arrives, we'll call our advertisers.

When the new product arrives, we'll send a special introductory offer to our best customers.

When the new product arrives, we'll have to stay late to pack it for shipping.

Groups of words may seem to be sentences because they contain subject and verb-type words, but beware of incomplete thoughts! In the initial example (When the new product arrives.), *product* seems to be the subject and *arrives* seems to be the verb, yet the example is still an incomplete thought.

As you read the following examples, decide if each has the subject and verb it needs:

1. Looking at the job market from a new perspective. (Hint: Beware of sentences that start with *-ing* ending words.)
2. My friend who teaches a wellness course.
3. Heading for the West Coast for a five-day vacation.
4. Your doctor's appointment scheduled for Tuesday.
5. When the man waiting to see you.

Let's take a look at what's missing. In the first example, who is looking at the job market? The subject is missing. The second example is tricky. *My friend* is the subject. The words *who teaches a wellness course* describe the friend. Still there is no verb. What does your friend do? Try this: My friend who teaches a wellness course drives 100 miles a day to get to her class. The verb is *drives*. In the third example, who was heading for the West Coast? The subject is missing. In the fourth example, the verb is missing. The fifth example needs an action to complete it.

Written Practice 1-1

Finish the following statements to make them complete sentences. There are several possible ways to complete the sentences; just be sure that each sentence has a subject and verb.

1. Before I leave for California _____ .
2. As soon as the rain stops _____ .

3. Because I'm trying to get a promotion _____ .

4. When I exercise several times a week _____ .

5. After I took a nutrition course _____ .

6. As soon as the rain stops and we have all the information we need about the weather _____ .

7. Before I started this job and when I was looking for one _____ .

8. Since you started working here and agreed to take the early shift

_____ .

9. After they serve lunch and we've stayed a while _____ .

10. Tom, whom everyone admires since he was precinct captain

_____ .

SENTENCE FRAGMENTS IN INFORMAL ENGLISH

When we're writing or speaking informally to friends and relatives, we do use fragments, and that's all right. However, the important word in the previous sentence is *informally*. Obviously, you need to know the difference between formal and informal occasions.

Informal: You say to your son, "Need money?" He says, "Sure." You both understand very well what those fragments mean.

In the workplace, informal English doesn't always work, especially in written communications. Look at this memo:

MEMO

From: Claire

To: Gino

Re: Office Supplies

Got enough supplies?

In this case, there have to be many questions in the reader's mind. What supplies is Claire asking about? For what period of time is Claire inquiring—this quarter, next month, this afternoon? Better:

MEMO

From:　Claire

To:　　Gino

Subject:　Office Supplies

We are ordering tomorrow for the third quarter. What office supplies will you need? Please include all paper goods as well as computer supplies and printer ink. Please e-mail me or place your order on my desk by 4 P.M.

Thanks,

Claire

RUN-ON SENTENCES

If fragments are pieces of sentences, run-ons are too many pieces running together. Have you ever seen or written a sentence such as the following?

Our new boss gave us his list of procedures some were already in our schedule.

Run-on sentences are very confusing to read since you don't know where one finishes and another starts. The two thoughts in this sentence could each stand alone:

Our new boss gave us his list of procedures. Some were already in our schedule.

Or since the thoughts are closely connected, they could be combined using a punctuation mark as shown in the following examples. (You'll learn much more about this in Chapter 4 and Chapter 5.)

Our new boss gave us his list of procedures; some were already in our schedule.

Our new boss gave us a list of procedures, but some were already in our schedule.

Another kind of sentence error is called a "comma fault" because sentences are strung together with the use of commas. For example:

We had to register we did, then we stood in line for an hour, then the line didn't move, we went home.

Note that removing the commas does not correct the problem, but results in a run-on sentence. You can, however, choose one of the following actions to correct the sentence:

1. Write separate sentences.
2. Change one or more commas to semicolons.
3. Insert a coordinating conjunction such as *and* or *but* following the comma.
4. Make one clause dependent upon the other.

All of these options will come into play in later chapters on building sentences and on punctuation.

Written Practice 1-2

Correct the following sentences.

1. My hours will be 9 A.M. to 5 P.M. yours will be 8 A.M. to 4 P.M.

   _____

2. Driving 230 difficult miles to our children's home is exhausting we really prefer to fly there.

   _____

3. We dread the Parkway portion of the trip, it's busy even during off-hours.

   _____

4. A medical myth states that we use only 10 percent of our brain, studies using imaging show that no part of the brain is completely inactive, don't believe everything you read or hear.

   _____

   _____

5. Larry says he'll be right on time tomorrow I'll believe it when I see it.

   _____

6. When you've finished unpacking.

   _____

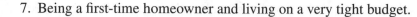

7. Being a first-time homeowner and living on a very tight budget.

   _____

8. The menacing figure walking swiftly through the park.

   _____

9. The community organized a march for food donations many people joined the march as it progressed we were too tired to do that.

   _____

   _____

10. I didn't buy enough yarn for my new knitting project, I turned around and went right back to the store.

    _____

    _____

FRAGMENTS AND RUN-ON SENTENCES IN E-MAIL

When should you be concerned about fragments and run-on sentences? Always. No matter what form of communication you use, be particularly careful to avoid the errors you found in the preceding practices. The level of formality in your writing will not always be the same. You know with whom you can be casual and who requires a more formal tone. Yet a caution regarding fragments and run-on sentences is always in order. This caution is particularly true when you use e-mail to communicate.

Written communication is no longer limited to letters. We now enjoy instant communication through e-mail. This development is a good thing: it speeds your message along and it can be more casual. Beware! Those positive aspects of e-mailing can also function to sabotage you. How is that possible? The answer, of course, is that whether you write a letter, a memo, a fax, or a report, if your name is on it, _you will be judged for the content_. Consequently, you should know that all the concepts in this chapter, and in this book, apply to e-mail as well.

If you send the following e-mail _to your best friend_, no one will comment on your omissions, fragments, and punctuation errors.

From: Holly Kimball

To: Liz Woods

Subject:

Liz—Lunch? what time?

H.

If, however, you send the following to a business contact, you risk changing that person's opinion of you. Again, don't forget that your name is on the e-mail. If the person who receives the e-mail stores all communications as a record, your e-mail becomes a plastic bottle: you write it in five minutes, but it's stored in the e-mail environment forever.

From: Joe Hidalgo

To: Harry Malcolm

Subject:

    Harry you and i talked about installing an air conditioning system in your plant are you ready to go ahead with it can you call me tommorow at 11AM to plan the project

Joe

How can you improve this e-mail? Start from the top. The subject line is blank. Should Harry, a very busy man, have to read through the entire e-mail to determine the subject? What specific subject would you include?

    Now look back at the body of the e-mail. Find the run-on sentence errors. How would you correct them? In the following example, you'll see one way of correcting the errors. Notice that spelling errors have been corrected as well. (Why didn't Joe at least use the spell-checker on his computer?)

From: Joe Hidalgo

To: Harry Malcolm

Subject: Date for installation of air-conditioner

    You and I talked about installing an air-conditioning system in your plant. Are you ready to go ahead with it? Can you call me tomorrow at 11 A.M. to plan the project?

Time and Number: Agreement Between Subject and Verb

In any list of common errors in English, lack of agreement between subject and verb ranks high. For example:

The berries in my cereal tastes so sweet.

To correct an agreement error, you need to identify both the subject and the verb. Whenever possible, start by identifying the verb. In the example sentence, the verb is *tastes*. Then you can ask, what tastes? The berries tastes. Oops! You just found the error. *Berries* is a plural subject and the verb must agree with it. Decide which is correct:

Berries tastes.

Berries taste.

Of course it is the latter. Later in this chapter, you will have an opportunity to learn more about this important concept.

In addition, just ahead, you will discover how the times (tenses) of verbs must be consistent and logical as verbs follow one another. What's wrong with the following?

Yesterday, I reprimanded the children when they *run* into the street.

Obviously, *yesterday* and *reprimanded* indicate past time, but *run* is in the present time. Change *run* to the past time—*ran*:

Yesterday, I reprimanded the children when they *ran* into the street.

Written Practice 1-3

In the following paragraphs, check the tenses of all the verbs for consistency of time. Find the one verb in each paragraph that needs to be corrected.

Paragraph 1

Children are not always happy to play alone. Does that mean that parents have to devote all their time to playing with their children? No, it didn't. Certain techniques work to encourage children to play on their own.

Paragraph 2

In 1999, The Academy of Pediatrics provided some guidelines for children and TV. They suggest that children under two years old should not watch TV. They advised that even older children should not watch TV before bedtime. Instead, they said that parents should read to children, or children might read to themselves and with their parents.

Written Practice 1-4

In each of the following sentences, find the verb (action word). Label each verb *present*, *past*, or *future*. The first one is done for you.

1. A consumer quickly learns that "living green" is not easy. _learns/present_

2. I will avoid plastic packaging as much as possible. _____

3. My family turned off the lights all over the house. _____

4. Toby decided to cycle to work. _____

5. Marilyn's child uses much less hand towels than my child does. _____

6. He eats lunch at the same time every day. _____

7. Our three children will play together tomorrow. _____

8. They ate lunch in the park. _____

9. I collected shells on the beach. _____

10. I keep a scrapbook for each child. _____

11. You will ask yourself some important questions before the election.

_____

12. The law student completed his final exam. _____

13. David played the guitar in the band Neville Blues. _____

14. Aidan will start school next year. _____

15. The car stops at every yellow light. _____

CONSISTENT VERB TENSE IN PARAGRAPHS

The verb tenses in the previous written practice section were likely easy to determine. You have just made decisions about tense in single sentences, and you can do this for verbs in paragraphs, too. There is one additional consideration: That is, is the tense consistent throughout the paragraph? Read the following paragraph, and decide if the writer was consistent.

> When I decide to ask for a raise at work, I do some homework first. First, I consult the *Occupational Outlook Handbook* from the U.S. Department of Labor to check recent salaries in my field. Then I gather my recent performance evaluations, and I reread them carefully to recall the list of my accomplishments. However, I still need to list accomplishments that have accrued since that evaluation. I always list higher sales, the number of sales calls, and the number of those calls that result in sales.

You probably realized that the writer was consistent in this paragraph. Some of the present tense verbs are *decide, do, consult, gather, reread,* and *need.* Now read this paragraph with the same task in mind. Is the tense consistent?

> Your company may not be in a position to offer you a raise. If the company was laying people off, it is probably not a good idea to ask for a raise at this time. Asking for a substantial raise can only make you seem unrealistic and untouched by what is going on around you. Instead, ask for something other than money, such as flex time, or a better office, or new equipment.

Here are some verbs: *offer, was laying off, ask.* Are they all in the same tense? Clearly, the writer meant to write in the present tense, but one verb does not conform: *was laying off* indicates the past; it should be *is laying off.*

Written Practice 1-5

In the following paragraph, choose the correct verb for each sentence. The first one (*opens*) is provided for you and sets the tense, or time, in the present.

> Every morning Maria opens the office and immediately (checks/checked) the fax machine for messages. It seems that each day more and more unsolicited faxes (will appear/appear). Now Maria (knows/knew) she will have to find a way to unlist the fax number.

SUBJECT AND VERB AGREEMENT IN NUMBER

As you read in the introduction to this section, a verb changes depending on whether the subject of the sentence is singular or plural. Look at the following examples:

The new *computer saves* me so much time.

The new *computers save* us so much time.

In the first sentence, the subject is *computer* and it is singular—there is only one. In the second sentence, the subject is *computers* and it is plural, meaning there is more than one. A singular noun, such as one *computer*, does not have an *s*; but a plural noun, such as two or more *computers*, uses the *s* to show there is more than one. Now look at the verb. One computer *saves* me so much time. The verb takes an *s* to accommodate a singular subject. Obviously, verbs don't work according to the same rules as nouns. With a verb, an added *s* means that it is singular, not plural.

One more complication: sometimes two words are used to form a plural subject:

A desk and a chair (plural subject) *stand* (plural verb—no *s*) in the corner of the room. Two things *stand* in the room.

A desk *stands* in the corner of the room. One thing *stands* in the room.

Once again, a plural subject is followed by a verb with no *s*. A singular subject is followed by a verb with an *s* ending.

Let's look at more examples:

Food and exercise (plural subject) comprise (plural verb—no *s*) an important part in any weight-loss program.

The two candidates (plural subject) address (plural verb—no *s*) the crowd.

My son and daughter (plural subject) live (plural verb—no *s*) on their own now.

Two cars (plural subject) vie (plural verb—no *s*) for that spot each morning.

Written Practice 1-6

For each of the following sentences, see if there is agreement in number between the subject and verb. Correct any errors in agreement.

1. House prices changes every month.

   _____

2. The Blake family go camping every summer.

   _____

3. The painter and his hired men takes time to do a very neat job.

   _____

4. Interferences such as a phone call or visitor keeps me from finishing my work.

   _____

5. My friend, with his children in tow, take a one-mile walk each morning.

   _____

6. An extraordinary new development in manufacturing clothes give us bamboo fiber.

   _____

7. Bamboo fiber rate very high not only as eco-friendly but for being revolutionary for many reasons.

   _____

8. Some of the advantages of bamboo fabric includes its strength and softness.

   _____

9. Bamboo fabric also pay great dividends to the environment.

   _____

10. As it grows, bamboo plants gives us clean air, consumes carbon dioxide, and returns oxygen to the environment.

    _____

Lack of agreement between subject and verb (e.g., *The contest winners was there to receive their awards.*) is one of the errors most often committed by speakers and writers. We frequently hear these errors as well as see them in writing. *Frequency*, however, does not give anyone a pass

Let's go back to Joe Hidalgo's e-mail history. He has some work to do on subject-verb agreement.

From: Joe Hidalgo

To: Harry Malcolm

Subject: New office designs

Harry,

I'm attaching the two designs you liked most. Your patience and consideration in waiting for their completion is very much appreciated. Carlos, Mark, and I, who have been assigned to this project, feels honored to have been chosen to work on this inquiry. Please feel free to ask us about any item that is unclear to you.

We look forward to working with you.

Joe Hidalgo

Did you see the subject-verb agreement errors in the e-mail? They occurred in the second and third sentences. Here are simple changes to correct the errors. Sentence 2 correction: Your patience and consideration . . . <u>are</u> very much appreciated.

The subject (*patience and consideration*) is plural. You cannot use the singular *is* with a plural subject; you can use the plural form *are*. Sentence 3 correction: Carlos, Mark, and I, who have been assigned to this project, <u>feel</u> . . . inquiry. The subject (*Carlos, Mark, and I*) is plural. You cannot use the singular *feels* with a plural subject. You can use the plural form *feel*.

DETERMINING AGREEMENT WITH PREPOSITIONAL PHRASES

When you speak or write a simple sentence, it's easy to match the correct verb to the subject:

A bully *threatens* the child.

In the preceding sentence, the verb is clear: *threatens*. Who did the threatening? The *bully*, or subject, did the threatening. A singular verb (*threatens*) agrees with a singular subject (*bully*). What happens when you add prepositional phrases, or interrupting words? The sentence becomes more complicated, and unless you are very observant, agreement is easily lost.

A bully who is in the same classes *threaten* the child.

A bully who is in the same classes *threatens* the child.

Some writers would be fooled by the closest word to the verb, that is, *classes*. *Classes* is plural, so the verb must be plural: *threaten*, right? No, you need to find the subject. Is the word *classes* the subject? Do they *threaten* the child? No, it's the *bully* (singular subject) who *threatens* the child.

Find the subject and the verb in the following example. Does the verb agree with the subject in number?

A woman in workout clothes *walk* into the gym.

What is the verb? *Walk* is the verb. Who walks: Does the woman walk? Or do the clothes walk? Of course, the woman walks. *Woman* is the singular subject. That fact makes the original sentence incorrect. The following is the correct sentence:

A woman in workout clothes *walks* into the gym.

When you are unsure if the verb should be singular or plural, use the following hint. Forget about all other elements of the sentence and do this: find the verb and then ask yourself who or what does that.

Today, forward-thinking organizations in this country focuses on customer service.

Let's think this through using the preceding hint. What is the verb? *Focuses* is the singular verb. What focuses? *Organizations* is the plural subject. Do we have an agreement issue? The answer is yes. The phrase *in this country* comes between the subject and verb, and since the word *country* is singular, we fall into the agreement trap.

In the next section of this book, you will learn much more about these prepositional phrases. Until then, just remember to find the verb first and the subject will fall into place.

Perfect Verb Tenses

You have been working with verbs in the present, the past, and the future tense. It's important to add one other verb formation to this list, and that is the perfect tense. We'll explore this even more later in the book, but for now, you should know that the three perfect tenses (present perfect, past perfect, and future perfect) are formed by adding *has*, *had*, or *have* to the past tense of the verb. Let's concentrate on the present perfect tense—a time that started in the past and continues into the present. Look at the verb *complain*:

I *complain*. (present)

I *complained*. (past)

I *will complain*. (future)

I *have complained* ever since we moved farther from town. (present perfect)

The last example conforms to the definition of the present perfect tense. The complaining started in the past and continues into the present. Look at one more example, using the verb *prepare*:

I *prepare* three meals a day. (present)

I *prepared* three meals a day. (past)

I *will prepare* three meals a day. (future)

I *have prepared* three meals a day since 2001. (present perfect)

Written Practice 1-7

Circle the verb in each sentence. Then identify the tense of the verb. Use the previous example sentences as your guide.

1. I expect a raise in October. _____
2. Last year I received less than the maximum. _____
3. I have expected a larger raise for the past two years. _____
4. You think my larger raise will come this year, don't you? _____
5. I have read every document in the company. _____
6. My feet slid across the newly polished floors. _____
7. Next time I will know when the floor is wet. _____
8. We wrote a list of safety instructions. _____
9. We will implement the ideas shortly. _____
10. I avoided a serious injury this time. _____

Irregular Verbs

If English is your first language, you probably switch from tense to tense with great ease—that is, with *regular* verbs. People are much more likely to have problems with the tenses of *irregular* verbs. The spellings of these verbs change to a greater degree to indicate tense—and English has quite a few of them.

Perhaps you've heard the following incorrect past-tense verbs:

I *brung* my lunch with me every day last week to save money.

I *hanged* my hat on the hook.

Now look at this partial list of irregular verbs, and find the correct past forms of *bring* and *hang*:

Irregular Verbs

Present	Past	Future	Present Perfect
begin	began	will begin	have begun
bend	bent	will bend	have bent
bet	bet	will bet	have bet
bite	bit	will bite	have bitten
bring	brought	will bring	have brought
burst	burst	will burst	have burst
buy	bought	will buy	have bought
choose	chose	will choose	have chosen
cost	cost	will cost	have cost
dig	dug	will dig	have dug
dive	dived *or* dove	will dive	have dived
drink	drank	will drink	have drunk
drive	drove	will drive	have driven
fling	flung	will fling	have flung
fly	flew	will fly	have flown
forbid	forbade	will forbid	have forbidden
forget	forgot	will forget	have forgotten
freeze	froze	will freeze	have frozen
get	got	will get	have gotten
grind	ground	will grind	have ground
hang	hung	will hang	have hung
have	had	will have	have had
know	knew	will know	have known
lay (place)	laid	will lay	have laid
lend	lent	will lend	have lent
lie (recline)	lay	will lie	have lain
mistake	mistook	will mistake	have mistaken

ride	rode	will ride	have ridden
ring	rang	will ring	have rung
run	ran	will run	have run
see	saw	will see	have seen
seek	sought	will seek	have sought
send	sent	will send	have sent
shake	shook	will shake	have shaken
shine	shone	will shine	have shone
shrink	shrank	will shrink	have shrunk
sing	sang	will sing	have sung
sink	sank	will sink	have sunk
slide	slid	will slide	have slid
speak	spoke	will speak	have spoken
spin	spun	will spin	have spun
spring	sprang	will spring	have sprung
steal	stole	will steal	have stolen
sting	stung	will sting	have stung
strike	struck	will strike	have struck
swear	swore	will swear	have sworn
swim	swam	will swim	have swum
swing	swung	will swing	have swung
take	took	will take	have taken
tear	tore	will tear	have taken
think	thought	will think	have thought
throw	threw	will throw	have thrown
wake	woke	will wake	have waken
weep	wept	will weep	have wept
wind	wound	will wind	have wound
wring	wrung	will wring	have wrung

Written Practice 1-8

In each of the following sentences, find and correct the error in verb form.

1. That dog will lay in the grass all day.

   _____

2. I waked up too late to eat breakfast

   _____

3. Mike swum the entire way.

_____

4. I layed my keys on the counter and now they're gone.

_____

5. The child reported that he had runned all the way home.

_____

We usually learn the correct use of irregular verbs very naturally as we learn to speak English. For some people it is more difficult than for others. We all need to keep checking our usages because it's so easy to forget some of the irregular forms in the list. If you ever hesitate as you're about to speak or write one of these verbs, it's a clue that you need to go back and review. For example, two of the most mis-used irregular verbs are *lay* (to place) and *lie* (to recline), but if we establish some clues to their usage, it will help. Notice that the verb *lay* has an *a* in the middle and the clue word, *place*, is spelled with an *a*. The verb *lie* has an *i* in the middle as does the clue word, *recline*. Those two clues will start you off correctly in the present tense. Now you need clues for the past and perfect tenses.

Written Practice 1-9

Choose the correct verb form for each sentence.

1. I have never (laid, lain) in bed all day.
2. Mort has (swim, swum) the canal each spring.
3. The hanger was (raised, rose) twenty feet to accommodate the new planes.
4. I had (payed, paid) that bill long before it was due.
5. The toddler's parents had (forbade, forbidden) him from going into the street alone.
6. I have (swinged, swung) on that gate since I was a child.
7. We have (chosen, chose) a place for our wedding reception.
8. I have (drank, drunk) too much at this party!
9. The child (threw, throwed) a perfect strike.
10. I had (seen, seed) him only one other time.

Written Practice 1-10

In each paragraph, find the one verb that is not consistent in tense. Circle those verbs.

Paragraph 1

About three days after Christmas, do your children say, "I'm bored. What should I do now?" The answer could be that the children need to play, but in a way that is different from what they've been doing. They may simply need to leave their new indoor toys, their computers, and the TV and went outside into open space.

Paragraph 2

If it's not dangerously cold outside, children should spend time exercising their muscles in the open atmosphere. Many opportunities existed in the outdoors, from bike and sled riding to building snow forts. All of these activities give children the chance to use both large and small muscles and to focus on totally different tasks.

QUIZ

Identify and correct the errors in each of the following sentences, following the provided example.

Assuming that we make the early train. _sentence fragment_

I will be home on time assuming that we make the early train.

1. If you decide on which route to take. _____

_____

2. Looking back at his childhood. _____

_____

3. You're ready don't hesitate. _____

_____

4. Mark and Amy runs a very organized household. _____

_____

5. Buying a new piece of clothing. _____

_____

6. If you had rode to work with us, you would have been on time. _____

_____

7. When my time on the meter ran out. _____

_____

8. I'll be there, the children will arrive later, we'll all have lunch. _____

_____

9. He complained, "These cars parks in the wrong spaces every day!" _____

_____

10. Because I had written, word-processed, corrected, and approved the report.

_____

CHAPTER 2

Introduction to the Parts of Speech

In this chapter you will learn:

Parts of Speech
Nouns
Verbs
Adjectives
Adverbs
Pronouns
Prepositions
Conjunctions
Interjections
Articles

Parts of Speech

Use the following chart to reacquaint yourself with the parts of speech.

Part of Speech	Function	Examples
Noun, pronoun	Names a person, place, or thing	Elliot, President Adams, cat, he, she, them
Verb	Provides the action or state of being	fly, stand, walk, count, is, are, be
Adjective	Modifies or describes a noun	tall, noisy, blue, hot
Adverb	Modifies or describes a verb, adjective, or other adverb	noisily, easily, hardly
Preposition	Introduces a relationship between a noun or pronoun and other words in a sentence	on, in, up, over, to
Conjunction	Joins words, phrases, and clauses	and, but, or, yet
Interjection	Expresses emotion	ah, oh, wow
Article	Identifies or points out a noun	a, an, the

One way to understand English grammar is to think of words as having two names: a grammatical name, called a part of speech, and a function name that tells what it does in the sentence. Look at the following sentence:

The tennis ball hit the opponent on his head.

Part of Speech:	Article	adjective	noun	verb	article	noun	preposition	pronoun	noun
	↓	↓	↓	↓	↓	↓	↓	↓	↓
	The	tennis	ball	hit	the	opponent	on	his	head.
	↑	↑	↑	↑	↑	↑	↑	↑	↑
Function:	Identifies	describes	subject	verb	identifies	object	introduces	describes	object

Why is it important to know and understand this concept? The simple answer is that correct English usage depends upon it. The following examples will explain this. First, think of the pronouns *he* and *him*. The pronoun *he* functions as the subject of a sentence. *Him* functions as an object. The different function categories of pronouns are explained later in this chapter.

He hit the opponent on the head. (*He* is the subject and *hit* is the verb.)

He hit *him* on the head. (*He* is the subject, *hit* is the verb, and *him* is the object who received the hit.)

As you can see in the following example, function is extremely important in choosing the correct pronoun.

Him hit he. (An object pronoun, *him*, cannot be used as a subject, and a subject pronoun, *he*, cannot be used as the object.)

You will have an opportunity to study the complete pronoun list and their functions later in the chapter. For now, you just need to remember that *I*, *he*, and *she* are subject pronouns and that *me*, *her*, and *him* are object pronouns.

COMMON ERRORS

One of the most persistent errors in English is the use of an object pronoun as the subject or a subject pronoun as the object:

Incorrect: The gift was for Michael and I.
Correct: The gift was for Michael and *me*.

Incorrect: Me and him are going to the movies.
Correct: *He and I* are going to the movies.

Written Practice 2-1

Write your correction for each sentence on the lines provided.

1. Him and me share a job. _____
2. Tim and him share a job. _____
3. This pizza is for Betsy and I. _____
4. The argument is between Marcus and I. _____
5. Tim and me are happy about the new arrangement. _____

VERSATILITY OF ENGLISH WORDS

You learned in Chapter 1 that a sentence must have a subject and a verb to be a complete sentence. You have seen that subjects are either nouns or pronouns. Look at the following examples:

James (noun) played the comical (adjective) part to perfection.

He (pronoun) played the comical (adjective) part to perfection.

Can you simply decide to have an adjective function in place of the noun or pronoun?

Comical played the James part to perfection.

Obviously you can't. *Comical* did not play the part; *James* did.

Interestingly, though, English words have great versatility. For example, consider the word *play*. How many different functions can it perform?

Subject: The play takes two hours to perform. (The noun *play* is what the sentence is about; it's what *takes* [verb] the time.)

Verb: James will play the lead part. (The verb *will play* tells what the subject will do.)

Modifier: The children love the play area. (The adjective *play* describes or modifies the noun *area*.)

Object: Tom made the best play of the game. (The noun *play* is the object of the verb *made*.)

Now experiment with the word *work*.

Subject: Work starts at 8 A.M. sharp. (The noun *work* is what the sentence is about; it's what *starts* [verb] at 8 A.M.)

Verb: Karra works fifty hours per week. (The verb *works* tells what *Karra* does.)

Object: Karra does many hours of work each week. (The noun *work* is the object of the preposition *of*; *of work* modifies *hours*.)

Adjective: The plumber's work permit allows him to install all new pipes. (The adjective *work* modifies or describes the noun *permit*.)

You probably agree that one English word can carry out many functions, depending upon the meaning of the sentence.

Written Practice 2-2

In each of the following sentences, identify the underlined word as *subject*, *verb*, *object*, or *modifier*. The first one is done for you.

1. You should <u>paint</u> the room white. *verb* _____
2. The <u>paint</u> comes in three shades of red. _____
3. The salesperson gave us a <u>paint</u> chart from which we chose a color.

   _____
4. Then she mixed the <u>paint</u>. _____
5. <u>Paint</u> is an easy solution to a decorating problem. _____
6. A <u>comment</u> appeared in our local newspaper. _____
7. Then the losing candidate made a <u>comment</u> about the voting equipment.

   _____
8. I don't <u>comment</u> on other people's parenting skills. _____
9. You can <u>nurse</u> that bird back to health and then release it in the forest.

   _____
10. A <u>release</u> regarding his decision appeared on his blog. _____

Nouns

You know nouns as words that stand for people, places, or things. People and places are easy enough to recognize: *Philip*, *Marcel*, *Pittsburgh*, the *Rosebowl*, *Radio City Music Hall*—and we could go on forever. Things are easy, too: *table*, *pens*, *candy*, and *TV* are just a few. More difficult to recognize are the words we call *abstract* nouns. These are ideas or qualities such as *honor*, *love*, *loyalty*, and *determination*. A good rule of thumb for recognizing a noun is this: If you can put *a*, *an*, or *the* in front of the word and it still makes sense, it's a noun.

Written Practice 2-3

Circle all the nouns in the following sentences.

1. Psychologists now believe that people who get what they want are not necessarily as happy as they thought they would be.
2. Dr. Daniel Gilbert, a Harvard psychologist, thinks that in the future we'll wonder why we made today's choices.
3. We may make perfectly good choices for ourselves today, but we don't know who we'll be in the future.
4. Credit cards are a great convenience until we overspend!
5. Check your credit at least once a year.
6. A lawyer testified on that case.
7. A renowned designer of glass is Dale Chihuly.
8. Carpet covered the entire space.
9. Environmentalists in our area planted clams in local ponds and had great success.
10. Lawmakers held hearings on the growing deficit.

Verbs

As you learned in Chapter 1, sentences are complete only if they contain both a subject and a verb. The verb is part of the backbone of any sentence, joining the noun or subject as one of two absolutely necessary elements of a complete sentence. The verb lives in what grammarians call the *predicate*, which contains the verb plus all the words that relate specifically to it. The verb gives the subject its action or expresses its state of being.

The doctor suggested that I take much more calcium.

The doctor is a believer in vitamin therapy.

In the first sentence, the subject is *doctor* and the verb or action is *suggested*. In the second sentence there is no action verb; rather, there is the linking or being verb *is*. Many prefer to call *is* a linking verb because that is what it does—it links a word in the predicate to the subject. In this case, it links *believer* to *doctor*. Later in this section, you will learn much more about *linking* or *being* verbs.

Written Practice 2-4

Circle all the verbs—both action and linking—in each of the following sentences.

1. Time flies.
2. The newly cleaned mirrors glitter and gleam.
3. My house is cold in the winter.
4. The child felt sad.
5. I am the president of our social club.
6. The company's eight stores closed in 2008.
7. My bank will merge with a larger one.
8. Bluefish and bass are abundant in Long Island Sound.
9. September 11, 2001, is a date seared in most memories.
10. A man, arrested for drunk driving, produced his identification.

LINKING/BEING VERBS

You've learned that action words are verbs, and they are easy to recognize:

The kite *crashed* into the field.

A car *sped* down the highway.

My cat *caught* a mouse.

The moving truck *lumbered* on its way.

Reading this last sentence, you can actually see in your mind's eye the action of the word *lumbered*.

What if the verb did not signal an action but worked to link the predicate (the verb half of the sentence) to the subject? That's what we expect linking verbs (also known as being verbs) to do. You can see this transformation in the following sentence:

The moving truck *was* huge and lumbering.

The being verb *was* does not provide a picture, but it does link the subject, *truck*, to words (adjectives *huge* and *lumbering*) that describe it. Now look at this example:

"Twinkle, Twinkle Little Star" *was* the first song I learned.

The linking verb is the same—*was*. But what does it link? In this case, the subject, *"Twinkle, Twinkle Little Star"* is linked to a noun that means the same as the subject. In fact, you can turn the sentence around and keep the same meaning:

The first song I learned was "Twinkle, Twinkle Little Star."

We can say, then, that linking verbs can function as equalizers: *"Twinkle, Twinkle Little Star"* equals a song.

Conclusion? Either nouns or adjectives that link the predicate to the subject follow linking verbs.

It's also interesting that some action verbs can be converted to linking verbs, depending on the verb's function and meaning of the sentence:

Mario *grows* tomatoes.

Each summer, Mario's family *grows* tired of eating tomatoes.

In the first sentence, *grows* is an action verb. In the second sentence, *grows* is a linking verb that links the subject *family* to the adjective *tired*. *Tired* is an adjective that describes the family.

Remember that each linking verb is subject to the same rules as action verbs: a linking verb must agree with its subject in number.

Here is a list of common linking verbs:

appear	am	are	be	become
feel	grow	is	look	remain
smell	sound	taste	was	were

Written Practice 2-5

For each of the following sentences, select the linking verb that expresses the correct number.

1. John Adams (was/were) President for one term.
2. The White House of Adams' time (appears/appear) very strange.

3. It (seems/seem) unfinished with no plaster in most of the rooms and no main staircase.

4. People (grows/grew) tired of seeing Mrs. Adams's laundry hung in the East Room.

5. The White House grounds (smell/smells) foul.

6. The grounds (was/were) littered with workers' shanties, stagnant water, and outhouses.

7. Today, the White House flowers (is/are) perfect.

8. The rooms (remain/remains) colorful and neat.

9. Visitors (seem/seems) delighted with their tour.

10. Our group (were/was) silent as the President approached.

As you work with linking verbs, you'll note that the past tense is easier to achieve than the present. In the present tense, the verb endings change. For example:

Present Time, Singular, and Plural

I *seem* taller than Jan.

You *seem* taller, also.

Jethro (He) *seems* tired after all that yard work.

Betsy (She) *seems* to have less back pain.

Their cat (It) *seems* unable to sleep alone.

Who *seems* the smartest in the group?

Marcel and I (We) *seem* rested after our vacation.

You and David (You) *seem* exhausted from your schedule.

Aidan and Elias (They) *seem* able to go without sleep.

Past Time, Singular, and Plural

I *seemed* taller than Jan.

You *seemed* taller, also.

Jethro *seemed* tired after all that yard work.

Betsy *seemed* to have less back pain.

Their cat *seemed* unable to sleep alone.

Who *seemed* the smartest in the group?

Marcel and I *seemed* rested after our vacation.

You and David *seemed* exhausted from your schedule.

Aidan and Elias *seemed* able to go without sleep.

BE: A LIFE OF ITS OWN

You saw a list of common linking verbs earlier. Indeed, one of them is the verb *be*. *Be* is more complicated than other verbs for two reasons: First, it has many different forms, depending upon tense and number (*am*, *is*, *are*, *was*, *were*). Second, it combines with the helping words *to*, *will*, *can*, *could*, *would*, or *should* in the following ways:

I *would be* grateful to you if you would vote for my candidate.

You *should be* more careful when you walk on the ice-covered streets.

I *can be* ready at 1 P.M.

Bess *could be* your greatest ally.

My children wanted *to be* helpful.

You *will be* expected to win.

Written Practice 2-6

Use a form of the linking verb *be* to fill each space in the following sentences. Your choice may be one word or two, depending upon the meaning of the sentence.

1. Her dog _____ a Pomeranian.
2. Her choice _____ a different one as well.
3. Yesterday, the gray clouds _____ thickening just as we left.

4. The picnic _____ rescheduled for sometime in June.

5. I _____ so happy that you remembered me.

6. The child expects that chair _____ hers.

7. As they bake, the cookies _____ so good!

8. They _____ delicious, too.

9. Alex and Jenna _____ always happy to eat dessert.

10. Next year, those two _____ my best friends.

Can the linking verb *be* be any more complicated? Yes, it can. Frequently, a linking verb combines with another word. The combination, called a contraction, requires dropping a letter in the verb and replacing it with an apostrophe:

She *is* the strongest runner I know.

She's the strongest runner I know. (The *i* is dropped.)

Written Practice 2-7

In the following sentences, convert the italicized words into contractions.

1. *We are* more determined than you think. _____

2. *Here is* your chance to shine. _____

3. *It is* about time you took charge! _____

4. Ron said that *you are* his favorite sitter. _____

5. *You will* find that *it is* an involved community. _____

6. *I am* your best friend. _____

7. *He is* in our carpool, too. _____

8. *They are* driving in front of us. _____

9. *You are* foolish if you think I'll pay for the gas. _____

10. *It is* time to go home. _____

NOTE: *Don't use an apostrophe in the word* its *when it indicates possession.*

The mother cat groomed *its* kitten.

There is one more combination you should know about, and that is the linking verb combined with *not*. Notice that in such a case, the word *not* is contracted.

are not = aren't

is not = isn't

was not = wasn't

were not = weren't

COMMON ERRORS

Note the following incorrect linking verb combinations and their corrections:

Incorrect: The bird built it's nest with twigs.
Correct: The bird built *its* nest with twigs.

Incorrect: James ain't leaving until the very end.
Correct: James *isn't* leaving until the very end.

Incorrect: There's two answers to that question.
Correct: *There are* two answers to that question.

Incorrect: Your one of the final candidates.
Correct: *You're* one of the final candidates

Adjectives

Adjectives describe nouns and pronouns, adding color and clarity to sentences. For the most part, you will find an adjective placed in front of the noun it modifies or describes:

A *playful* beagle won the competition. *Playful* is the adjective that describes the noun, *beagle*.

When two adjectives (*playful*, *tan*) describe a noun, they are usually separated by a comma:

A *playful*, *tan* beagle won the competition.

But adjectives may also come after the noun, as they do in the following sentence:

A beagle, *playful* and *tan*, won the competition.

Notice two things: The commas are outside the two adjectives, and they are joined by *and*. Also notable is the fact that this form puts more emphasis on the adjectives.

Adjectives can appear in a third place, which is after a linking verb. You will read much more about this in the section on linking verbs, but for now recall that a linking verb links to another word in the subject:

The beagle is *playful*.

Playful, the adjective, describes the subject, *beagle*. *Playful* is linked to the subject by the linking verb *is*.

Written Practice 2-8

Circle all the adjectives in the following sentences.

1. The smooth-haired dog is a beagle.
2. Lise is organized.
3. I have a well-informed friend.
4. Richard, tall and tan, returned from a long vacation.
5. A sleek car arrived at the front door.
6. The strapping quarterback fell to the ground.
7. His right knee was injured badly.
8. The loud, pulsing music tore through the small space.
9. An angry landlord rushed upstairs to complain.
10. A friend, gesturing and smiling, left the auction.

COMPARISON OF ADJECTIVES

Descriptive words follow a pattern when they are used in comparisons. For example:

One house is *near.*

A second house is *nearer.*

A third house is *nearest.*

The adjective *near* follows a linking verb, *is,* and describes the subject, *house.* In the second sentence, two houses are compared and the adjective's spelling changes: *-er* is added. In the third sentence, three houses are compared. The spelling changes again: *-est* is added to indicate more than two.

So the changes for comparisons are simple. Just add *-er* for a comparison of two or *-est* for a comparison of more than two. For example:

Describing Word	Comparison of Two	Comparison of More than Two
soon	sooner	soonest
funny	funnier	funniest
loud	louder	loudest
short	shorter	shortest

The preceding transformations were quite simple. The complication occurs when the adjective has more than two syllables:

wonderful	wonderfuler	wonderfulest

Sound strange? Most people would say these do. That is why we use the words *more* and *most* instead of the awkward suffixes, *-fuler* and *-fulest*:

wonderful	more wonderful	most wonderful

Now compare the adjectives in the following chart.

Describing Word	Comparison of Two	Comparison of More than Two
difficult	more difficult	most difficult
valuable	more valuable	most valuable
legible	more legible	most legible
sympathetic	more sympathetic	most sympathetic

Finally, some adjectives take completely different forms to express comparisons:

Describing Word	Comparison of Two	Comparison of More than Two
good	better	best
bad	worse	worst
little (size)	smaller	smallest
little (amount)	less	least
much	more	most
far	further	furthest

Written Practice 2-9

Correct the awkward forms in each of the following sentences.

1. My car is valuabler than hers.

   _____

2. This is the efficientest furnace we've ever owned.

   _____

3. Of all the grapes in the bunch, this is the worse.

   _____

4. On the other hand, the green grapes are the goodest.

   _____

5. Once I learned the first piece, my piano teacher gave me a difficulter piece to practice.

   _____

6. This is the enormousest house in the neighborhood.

   _____

7. In my family, I have the legiblist handwriting.

   _____

8. To win, you'll have to be tenaciouser.

   _____

9. Ted is sympatheticer than Juan.

_____

10. That dress is the beautifulest in my closet.

_____

Adverbs

Using adverbs is another way of adding interest and color to your sentences. Adverbs are frequently formed by adding -ly to an adjective. Add an -ly to the adjective *sincere*, and you have formed an adverb: *sincerely*. However, not all adverbs end in -ly. *Very*, *almost*, *quite*, *always*, and *often* are adverbs as well. Like an adjective, the adverb modifies or describes another word. The difference between the two is that the adverb describes a verb, an adjective, or another adverb. Adverbs usually follow the verbs they describe:

The beam tilted *slightly* to the left.

The adverb *slightly* describes the verb *tilted*.

The *slightly* faded shirt lay on the dresser.

The adverb *slightly* describes the adjective *faded*.

The very *slightly* faded shirt could still be worn.

The adverb *very* describes the adverb *slightly*.
We are accustomed to changing adjectives into adverbs simply by adding -ly: *simple*, *simply*.

That is a *simple* dress.

Simple describes the noun *dress*.

I *simply* want to dress for the occasion.

Simply describes the verb *want*.

Unfortunately, some adverbs don't follow the -*ly* rule. They keep the same spelling. The words that are often misused are *fast* and *hard*:

I run fast.

Fast is an adverb in this sentence; it describes the verb *run*.

Mel is a fast runner.

In this sentence, *fast* is an adjective that modifies the noun *runner*.

Mel runs hard.

Hard is the adverb that describes the verb *runs*.

Mel loves hard tasks.

Hard is the adjective that describes the noun *tasks*.

COMMON ERRORS

One of the most common errors occurs when people struggle to make the choice between *good* and *well*. Because it is an adjective, the word *good* describes people, places, or things—nouns. *Good* never describes an action. *Well* is the adverb form of *good*, so it describes an action. The only exception occurs when referring to someone's health:

Incorrect: We heard a very well speaker
Correct: We heard a very *good* speaker.

Incorrect: Chuck plays the guitar so good.
Correct: Chuck plays the guitar so *well*.

Incorrect: Chuck doesn't feel so good today.
Correct: Chuck doesn't feel *well* today. (*Well* refers to Chuck's health.)

Written Practice 2-10

Circle the correct word to complete each sentence.

1. He plays basketball (good/well).
2. The (good/well) weather encouraged us to take a long walk.
3. Nina hasn't been (good/well) since she left the office with a fever.
4. It's a (good/well) thing she went home.
5. Fortunately, everyone in the office has stayed (good/well).
6. Billy cleaned the floor and did such a (good/well) job!
7. He works on his own very (good/well).
8. After having the flu, I didn't feel (good/well) for three weeks.
9. When Jenna was a toddler, she was so (good/well) at playing alone.
10. I saw such a (good/well) movie this weekend.

Pronouns

Pronouns are small words that give people big problems. Pronouns cause some of the most common errors in English. Look back to the earlier Common Errors section for more examples:

Me and Tad wait impatiently for summer.

From what you've learned, you know that this sentence contains a plural subject: *Me and Tad. Wait* is the plural verb. What's wrong with the sentence? The pronoun *me* is wrong. Remember that the function of the pronoun in the sentence dictates the form you choose. In this incorrect sentence, *me* is used as a part of the plural subject, but it is not a subject pronoun. How can you know that? Look at the following chart, which will solve most of your pronoun problems.

Subject Pronouns	Object Pronouns Receive the Action	Ownership Pronouns
I	me	my, mine
you	you	your, yours
he	him	his
she	her	her, hers
it	it	its
we	us	our, ours
they	them	their, theirs
who	whom	

Now go back to the incorrect sentence. Remember that *function is key*!

  Me and Tad wait impatiently for summer.

What is the subject? It is *Me and Tad*. Look for the pronoun *me* in the previous chart. It is in the column titled Object Pronouns Receive the Action. Does the pronoun *me* receive the action of the verb *wait*? No, it's trying to act as the subject of *wait* (as *Tad* is). Object pronouns cannot do that. Correction: *Tad and I* wait impatiently for summer. Also, remember to mention yourself second.

Written Practice 2-11

Correct the pronoun errors in each of the following sentences.

1. Me and my friends meet one night a month for dinner.

   _____

2. Him and me are best friends.

   _____

3. My boss gave he and I the same raise.

   _____

4. Send the letter to he by express mail.

   _____

5. That gift is from Alex and I.

   _____

As incredible as it may seem, there is much more to learn about the correct use of pronouns, so you will find more instruction and practice in a later chapter. However, this section serves as an excellent introduction to what is to come.

Prepositions

Prepositions link, or relate, nouns, pronouns, and phrases to other words in a sentence. The word or phrase the preposition introduces is called the object of the preposition.

Common prepositions include:

about	above	after	along	against
among	around	at	before	beside
between	for	from	in	into
near	like	on	of	over
under	up	with		

Now take a look at some examples:

The child held the toy *over her head.*

The preposition *over* introduces the phrase *over her head. Head* is the object of the preposition. You can see that the phrase *over her head* tells where the child held the toy, so it acts as an adverb that describes the verb *held.*

The officers in the boardroom prepared for a long meeting.

The preposition *in* introduces the phrase *in the boardroom.* The phrase describes which officers are being talked about. The word *officers* is a noun. What part of speech describes a noun? An adjective does, and therefore this prepositional phrase acts as an adjective, describing a noun.

We met in the boardroom.

The preposition *in* introduces the phrase *in the boardroom. In the boardroom* describes where we met. The prepositional phrase acts as an adverb, describing *met.*

We found termites under the porch.

The preposition *under* introduces the phrase *under the porch*. What does this prepositional phrase tell you? It tells you where the termites were found. The prepositional phrase describes the verb *found*; thus it acts as an adverb.

Written Practice 2-12

Find the prepositional phrase in each of the following sentences. Tell which word the prepositional phrase describes. The first one is done for you.

1. A new bank opened in town.
   in town describes *opened*

2. Don't position all the furniture against the walls.

   _____

3. One bottle inside the carton was smashed.

   _____

4. Please place the key between the doors.

   _____

5. I opened the car door and left my coffee cup on top.

   _____

6. Please tell me more about Larry.

   _____

7. I'm teaching a class in the adult school.

   _____

8. We heard children laugh at the park.

   _____

9. The new program on TV has a huge audience.

   _____

10. The logs in the fireplace burned brightly.

    _____

We'll return to prepositional phrases in a later chapter. They are often the source of common errors in sentences because they come between the subject and the verb.

Written Practice 2-13

In the following sentences, first find the subject (it is not in the prepositional phrase); then decide if it is singular or plural. Does the verb match the subject in number? If not, correct the verb. The first sentence is done for you.

1. The bottles inside the carton *is* all broken. <u>The word *bottles* is the subject and it is plural. The verb *is* is a singular verb. Change the singular *is* to its plural form, *are*.</u>
2. The newspaper between the doors *are* old.
3. The paint cans against the walls *was* left open.
4. My friend, among all my classmates, *are* the smartest.
5. The most exciting movies in the list *is* adventure movies.

Conjunctions

The word *conjunction* means "to join with," and that is exactly what this part of speech does. Common conjunctions *and*, *or*, and *but* join or coordinate our thoughts. They connect words to other words:

Lise and Gregor came to America a few years ago.

The two parts of the subject, that is, Lise and Gregor, are connected by *and*.
Which words are connected in the following sentences?

I couldn't decide whether I should read a book or clean the house.

The phrases *read a book* and *clean the house* are connected by *or*.

Dave had always been short, but he finally grew as a teenager.

The clauses before and after the comma are connected by *but*.
For, and, nor, but, or, yet, and *so* all coordinate words, phrases, and clauses. You can use the acronym *FANBOYS* to remember these conjunctions. Because of their function, they are called coordinating conjunctions.
There is another way of connecting equal parts of a sentence: using *correlative conjunctions*. The difference between correlative and coordinating conjunctions is

that correlative conjunctions come in pairs that relate to one another. Examples are *either/or*, *neither/nor*, *both/and*, *not only/but also*:

Either I will pass the test, *or* I won't be driving.

The rain ruined *not only* the flowers, *but also* the grass.

Finally, *subordinating conjunctions* function to connect or link dependent and independent clauses. You can identify the independent clause by finding the part of each sentence that can stand alone. For example:

Until I leave, I'll be in charge. (independent clause: I'll be in charge)

When you call me, I'll put dinner in the oven. (independent clause: I'll put dinner in the oven)

Zeke died a lonely man because he never tried to make friends. (independent clause: Zeke died a lonely man)

In the preceding sentences, the subordinating conjunctions are *until*, *when*, and *because*. Here is a more complete list of subordinating conjunctions:

after	as	as if	as long as	because
before	but that	even if	except that	ever since
if	if only	in case	just as	since
until	when	whenever	while	

A later section will show how important it is to coordinate or subordinate thoughts with the use of conjunctions, since they add interest, meaning, and contrast to writing.

Written Practice 2 14

In each of the following sentences, circle the conjunctions and decide what kind it is—coordinating, correlative, or subordinating.

1. Abby and Michael are siblings.

   _____

2. I had to decide between having a big breakfast or saving room for lunch.

   _____

3. Karra had always loved sewing, but she didn't take sewing lessons until she was in her thirties.

4. Neither the new computer nor the old one is working now.

5. Until the clock strikes 5 P.M., we'll work!

6. Because it is so hot, we've run the air-conditioning for days.

7. Your comment was neither funny nor helpful.

8. Our relationship is not only warm, but also encouraging.

9. You join the group first, and I will follow.

10. Since the candidate addressed our issues, we voted for her.

Interjections

We emphasize and exclaim with interjections: *Wow! Whew! Oh no! Hey! Great!* There's nothing much more to say about them; there are no rules. Just don't use them too much.

Articles

Articles *a, an,* and *the* point to nouns:

The movie starts at 8 P.M. (*The* points to the noun *movie.*)

A fruit drink may or may not be good for your diet. (*A* points to the noun *drink.*)

An old friend came by to visit. (*An* points to the noun *friend.*)

Articles are considered either definite or indefinite. In the first example sentence, the article *the* points to a specific movie, that is, the one at 8 P.M. In this case, *the* is a definite article. On the other hand, *a* fruit drink may be any you can think of, not definite but indefinite. The same is true of *an* old friend; *an* does not point out Harry, Lois, or Gabe, but any friend. *An* acts as an indefinite article.

We often think of articles functioning as adjectives because they do what adjectives do—describe the nouns they introduce.

QUIZ

Find and correct the errors in the following sentences.

1. Her and me share a healthful lunch every day.

   _____

2. I run really good in a race.

   _____

3. Mel doesn't feel good today.

   _____

4. Me and Ted shares a locker at the gym.

   _____

5. The gym gave a discount to Ted and I.

   _____

6. This cereal, of all the cereals I've tried, are the best.

   _____

7. Until you call me or I receive your message.

   _____

8. A project w'ere doing now will furnish a shelter.

   _____

9. Wow. Youve broken the all-time record.

   _____

10. Ain't spring your favorite season?

   _____

CHAPTER 3

More About Verbs, Prepositions, and Pronouns

In this chapter you will learn:

Perfect Tenses

Every time you write a sentence, you use a verb to express time:

Present time: My best friend visits us from time to time.

Past time: She visited four times last year.

Future time: She will visit us again next week.

These are the simplest expressions of time, but as you read in Chapter 1, ideas are occasionally more complicated and require a different use of verbs.

PRESENT PERFECT TENSE

How do you express an action that started in the past but continues into the present time? In Chapter 1, you learned this simple answer: You add a helping word *has* or *have* to the past tense of the verb. Take the previous example:

My best friend *has visited* us from time to time.

The verb *has visited* tells us that the visiting started in the past but continues in the present.

Written Practice 3-1

Using the preceding information, find and correct the past-perfect verb errors in the following sentences. The first one is done for you.

1. Lacey banked at Yardley Trust for four years, but she's considering a change of banks.

   Lacey has banked . . .

2. I banked at Yardley Trust for one year, and I'm planning on staying there.

3. I am writing business manuals for twenty years. (Tricky! Remember that *am* is a form of *be*.)

_____

4. The Tomkins owned the pharmacy for ten years and are now starting to renovate it.

_____

5. I watched baseball on TV year after year, but now I'm reserving seats at the stadium.

_____

PAST PERFECT TENSE

On occasion, one past action occurs before another past action. For example:

My friend had visited us from time to time before he moved to Seattle.

Both verbs are in the past (*visited*, *moved*), but the visiting took place in the past before the moving. The challenge is to always make clear which action occurred first. The helping verb *had* makes that clear. For example:

Jackie had eaten alone before I invited him to join us.

COMMON ERRORS

Remember that too much *had* is not a good thing!

After we *had* bought the furniture, we *had* found a better sale.
Unbelievably, I *had* walked on that foot for days before I *had* realized it was broken.

Only one verb should include the helping verb *had*. Which action came first in each sentence? That's the verb that should be accompanied by *had*:

After we *had bought* the furniture, we found a better sale.
Unbelievably, I *had walked* on that foot for days before I realized it was broken.

The addition of the helping verb *had* shows that Jackie ate alone before someone invited him to join a group.

Written Practice 3-2

In each of the following sentences, indicate the present or past perfect tense by inserting a helping verb where needed. The first one is done for you.

1. Before I finished my second dessert, my mother brought the main course.

   Before I had finished . . .

2. I took yoga for three years before I heard about Pilates.

   _____

3. I never saw a vineyard before I went to California.

   _____

4. If you remembered your diet plan, you definitely would not have started with dessert!

   _____

5. I chose the menu, but I still didn't take the blame.

   _____

6. Bill said, "If you screamed, I would have come running."

   _____

7. I owned a small car for years before I actually needed to save on gas.

   _____

8. My niece participated in the Iron Man Competition for several years before she stopped running.

   _____

9. I worked at ABC Management for four years before I received a promotion!

   _____

10. Eli and Eleanor ate at that restaurant many times before it closed.

   _____

FUTURE PERFECT TENSE

What if you want to express one future action before another future action? For example:

> I will have visited my grandchildren a number of times before they stay with me in the summer.

The words *will have* show that the visiting will be completed before the staying occurs in the summer. In other words, a future action—*visiting*—will be completed before another future action, *staying*, happens.

Written Practice 3-3

Correct the verb tense errors in the following sentences. The first one is done for you.

1. I will have planted a hundred bulbs before I will have considered stopping.

   . . . before I consider stopping

2. I will have flown one million miles before I will have retired.

   _____

3. I will fly one million miles before I will have retired.

   _____

4. By the time you will have arrived, I will bake the cake.

   _____

5. The exterior house painting will have been done before you will have moved in.

   _____

SIMULTANEOUS ACTIONS

Consider one more: the use of time in a sentence that expresses *simultaneous actions*.

As the baseball hero walked into the stadium, the ecstatic fans cheered.

Two actions happened at the same time: (1) *The baseball hero walked* and (2) *the ecstatic fans cheered*. When two actions occur simultaneously, *neither* action word is accompanied by *had*.

Written Practice 3-4

Choose the correct verb for each of the following sentences.

1. When the singer appeared to sing the National Anthem, everyone (rose/had risen).
2. I (will have commuted/commuted) one million miles by air by the time I retire.
3. The music (swelled/has swelled) and the movie began.
4. As I lifted the Sunday newspaper, I (saw/had seen) my missing pen.
5. By the time I leave the house, my bus (will have left/left).
6. The court (decided/had decided) that the driver was wrong.
7. As we (filed/had filed) out of the room, the lights went out.
8. I (picked/had picked) up my personal mail before I arrived at work.
9. When the electric lines fell, our lights (went out/had gone out).
10. Before she goes up to the platform, she (will have prepared/prepared) her talking points.

Written Practice 3-5

This practice reviews all the types of verbs taught in Chapter 3. Find an incorrect verb form in each of the following sentences. Write your correction on the line provided.

1. Even busy children loves to read a good book.

   _____

2. My son read for at least a year before he went to school.

   _____

3. After he had started school, we had started going to reading hour at the library.

_____

4. If we known about story hour, we would have started sooner.

_____

5. Manny and I had shopped at Wizardry for many years before we had met the owner.

_____

6. Before Lise has climbed to the diving board, she visualizes her first dive.

_____

7. As we had walked to the graduation march, the music started.

_____

8. Marian will visit us four times before the year is over.

_____

9. After we had watched four hours of baseball, we had learned that a football special was on simultaneously.

_____

10. He will have failed before he will have realized his mistake in not working harder.

_____

Prepositional Phrases

As you learned in Chapter 2, prepositions link or relate nouns, pronouns, and phrases to other words in a sentence. The word or phrase the preposition introduces is called the prepositional phrase. In the phrase, you find the object of the preposition. You can find a list of common prepositions in Chapter 2.

To write sentences correctly, you need to have one very important fact in mind: the subject of a verb will never be part of a prepositional phrase. A prepositional phrase begins with a preposition, such as *in*, *on*, *at*, *between*, or *among*, and ends with a noun, pronoun, or gerund. Look at the following examples of prepositional phrases:

in the dirty pail	on the smooth highway
at home	between us
among the empty pizza boxes	without crying

Sometimes a prepositional phrase seems to be either the subject itself or part of the subject. Read the example that follows:

Neither of these boys wants a low-paying job this summer.

In this sentence, the boys seem to be the ones who do not want the low-paying job, but because they are part of a prepositional phrase, *of these boys*, they are *not* the subject. The word *Neither* is the actual subject. Here is another example:

My dog, along with her seven puppies, has chewed all of the stuffing out of the sofa cushions.

In this sentence, both my *dog* and her *seven puppies* are chewing on the sofa, but because the puppies are part of the prepositional phrase *along with her seven puppies*, the only word that counts as the subject is *dog*.

Prepositional phrases are the source of common mistakes in sentences because they come between the subject and the verb, causing errors in agreement between subject and verb. For example:

The bottles inside the carton (is/are) all broken.

How do you correctly choose the verb in this sentence? Start by placing parentheses around the prepositional phrase *inside the carton*:

The bottles (inside the carton) is/are all broken.

The prepositional phrase does not determine the number—singular or plural—of the verb. Rather, identify the subject of the sentence, which is *bottles*. Does the subject *bottles* need a singular or plural verb? The answer, of course, is plural. Now you can choose the verb form *are*.

Written Practice 3-6

In each of the following sentences, place parentheses around the prepositional phrase. Then find the subject and correct the verb form.

1. The bottles inside the carton is all broken.

   _____

2. The newspaper between the doors are old.

   _____

3. The paint cans against the walls was left open.

   _____

4. My friend among all my classmates are the smartest.

   _____

5. The most exciting movies in the list is adventure movies.

   _____

Another common error has to do with the placement of a prepositional phrase in a sentence. Which of the following two sentences is the more precise one?

The boy ran down the stairs *in the yellow boots*.

The boy *in the yellow boots* ran down the stairs.

The answer, of course, depends on whether the stairs are actually wearing yellow boots. If not, the second sentence is correct. What general rule can you conclude from this error? Place a prepositional phrase as close as possible to the word it describes. For example:

The man was late for his train *on the cell phone*.

Logic tells us that the train was not on a cell phone, but the sentence is not that clear. How can you make it clear that the man is using a cell phone? Simply place the prepositional phrase where it belongs:

The man *on the cell phone* was late for his train.

Written Practice 3-7

In each of the following sentences, put the prepositional phrases in the correct place.

1. I did not see down the road a huge crash.

   _____

2. The hamster belongs to Tommy with the shortest legs.

   _____

3. That antique roadster is in the garage with 50,000 miles on it.

   _____

4. The prospective voters on the table completed their registration for the election.

   _____

5. You should hang on the wall some of your new artwork.

   _____

6. The banana-nut bread smells wonderful in the oven.

   _____

7. Ned, under the deck, lined up furniture and boxes.

   _____

8. You probably received a letter about the dangers of contaminated water in the mail.

   _____

9. We drove along the endless highway toward the setting sun in a red convertible.

   _____

10. Remove the filter from the furnace with the pliers.

    _____

More About Pronouns

There are a number of different types of pronouns that you should know about. The chart in Chapter 2 must be expanded to include all of the pronouns. This chapter discusses six types of pronouns. Review the following new pronoun list before you continue:

Personal (subject): I, you, he, she, it, we, they, who
Personal (object): me, you, him, her, it, us, them, whom
Mirror: myself, yourself, himself, herself, itself, ourselves, yourselves, themselves
Relative: which, that, who, whom, what, whatever, whomever
Pointing: this, these
Indefinite: all, any, anybody, anything, both, each, either, enough, everybody, few, less, many, more, much, neither, none, nothing, one, plenty, several, some, someone
Ownership: my, mine, your, yours, his, hers, its, our, ours, their, theirs

Personal Pronouns

Earlier in the chapter, you learned to choose the correct pronoun according to its function. Personal pronouns are used as both subjects and objects. Look at the following incorrect example:

   Incorrect: *Me* walks a mile every morning.

Me cannot be used as the subject; it is an object pronoun. *I* is the subject pronoun.

   Correct: *I* walk a mile every morning.

Take a look at a correct use of *me*:

   You should give your phone number to me for emergencies.

In this sentence, the pronoun *me* is the object of the preposition *to*.
   At times you may have trouble deciding whether to use a subject or object pronoun. Here's a trick you should know when you have a choice between two pro-

nouns: Try one pronoun at a time. For example, what would you do if you couldn't decide between these two pronouns?

I ran into Jack and (he/him) at the mall.

Using the previously mentioned trick, you would eliminate one pronoun and say the sentence, preferably out loud.

I ran into *he* at the mall.

I ran into *him* at the mall.

Which sounds better to you? Undoubtedly, you would say the second sentence sounds correct, and it is. The pronoun chart at the beginning of this section tells you that *he* is a subject pronoun, which cannot be used in this object position. By the way, *Jack* and *him* are objects of the preposition *into*.

Consider this issue another way:

Jack and (he/him) ran into Mel at the mall.

Which pronoun will you use? First, decide what the pronoun's function is in this sentence. You probably realize that you are choosing a subject pronoun. You can look at the pronoun chart to confirm your choice, or once again, you can eliminate one word in the subject to find the answer.

Him ran into Mel at the mall.

He ran into Mel at the mall.

Say it out loud, and your ear will tell you the correct statement.

Subject and object pronouns are also involved in comparisons. It's very easy to make a pronoun error when you say or write a comparison. For example:

Cindy liked the movie more than (she/her).

The first thing you have to know is that this is an *unfinished comparison*. The sentence means that Cindy liked the movie more than someone else did. In fact, the verb *did* is understood although not stated. Consequently, if you add *did* to the end of the sentence, which would you choose, *she* or *her*?

Cindy liked the movie more than (she/her) did.

The answer is now obvious to you:

Cindy liked the movie more than *she* did.

Keep this in mind: finishing the sentence also avoids any misunderstanding due to ambiguity. What else could the sentence mean? Cindy liked the movie more than her, meaning "her friend Lee"? Did Cindy like movies more than she liked her friend Lee? No, this is not the intention. When in doubt, finish the sentence.

Written Practice 3-8

Correct the pronoun errors in each of the following sentences.

1. Mac and me, and our families, share a camper.

   _____

2. I sent a letter of complaint to the salesperson and she.

   _____

3. I ate much more at dinner than her.

   _____

4. Give the results to Bonnie and she.

   _____

5. You and them play cards every weekend, don't you?

   _____

6. Shelley has voted in more elections than him.

   _____

7. You could give he your house key.

   _____

8. The cat and him are under the bed.

   _____

9. Blame it on him and I.

_____

10. She takes the children to the playground more than him.

_____

Ownership Pronouns

When pronouns seem to take the role of adjectives, that is, modifying or describing another word, they can cause confusion. Let's clear that up right now. The fact is that a personal pronoun sometimes shows ownership:

Our choosing a car became a difficult issue.

Whose choice of cars was it? It was _ours_.

Your losing weight is the only thing we talk about!

Whose loss of weight was it? It was _yours_.

I know that you oppose _my_ leaving the meeting early.

Whose leaving was it? It was _my_ leaving.

What do the phrases _our choosing_, _your losing_, and _my leaving_ have in common? They are all introduced by a personal ownership pronoun that is then followed by an -_ing_ ending verb known to grammarians as gerunds. What is so interesting about English is that you can take a verb that ends in -_ing_ and have it perform as a noun would. For example:

Our choosing a car became a difficult issue.

In the preceding sentence, what is the subject? If you said _Our choosing_, you won the grammar prize! The gerund phrase acts as a noun and functions as the subject. The ownership pronoun, _Our_, does the job of an adjective and modifies _choosing_. Look at the rest of the sentence. What is the verb in the sentence? It is _became_.

Written Practice 3-9

Refer to the list at the top of page 61 to find the ownership pronouns. Then correct the pronoun errors in each of the following sentences.

1. Me buying a car without consulting you was a mistake.

   _____

2. Them charging me too much was also a mistake.

   _____

3. Jorge was thrilled about she choosing me to lead the discussion.

   _____

4. She staying one extra day was no problem to the Santos family.

   _____

5. Them fighting all the time gave all of us a headache.

   _____

Mirror Pronouns

The mirror pronouns are used for emphasis. They reflect the action back to the subject. For example:

Melania *herself* caused the problem.

This sentence makes it clear that the problem was caused exclusively by the subject, Melania. You just need to remember two things: Don't overuse this kind of pronoun, and when you do use one, choose the correct form. You can review the mirror pronouns in the chart provided earlier. The following usage is correct:

You *yourself* asked me to take on this project.

Yourself reflects the asking back to the subject, *you.*

The following example is incorrect:

My boss suggested the project to Harry and *myself.*

This sentence is an example of the overused mirror pronoun. What's wrong with this use of *myself*? Locate the subject and verb: *boss* (subject), *suggested* (verb). *Project* is the object of the verb suggested. Is there any word that *myself* can logically mirror? No. Also, if you recall, the word *to* is a preposition and it can be used to introduce a prepositional phrase (*to Harry and myself*). If written correctly, a prepositional phrase ends with an object noun or pronoun. As the pronoun chart indicates, *me* is the object pronoun required in this phrase. The sentence should read:

My boss suggested the project to Harry and me.

COMMON ERRORS

Do not *ever* use the words *hisself* or *theirselves.* They are examples of nonstandard English.

Incorrect: He hisself answered the door.
Correct: He *himself* answered the door.

Incorrect: They moved the couch theirselves.
Correct: They moved the couch *themselves.*

Written Practice 3-10

Delete the incorrect pronoun and insert the correct one in each of the following sentences.

1. They took their cat and theirselves to the beach.

   _____

2. Larry and myself eat lunch together every day.

   _____

3. Marty asked hisself an important question.

   _____

4. All of you yourself have to make that decision.

_____

5. Ken sent an email to the team leader and ourself.

_____

Relative Pronouns

Relative pronouns allow you to show the relationship between a subordinate clause and the main clause. The main clause is always the one that can stand alone, while the subordinate clause cannot. A relative pronoun links the two. Of course, since these words are pronouns, they—just as all other pronouns—can stand in for nouns. For example:

Willie left the office to visit Mike, who was recovering in the hospital.

The relative pronoun _who_ links the main clause, _Willie left the office to visit Mike_, to the subordinate clause, _who was recovering in the hospital._

Recalling Chapter 1, you realize that the subordinate clause is a fragment if it stands alone:

Can stand alone: Willie left the office to visit Mike.

Cannot stand alone: who was recovering in the hospital.

Relative pronouns include both _definite_ and _indefinite_ varieties. Definite pronouns are _which_, _that_, and _who_ or _whom_. Indefinite pronouns include _what_, _which_, _who_, _whatever_, _whoever_, and _whomever_. The major difference between definite and indefinite pronouns is that, once again, the choice is ruled by the word's function. Definite pronouns can stand in for a noun in the sentence:

Jorge married Marielle, who had a child from her first marriage.

In this sentence, _who_ stands in for _Marielle_. In addition, you should know that the name Marielle is the antecedent, which is the word that comes before and relates to the pronoun—in this case, _who_.

Who, Whom, That, or *Which*?

Remember a few simple rules regarding the pronouns *who, whom, that,* and *which*. Once again, some pronouns can be used as subjects, while others are objects. Remember this when you are trying to choose between *who* and *whom*:

Who is the CEO of the company? (*Who* is the subject of the sentence.)

Whom did you vote for in the election? (Turn the question around: You did vote for whom in the election? *You* is the subject, *did vote* is the verb, and *whom* is the object of the preposition *for*.)

It may not be much consolation, but many, many people confuse the use of the words *who* and *whom*. Your goal should be to use them correctly, but don't be surprised if you frequently hear and see them used incorrectly.

Here are other important rules:

1. Use *who* and *whom* to refer to people: I didn't know *who* you were until yesterday.
2. Use *that* to refer to people, animals, and things: The trip *that* I loved took us to Italy.

If you want to ask a question, you will at some point need to use a question pronoun—*what, which, who,* or *whom*. For example:

Who took my pen?

What is today, Saturday or Sunday?

Who knows?

Whom do you ask for advice? (Notice the objective form, *whom*. Turn the sentence around to distinguish between the subject and the object: You do ask *whom* for advice? *You* is the subject and *whom* is the object.)

Consider which question pronoun is correct in each of the following sentences:

(Who/Whom) left early?

Who is correct because it is the subject of the sentence.

COMMON ERRORS

Never use *which* to refer to people. For example:

Incorrect: The person which is in charge is my least favorite woman in the group.
Correct: The person who (or that) is in charge is my least favorite woman in the group.

About (who/whom) were you speaking?

Whom is correct because it is the object of the preposition *about*.

Distinguish between *that* and *which*—a frequent error—according to the kind of clause you use, one that is critical and necessary to the sentence or one that is not. *Which* clauses require commas to show that this part of the sentence could be left out:

Her dog, which barks every morning at 5 A.M., should live on a farm.

In this sentence, the clause, *which barks every morning*, is not absolutely critical to the meaning of the sentence. The main part of the sentence could stand on its own:

Her dog should live on a farm.

The pronoun *which* is called parenthetical: as you can see, it is incidental and can be left out of the sentence without affecting the meaning. Other examples:

The coat, *which is Robert's*, was found in the theater.

The coat—whether or not it belongs to Robert—was found in the theater.

The house, *which my brother designed*, will be ready for spring occupancy.

The house—whether or not my brother designed it—will be ready for spring occupancy.

On the other hand, *that* clauses are critical to the meaning of a sentence:

The dress *that* Avi designed sold the most.

The word *that* tells who designed the dress that sold the most.

The computer *that* is on Inga's desk is the next to be updated.

The word *that* tells which computer of all the ones in the office is next to be updated.

Demonstrative Pronouns

That, *those*, *these*, and *this* are pronouns that point to the thing being talked about. Again, the demonstrative pronoun has to be able to take the place of a noun, just as all pronouns do. In some contexts, however, the demonstrative pronoun does the job of an adjective; it describes the noun. For example:

Those are my choices for the dinner menu. (*Those* means the same as the word *choices* and can stand in for it.)

Other examples:

Pronoun: *This* is my new computer. (*This* means the same as the word *computer* and can stand in for it.)

Adjective: *This* computer has so much more memory. (*This* describes *computer* and acts like an adjective.)

Written Practice 3-11

For each of the following sentences, decide whether the demonstrative pronoun functions as a pronoun or an adjective.

1. These are the CDs I just bought. _____

2. Those CDs were not my first choice. _____

3. I gave this same schedule to everyone. _____

4. That is a very big job! _____

5. This is my first project for the company. _____

Indefinite Pronouns

Indefinite pronouns are just that—unclear. They replace nouns without specifying which ones they replace. In other words, they do not take the place of particular nouns.

Singular indefinite pronouns: another, anybody, anyone, anything, each, either, everybody, everyone, everything, little, much, neither, nobody, no one, nothing, one, other, somebody, someone, something

Plural indefinite pronouns: both, few, many, others, several

Singular or plural indefinite pronouns: all, any, more, most, none, some

The confusion surrounding indefinite pronouns has to do with deciding their number and gender. Singular indefinite pronouns take singular verbs or singular personal pronouns. For example:

Incorrect: Each of the members have one vote.

Correct: Each of the members has one vote.

Because the subject *each* is singular, *has* is correct.

Incorrect: One of the girls gave up their seat.

Correct: One of the girls gave up her seat.

Because *her* refers to *one*, it is singular.

As you would expect, plural indefinite pronouns take plural verbs or plural personal pronouns:

Correct: A few of the teenagers were voicing their disapproval.

Because the subject *few* is plural, so are the verbs *were* and *their*.

Because some indefinite pronouns can be singular or plural, your choice depends on what the indefinite pronoun refers to:

Correct: All of the people clapped their hands.

Because *all* refers to *people*, which is plural, use *their*, a plural pronoun.

Correct: All of the delivery was soaked.

Because *all* refers to *delivery*, which is singular, use a singular verb, *was*.
The pronouns that end with *-body* or *-one*, such as *anybody*, *somebody*, *no one*, or *anyone*, are singular. *Each* and *every* are singular, while words such as *all* or *some* may be singular. That means that a possessive pronoun referring to these singular words must also be singular:

Each boy received *his* gift as he left the party.

In former times, standard written English allowed the use of the pronoun *his* to refer to a singular indefinite pronoun whether or not genders were clear:

Each received *his* gift as *he* left the party.

Today, if you don't know whether all who attended were male, you need to write *his or hers*:

Each received *his or her* gift as *he or she* left the party.

This makes an awkward sentence. A better alternative is to rewrite the sentence:

Upon leaving, *each* guest received a gift. (Each guest could be male or female.)

Upon leaving, guests received *their* gifts.

Guests, plural, could be male or female. Plural personal pronouns, such as *their*, in English are neither masculine nor feminine.
Be sure to use singular indefinite pronouns with singular verbs or singular personal pronouns.

Written Practice 3-12

Correct the pronoun in each of the following sentences. Review the previous explanations as you make your choices.

1. Whom is your brother?

   _____

2. The food which I eat every night must contain protein.

   _____

3. This is her brother Timothy who I have known for years.

   _____

4. The medicines which arrived in the mail are not the ones I need.

   _____

5. Whom is the new president of the board?

   _____

6. One of the men lift 200 lbs.

   _____

7. All of the groceries which arrive every afternoon are from ACE Market.

   _____

8. The puppy whom we chose was four months old.

   _____

9. Everybody in the community receive free coupons from that company.

   _____

10. At the end of the meeting each participant received his certificate.

    _____

Written Practice 3-13

In each of the following sentences, circle the incorrect pronoun. Then write your correction on the line provided.

1. Jose and me have a lot in common.

   _____

2. Every morning, Jamie brings coffee for Samantha and I.

   _____

3. Please don't give me nothing for Christmas!

   _____

4. Me and Cari can't return the favor.

   _____

5. We ran into Jesse and she at the elementary school.

   _____

6. Abby bakes better than her.

   _____

7. The police were very upset about me leaving the scene.

   _____

8. My friend Marilyn suggested a menu to myself.

   _____

9. One of the club members had to give up their membership.

   _____

10. Whom is in charge here?

   _____

QUIZ

Choose the correct word or phrase in each of the following sentences.

1. Antonio (had driven/drove) for us before we hired someone new.
2. I (will have word processed/had word processed) for twenty-six hours by the time I finish for the week.

3. Lightning struck and we (had smelled/smelled) smoke immediately.

4. We think our dog of all the dogs we know (is/are) the smartest.

5. (We/Us) are in charge of the Halloween party this year.

6. (Him/He) and (me/I) do this every October.

7. You shouldn't make a decision dependent upon (me/my) going.

8. Kenny (hisself/himself) is responsible for our downfall.

9. Lawrence left the studio (which/that) is to the left of the gym to conduct a Pilates class.

10. (Whom/Who) is talented enough to direct the play?

Circle the letter of the word or phrase that best completes or corrects each sentence.

1. It looks as if we will be working together on this soon, they asked me about it the other day.

   (a) soon. they

   (b) soon. They

   (c) soon? They

   (d) soon? they

2. The deer run in our yard with the longest antlers.

   (a) The deer in the yard with the longest antlers run.

   (b) The deer ran in our yard with the longest antlers.

   (c) The deer with the longest antlers run in our yard.

   (d) Many deer was running in our yard with the longest antlers.

3. You have all the measurements now I'm going to call John to hear what he has to say.

   (a) measurements; now

   (b) measurements, now

   (c) measurements. Now

   (d) both a and c

4. Your house, in this group of seven houses, look the best.

   (a) is looking the best.

   (b) looks the best

   (c) has been looking the best.

   (d) had been looking the best.

5. Looking at our new furniture when it arrived.

   (a) Looking at our new furniture; when it arrived!

   (b) Looking at our new furniture when it arrived made me happy!

    (c) Looking at our new furniture when it arrived and making me doubt my choice.

    (d) Looking at our new furniture. When it arrived!

6. The children in our family rides bikes.

    (a) ride's

    (b) ride

    (c) riding

    (d) ridding

7. Yesterday we went to the local market and shop for fresh vegetables.

    (a) shoped

    (b) shops

    (c) shopped

    (d) shopping

8. Gas in our cars disappear very quickly.

    (a) disappears

    (b) will be disappeared

    (c) was disappeared

    (d) should be disappeared

9. Each day I consult my horoscope, and if I liked it, I carry it with me.

    (a) liking it,

    (b) have been liking it,

    (c) have liked it,

    (d) like it,

10. Me arriving late threw the schedule off completely.

    (a) Me arriving late cleared the schedule completely.

    (b) Me having arrived late threw the schedule off completely.

    (c) Me and him having arrived late threw the schedule off completely.

    (d) My arriving late threw the schedule off completely.

11. The guests lingers at the door.

    (a) lingering

    (b) are lingered

    (c) is lingering

    (d) linger

12. We have chose chocolate ice cream for the last time.

    (a) has chose

    (b) have chosen

    (c) has chosen

    (d) have choosing

13. All ten candidates for the office presents their positions today.

    (a) has presents

    (b) have presents

    (c) present

    (d) presenting

14. Her collection of stamps include many from around the world.

    (a) was including

    (b) am included

    (c) is including

    (d) includes

15. The last book on the shelves fall to the floor every day.

    (a) falls

    (b) falled

    (c) felled

    (d) was falled

16. She walked on the treadmill for thirty minutes every day for a month.

    (a) have walked

    (b) has walked

(c) have been walking

(d) walks

17. They should have came out to meet us.
    (a) comes
    (b) have come
    (c) have coming
    (d) have comes

18. The money was returned to her and myself.
    (a) to her and himself
    (b) to her and hisself
    (c) to her and mine
    (d) to her and me

19. She should have went home.
    (a) should've went
    (b) should have been
    (c) should have gone
    (d) should have came

20. If you wanted to save money, you should have rode the bus.
    (a) having ridden
    (b) have ridden
    (c) have always rode
    (d) have rided

21. Him and me bought a motorcycle together.
    (a) Me and him
    (b) He and I
    (c) He and me
    (d) I and him

22. This is the worse meal I've ever had.

    (a) better

    (b) worser

    (c) worst

    (d) baddest

23. Admit that his is the beautifulest car you've ever seen!

    (a) beautifuler

    (b) most beautifulest

    (c) more beautifuler

    (d) most beautiful

24. I haven't felt good since the weather changed.

    (a) felt as good

    (b) haven't been good

    (c) felt well

    (d) felt so good

25. Daniella plays golf so good.

    (a) so well

    (b) really good

    (c) real good

    (d) really goodly

26. The puppies in the doghouse is adorable.

    (a) has been adorable

    (b) are adorable

    (c) is being adorable

    (d) was adorable

27. The guests in the living room seems uncomfortable.

    (a) do seems

    (b) are seeming

(c) they seems

(d) seem

28. Its about time we went home.

(a) Its'

(b) It's

(c) Its almost

(d) I'ts

29. It ain't ever late enough to go home!

(a) is'nt

(b) aint'

(c) isn't

(d) ain't never

30. The dog moved it's puppies every time we came near.

(a) its'

(b) it's own

(c) its

(d) I'ts

31. I dieted for six months, and I'm still waging the battle.

(a) have dieted

(b) was dieted

(c) was dieting

(d) having

32. Before I concluded the first page of my report, I knew it was inadequate.

(a) am concluding

(b) had concluded

(c) I having concluded

(d) are concluding

33. When the popular singer came on stage, the audience had roared.

    (a) audience be roaring

    (b) had been roaring

    (c) audience roared

    (d) will be roaring

34. Our group of eight people were waiting for the train.

    (a) are waiting

    (b) weren't waiting

    (c) was waiting

    (d) aren't waiting

35. The puppy belongs to Anton with the brown and white spots.

    (a) The puppy with the brown and white spots belongs to Anton.

    (b) The puppy and the white spots belong to Anton.

    (c) The puppy with the brown and white spots belong to Anton.

    (d) The puppy with the brown and white spots belonging to Anton.

36. Us and our neighbors share the driving.

    (a) Us and them share the driving.

    (b) Our neighbors and us share the driving.

    (c) Them neighbors share the driving with us.

    (d) Our neighbors and we share the driving.

37. I like classical music much more than her.

    (a) I like classical music more than she.

    (b) I like classical music much more than her, don't I.

    (c) I like classical music much more than she does.

    (d) I like classical music much more than her does.

38. Them and you go bowling once a week, don't you?

    (a) You and them go bowling once a week, don't you?

    (b) Them and you go bowling once a week, don't you?

     (c) They and you go bowling once a week, don't you?

     (d) Them and you go bowling once a week, don't they?

39. Him working late every night became a problem for the family.

     (a) Him working late every night becomed a problem for the family.

     (b) Him working late every night becomes a problem for the family.

     (c) Him working late every night became a problem for him and the family.

     (d) His working late every night became a problem for the family.

40. Them lighting the Christmas tree was fine with us.

     (a) Them lighted the Christmas tree was fine with us.

     (b) His lighting the Christmas tree was fine with us.

     (c) Him and her lighting the Christmas tree was fine with us.

     (d) Them and their family lighting the Christmas tree was fine with us.

41. John took the whole problem on hisself.

     (a) John took the whole problem on himself.

     (b) John and Dina took the whole problem on theirselves.

     (c) John took the whole problem on hiself.

     (d) On hisself, John took the whole problem.

42. Jamie and myself usually solve the problems easily.

     (a) Jamie and me usually solve the problems easily.

     (b) Jamie and myself usually solve the problems easy.

     (c) Jamie and theirselves usually solve the problems easily.

     (d) Jamie and I usually solve the problems easily.

43. Each of your choices were the right ones.

     (a) Each of your choices was the right ones.

     (b) Each and every of your choices were the right ones.

     (c) Each of your choices was the right one.

     (d) All of your choices was the right ones.

44. Whom left the lid off the jar?

    (a) Whom was it who left the lid off with you?

    (b) Who left the lid off the jar?

    (c) Whom lifted the lid off the jar?

    (d) Whom used the jar last?

45. Living in the mountains has been invigorating so we've decided to build a cabin here.

    (a) . . . invigorating? so we've decided . . .

    (b) . . . invigorating; so we've decided . . .

    (c) . . . invigorating. so we've decided . . .

    (d) . . . invigorating, so we've decided . . .

46. The weather both wet and gray for a week.

    (a) The weather wet, gray, and dismal for a week.

    (b) The weather, wet, gray, and dismal, wearing us down.

    (c) The weather, wet, gray and dismal, has worn us down.

    (d) The weather wet and dismal wearing us down.

47. I want to take a class at the adult school getting out of the house at night is frequently a problem my young children don't always cooperate.

    (a) I want to take a class at the adult school getting out of the house at night is frequently a problem. My young children don't always cooperate.

    (b) I want to take a class at the adult school. Getting out of the house at night is frequently a problem. My young children don't always cooperate.

    (c) I want to take a class at the adult school. Getting out of the house at night is frequently a problem my young children don't always cooperate.

    (d) I want to take a class at the adult school, getting out of the house at night is frequently a problem, my young children don't always cooperate.

48. The child ran into the classroom shouting, "I brung my lunch today! I choosed a peanut butter and jelly sandwich."

    (a) The child ran into the classroom shouting, "I bringed my lunch today! I choosed a peanut butter and jelly sandwich."

    (b) The child ran into the classroom shouting, "I brung my lunch today! I chose a peanut butter and jelly sandwich."

    (c) The child ran into the classroom shouting, "I packed my lunch today! I choosed a peanut butter and jelly sandwich."

    (d) The child ran into the classroom shouting, "I brought my lunch today! I chose a peanut butter and jelly sandwich."

49. Every day this week I lay my car keys on the kitchen counter when I came home.

    (a) Every day this week, I laid my car keys on the kitchen counter when I came home.

    (b) Every day this week, I lied my car keys on the kitchen counter when I came home.

    (c) Every day this week, I lain my car keys on the kitchen counter when I came home.

    (d) Every day this week, I have lain my car keys on the kitchen counter when I have come home.

50. Elliot had to remind hisself to set his alarm each night.

    (a) Elliot had to say to hisself to set his alarm each night.

    (b) Elliot had to say to hisself, "set this alarm each night."

    (c) Elliot had to remind himself to set his alarm each night.

    (d) Elliot had to remind hisself and it was to set his alarm each night.

ALL ABOUT PUNCTUATION AND CAPITALIZATION

CHAPTER 4

Punctuation: End Marks and Commas

In this chapter, you will learn:

Brief History of Punctuation
Period
Question Mark
Exclamation Point
Comma

Brief History of Punctuation

GobackmanyyearstotheGreeksandRomansthisiswhatyouwouldhaveread

After reading the preceding sentence, are you convinced that punctuation and spacing are absolute necessities? In fact, it has taken many, many years to reach this conclusion. Indeed, before the ninth century A.D., very early writing did not even require space between words. Some credit the Romans with using dots between words, while medieval scribes used pictures of birds, flowers, and daggers or other marks to indicate a pause. Since rhetoric, the study of oratory or public speaking, was an important course of study, early punctuation was not based on sentence structure, but rather on how a manuscript could be made readable.

The invention of the printing press by Johannes Gutenberg in 1436 was the stimulus for a new system of punctuation. To reach larger and larger audiences, books needed to be readable. Although earlier medieval writers used marks to show where a reader might pause, their punctuation was different from today's punctuation. One slash mark indicated a short pause and three indicated a long pause. Aldus Manutius (1449–1515), the Renaissance printer, used a period to indicate a full stop at the end of a sentence and a diagonal slash to represent a pause. For another two hundred years, printers experimented with various symbols, but it was not until the late 1600s and early 1700s that punctuation became consistent. Dr. Ben Jonson, a dramatist, authored *English Grammar* in 1617 (published in 1640 after his death), in which punctuation was used syntactically, or according to sentence structure. Although the way Dr. Jonson explained the need for punctuation might not be very clear today, it is instructive:

> For, whereas our breath is by nature so short, that we cannot continue without a stay to speake long together; it was thought necessarie, as well as for the speakers ease, as for the plainer deliverance of things spoken, to invent this meanes, whereby men pausing a pretty while, the whole speech might never the worse be understood.

Translation: Punctuation makes a sentence easier to understand.

That brings us to a particular, present-day problem. Is it acceptable to send an e-mail without proper punctuation and capitalization? It all depends upon whether you care what the recipient thinks about you as he or she reads your message. Lack of punctuation and capitalization may speak to some recipients as a lack of education, intelligence, and professionalism. You need to decide if this matters to you. Certainly, any business e-mail you send should have the same high standards you maintain in anything else you might write and sign. So let's start where the elders started—with end marks.

Period

The period is used to indicate a complete pause in thought.

RULES FOR USING A PERIOD

1. End a sentence with a period.

   Correct punctuation promotes comprehension.

2. Put a period after abbreviations.

   Jan. 1st, Mr. Letterman, A.M., 97 Main St., e.g.

3. Place a period inside quotation marks.

   Mack said, "I'll be back at 9 P.M. to pick you up."

4. Do not end a sentence with a period if it already ends with another end mark such as an exclamation point or question mark.

   Will you leave for training soon?

5. Do not use a period at the end of a sentence that is enclosed in parentheses and embedded in another sentence.

   When the trainee heard that she was accepted into the program (she had harbored no hope at all), she was very excited.

6. Use a period at the end of a sentence that is enclosed in parentheses but stands alone.

   When the trainee heard that she was accepted into the program, she was very excited. (She had harbored no hope at all.)

7. Use only one period at the end of a sentence when the sentence ends in an abbreviation.

   After school, I'm going to work for All Things Computer, Inc.

NOTE: *Some widely known acronyms (short forms of names or organizations) do not require periods:*

NBC, UNICEF, NFL, YWCA, CIA, FBI

This also applies to two-letter state abbreviations in zip codes:

NY, NJ, CA, MA

In the practice that follows, apply what you have just reviewed in the preceding seven rules. If you are in doubt about any answer, return to the rules for guidance.

Written Practice 4-1

For each of the following sentences, insert periods wherever necessary.

1. When I exercise, I want to see results
2. Ted and Amy enjoy the new bike path in their state
3. Music is an important part of my life (as I'm sure you know)
4. Finally, add 1 tbsp of butter and 1 tsp of salt
5. According to my coach, I need more confidence in order to pitch a good game
6. She said, "Don't run over the bike" (She was thinking of her shrinking budget)
7. I'm going to the YWCA after school, but I'll be home by 6 PM
8. Mr and Mrs Levitt met us for lunch
9. Mike and Mary are known as Capt and Mrs Murphy
10. Go to 77 Long Rd and wait for me

Written Practice 4-2

Of course, you need to use correct punctuation in paragraph forms. Look carefully as you read from one sentence to the next, and it will be clear where end marks are needed. Read the following paragraphs, and insert periods wherever they are needed.

Paragraph 1

Scientists have reached important conclusions regarding the connection between children's social disadvantages and their health risks Doctors considered three main social disadvantages: poverty, low parental education, and single parent household According to Dr Ruth S Stein, children with all three risk factors were twice as

likely as children with none to have a chronic health condition such as diabetes, asthma, or mental retardation

Paragraph 2

Where does chocolate come from? Actually, it *does* grow on trees It all starts with a small tropical tree, the Theobroma cacao, usually simply called "cacao" (It is pronounced ka-KOW *Theobroma* is Greek for "food of the gods") Cacao is native to Central America and South America, but it is grown commercially throughout the tropics About 70 percent of the world's cacao is grown in Africa

A cacao tree can produce close to two thousand pods per year The ridged, football-shaped pod, or fruit, of the cacao grows from the branches and, oddly, straight out of the trunk The pods, which mature throughout the year, encase a sticky, white pulp and about thirty or forty seeds The pulp is both sweet and tart; it is eaten and used in making drinks The seeds, were you to bite into one straight out of the pod, are incredibly bitter Not at all like the chocolate that comes from them

It's actually a perfect design The fruit attracts forest animals, like monkeys, who eat the fruit but cast the seeds aside, dispersing them and allowing new trees to sprout up (One of my favorite memories of a recent trip to Costa Rica was watching monkeys eating in a "chocolate" tree) It's hard to imagine why humans ever thought to do anything with the seeds.*

Question Mark

The question mark, another end mark, has an obvious use: It is used to ask a question or make an inquiry:

Are you coming?

Did Jack say you were coming?

Again, when you use a question mark, do not use any other end mark. The exception, of course, is when an abbreviation precedes the question mark. For example:

Did you say that Jack is starting his job at All Things Computer, Inc.?

---

*Adapted with permission from facts-about-chocolate.com.

When question marks are used with quotations, their usage is a bit more complicated, but very logical. Look at the following examples:

Did you know that Gwen said, "I'm a totally different person than the one I was as a teen"?

Gwen said, "Did you know that I'm a totally different person than the one I was as a teen?"

In the first sentence, the question refers to the entire sentence, not just the quoted part, so the question mark is placed outside the quotes. In the second sentence, the quoted portion is the question, so the question mark is placed inside the closing quotation marks.

For the following exercises, review the previous examples and information to confirm the correct use of a question mark.

Written Practice 4-3

In each of the following sentences, find and correct the errors in the use of question marks.

1. Was it Marco who said, "Our train leaves at 10 P.M.?"
2. "Do you think the weather is warm enough to plant flowers," Elsa asked?
3. The doctor's assistant asked, "May I have your insurance card."?
4. The patient wondered if the secretary would require some form of ID as well?
5. I asked my daughter, "When will you ever be on time for our appointments"?

Written Practice 4-4

In the following paragraphs, insert or delete question marks wherever necessary.

Paragraph 1

My friend asked, "Have you heard about the link of lead exposure to Alzheimer's disease" She had just read the study from the University of Rhode Island that found a link between early exposure to lead in the environment and the onset of Alzheimer's disease much later in life? The scientists cautioned lead poisoning patients not to fear that their lead exposure would definitely lead to Alzheimer's disease. They said, "There are, after all, many other things that can affect a person between youth and old age, aren't there"?

Paragraph 2

Do you see the world around you going green Has your supermarket started charging for bags—either plastic or paper. Will you finally decide to ride your bicycle to the office to help reduce carbon emissions (not even considering the cost of gas.) Did you remember to turn off the lights before you left home (And if you didn't, will it bother you all day) Surely, you have switched to energy-efficient lightbulbs, or have you I guess we can agree that going green is not an easy thing to do, or can we There's a popular children's song that says it all: It's not easy being green!

Exclamation Point

The exclamation point is probably the simplest of all end marks. The only challenge is to *not overuse it*.

The detective cried, "This was definitely murder!"

Don't bother me!

I will never forget seeing the movie *The Great Houdini*!

The company had the nerve to say, "We won't cover that loss"!

Once again, note the use of the end mark either inside the quotation marks (e.g., the first example) or outside the quotation marks (e.g., the fourth example) depending upon the meaning of the sentence.

Written Practice 4-5

In each of the following sentences, insert an exclamation point or a question mark wherever one is needed.

1. "Are you absolutely certain that the food has no nuts in it" Rosa asked.
2. "You know that I would never give you anything that would harm you" her sister shouted.

3. Where's the nearest restaurant I'm starving.

4. Will you check the windshield wiper fluid before we leave.

5. "She infuriated me with all her requests" the teacher yelled.

6. Did you really mean to leave your purse in the car.

7. I'm going back for mine, are you.

8. My doctor asked me if I was taking vitamin D?

9. I lost the game Isn't that sad

10. You have finally learned to use question marks correctly Yeah

Written Practice 4-6

In each of the following sentences, insert or delete the period, question mark, or exclamation where necessary.

1. All national elections bring change; the 2008 presidential election was historic in bringing an African-American into the White House Oval Office

2. We kept hearing people ask, "Did you vote"

3. Don't you think that this was one of the most important statements uttered by President-Elect Obama: "I will always be honest with you about the challenges we face?"

4. When we went camping last summer, we saw a bear. We wanted to scream, "Run"!

5. When we finally agreed to go (remember my reservations.), it was too late in the day.

6. "Wait" he cried, "There's contamination in there."

7. Chef Antonia said, "I'll be back at 6 PM to serve the main course Don't disappoint me"!

8. If you're really late, you'll find us at 100 Linden St

9. Address that letter to Newark, N.J.

10. We left a note on the door regarding suspending deliveries (Anyone would understand not to leave packages while we were away)

Comma

The comma is the most misused punctuation mark. Since there are so many comma rules, it is understandable why people become confused about their use. Commas are supposed to help clarify sentences and note the logical pauses. Speaking of clarifying, how would you interpret the following sentence?

She stole money from me and Ralph who lived in the other room complained.

Whom did she steal money from? If the writer meant that he had money stolen from him or her, then the sentence would be clearer if a comma were inserted after *me*. Then we understand that Ralph had no money stolen from him. He just complained.

The following are some rules you need to know to use the comma correctly.

RULES FOR USING THE COMMA

1. To ensure clarity, use commas to separate items in a series.

   Clear the bushes, pull the weeds, and plant the spring flowers.

2. Use commas to separate words or groups of words that interrupt the flow of the sentence.

   Hubert Humphrey, presidential hopeful, lost the election to
   Richard Nixon.

   Humphrey lost the election, if you recall, by only 1 percent of the
   popular vote.

3. Use a comma to separate more than one adjective describing the same word.

   The flourishing, bright, and imaginative summer garden lasts only a
   short while.

NOTE: *If the word* and *can be used between the adjectives, you need to use commas.*

   He wore a heavyweight business suit.

   In this example, you cannot use the word *and* between the adjectives *heavyweight* and *business*. Consequently, you should not insert a comma between the two words.

4. Use a comma to separate introductory words from the main part of the sentence, that is, from the part that can stand alone.

> Before Michael Jordan retired from basketball, he was my favorite player.

5. Insert a comma when the words *nevertheless*, *however*, *inasmuch as*, and *therefore* interrupt a complete thought.

> Unfortunately for Hubert Humphrey, however, his views on Vietnam alienated him from his former supporters.

> Will we ever, therefore, find a way to rationalize that war?

Written Practice 4-7

In each of the following sentences, insert commas where necessary.

1. Having a new sleek sports car is still just a dream.
2. This summer I'm going to paint the house get estimates for a fence and lose ten pounds.
3. While I waited for the estimator to arrive I looked at many paint colors.
4. A friend of mine a recent graduate is working hard to write an excellent résumé.
5. Your job however will be to finish cleaning the basement.

MORE COMMA RULES

6. Insert a comma to separate two complete thoughts (independent clauses) that are connected by a word such as *and*, *but*, *nor*, *yet*, *for*, and *or*.

> The sun rises in the morning, and it sets in the evening.

> We had an invitation to an elegant party, but we cancelled when we both got the flu.

NOTE: *When the clauses on both sides of the comma are complete thoughts, each could stand alone.*

7. Use a comma to separate a direct quotation from the rest of the sentence.

   "When it started raining, did you offer your friends a ride home?"
   she asked.

   He replied, "No, but I waited with them until their bus arrived."
   "I can understand why you didn't want to insist," she said, "but
   next time, see if you can convince them to go with you."

8. Use commas to separate the day from the year and the year from the rest of
   the sentence.

   Do you expect to graduate on June 23, 2009?

   I graduated on June 23, 2009, and went directly into the Air Force.

9. Use a comma to separate the name of a city from the name of a state
   or country.

   We grew up in Austin, Texas.

   My favorite trip was to London, England.

10. A comma is used in both the salutation and the closing of a friendly letter.

    Dear Elizabeth,

    Sincerely,

    Rebecca

11. When a sentence *begins* with a complete thought followed by an incomplete
    thought, a comma is *not* necessary,

    Incorrect: I always eat a hearty breakfast, before any activity.

    Correct: I always eat a hearty breakfast before any activity.

12. When a sentence has one subject, a comma is not necessary to separate two
    verbs.

    Incorrect: Harry returned to the polling place, and picked up the car
    keys he had left in the booth.

    Correct: Harry returned to the polling place and picked up the car
    keys he had left in the booth.

    Note: Harry is the subject. He did two things, that is, he *returned* and *picked up*.

Once again, refer to the preceding rules if you have a question about comma use in the next two exercises. When you reach the final Written Practice, however, try to make all the changes and additions on your own. Of course, check the Answer Key to see how well you did.

Written Practice 4-8

In each of the following sentences, insert commas where needed.

1. I will finish this course on August 15 2010.
2. My best friend lives in Bend Oregon.
3. "I'm telling you to clean your room" Mother insisted.
4. Dear Eileen

    I know that you are eager to hear about my job search so I'll call you on Saturday.
    My best
    Pat
5. When I talked to Tom and Andy I asked them to be in charge of the flashlight batteries barbecue and tent.
6. A detailed lengthy letter explained his options.
7. March a month just before real spring is usually quite cold in New England.
8. Max was nevertheless our best choice for the job.
9. Unfortunately for W.H. Auden however his poems have been misquoted in modern novels.
10. Before our next book club meeting let's read all of his poems.

Written Practice 4-9

In the following paragraphs, insert or delete commas where necessary.

Paragraph 1

Founded in 1981 as Students Against Driving Drunk SADD's focus initially was to combat teen deaths due to drinking and driving. SADD has expanded its mission and name and now sponsors chapters called Students Against Destructive Decisions. SADD now focuses on prevention of all destructive behaviors and attitudes that are harmful to young people, including underage drinking substance abuse violence reckless driving depression and suicide. SADD's unique approach involves young people delivering education and prevention programming to their peers through school- and community-wide activities and campaigns responsive to the needs of their particular locations. Since its formation SADD has spread to all fifty states Canada New Zealand and many other international locations.*

Paragraph 2

Are you ready for a substitute for the mind-bending compelling puzzle Sudoku? Psychologists now assure us that ten minutes of talking visiting and establishing social contacts boost intellectual performance as much as doing crossword puzzles. A team of researchers asked more than 3,500 people between 24 and 96 years old about their social interactions and tested their memories. One researcher offered "We found the more the social contacts the higher the level of mental functioning."

Paragraph 3

You've heard the 30-minutes-of-exercise-per-day recommendation for some time but you can't seem to fit that into your schedule. Is all hope lost? No say the experts. Will short, spurts of moderate exercise help your fitness level? If you're doing nothing and you decide to walk briskly five days a week or even three days a week for 30 minutes, you will experience positive results. In addition you can do the 30 minutes all at once or in shorter segments of at least 10 minutes each. After three months you'll probably experience lower blood pressure and a smaller waistline.

Written Practice 4-10

In each of the following sentences, insert or delete commas where necessary.

1. Jim Hanfry a weekly player finally won the office lottery.
2. My summer garden always includes squash tomatoes and cucumbers.
3. Can we therefore consider the matter closed?
4. The oldest theater in town was torn down and a parking lot was built in its place.
5. Before the cold weather arrives I turn off the outdoor water spout.
6. You will have driven 1,500 miles by the time you reach Detroit Michigan.

---

*Adapted from healthfinder.gov/orgs/HR2094.htm.

7. "I understand how you feel about homework" Miss Emry said "but I still have to assign it."

8. When Lenny arrived the party became lively.

9. We had accepted the invitation a week earlier but we cancelled when two of our children became ill.

10. Send us a current skill-related résumé and we will schedule an interview for you.

QUIZ

Find and correct the punctuation errors in each of the following sentences.

1. John my friend will march at the wedding

2. "I would like to pay for everyone's expenses but I can't" Mona said

3. Callie will be stationed in Seoul South Korea

4. We first met however in Nashville Tennessee

5. That was on November 25 2008

6. Are you my friend or not

7. "Run for your lives" he screamed as we raced out of the building

8. Our itinerary included a long walk in the Muir Woods a kayak ride and a mountain-climbing expedition Whew That was a long day

9. After our two-week vacation we needed a rest

10. After all the investigation of global warming can we therefore call this Arctic melting a nonexistent problem

CHAPTER 5

More About Punctuation

In this chapter you will learn about:

Semicolon

Quotation Marks

Colon

Apostrophe

Dash and Hyphen

Parentheses and Brackets

Semicolon

Ben Jonson (1572–1637), the English playwright, poet, and competitor to William Shakespeare, was the first notable writer from England to use the semicolon systematically. The semicolon is a strong mark of punctuation—stronger than the comma, but weaker than the period. The semicolon can be used to bring together complete thoughts that are closely related. The relationship between the two thoughts must be so clear that the reader immediately understands why the sentences are linked.

HOW TO USE A SEMICOLON

1. Use a semicolon between closely related independent clauses not joined by a coordinating conjunction.

    We've had extremely cold and wet weather this spring; my annual flowers are a month behind in growth.

    The new position makes weekend work mandatory; no one applied for the job.

2. Use a semicolon to connect independent clauses linked with a conjunctive adverb.

    I can't finish preparing the feast in one day; indeed, I may not be done in three days.

    I won't be able to take any time off; however, that doesn't mean you can't.

3. The semicolon is also used to connect other elements of equal weight. For example, use a semicolon between items in a series when the series contains internal punctuation.

    My territory includes Detroit, Michigan; San Jose, California; and Jacksonville, Florida.

    Among the conferees were John Litton, president of the Sun Awning Corporation; Leslie Martin, president of Paragon Computer; and Sue Daley, CEO of Environmental Sciences.

4. For clarity, use a semicolon to separate independent clauses that are joined by coordinating conjunctions when the clauses have internal punctuation that might lead to confusion.

> In most cases, the counselor in charge will communicate with the
>   parents; but on weekends, however, if the counselor in charge is
>   not available, Dr. Alper will take that responsibility.

Remember that semicolons are always followed by a lowercase letter, unless that letter begins a proper noun.

JOINING COMPLETE THOUGHTS WITH A SEMICOLON

A semicolon is a strong mark of punctuation that, unlike the period, can be used in the middle of a sentence to join two complete thoughts. Semicolons join independent clauses. You may recall that an independent clause is a group of words that contains a subject and a verb and expresses a complete thought.

You may recall the quote from John Kennedy's inaugural speech (cited in Chapter 7):

> Ask not what your country can do for you; ask what you can do for your
>   country.

Obviously, President Kennedy wanted the listener (reader) to fully appreciate how closely related the two thoughts were, that two requests existed simultaneously. In this case, a semicolon achieves this better than a period.

Go back much further to the King James Version of the Bible (1611) at Genesis. Read the first part of the second verse in Genesis:

> "And the earth was without form, and void; and darkness was upon the face of
>   the deep . . ."

In this verse, the semicolon allows the reader to explore and add a deeper meaning to the first clause. The basic idea here is that ". . . the earth was without form, and void." The next clause, "and darkness was upon the face of the deep," gives the reader further detail, a clearer idea of what the formless earth looked like.

Other examples:

> Two people started this project; only one person remains.

> Bindu has a four-year-old daughter; the child is being raised according to her
>   Indian heritage.

Either half of the Kennedy sentence as well as the preceding sentences could stand independently. Sometimes, however, for variety, we want to join thoughts that are closely related; we use a semicolon to do that. Otherwise, we might have a long series of not-too-interesting short sentences.

Notice that a comma would not work in place of the semicolon in the following sentence. In fact, you would create a common, serious error that is covered in Chapter 1: the run-on sentence. You cannot separate two complete thoughts with a comma:

Incorrect: Two people started this project, only one person remains.

You can, however, separate two thoughts with a comma and a conjunction in place of the semicolon. (Do you remember the conjunctions *for, and, but, or, yet,* and *so* introduced in Chapter 2?)

Correct: Two people started this project, *but* only one person remains.

In summary, you can write one sentence three ways, each being correct:

I don't like the terms of the contract. I will not sign it.

I don't like the terms of the contract; I will not sign it.

I don't like the terms of the contract, so I will not sign it.

Remember that you need a complete sentence on both sides of a semicolon:

Incorrect: While I've read through the complaint once; I'm not ready to sign it.

Correct: I've read through the complaint once; I'm not ready to sign it.

Which word in the first sentence makes the punctuation incorrect? The word *while* makes the first half of the sentence an incomplete thought. When you say the first sentence aloud, you want to ask, "What then?" Consequently, you can't use a semicolon. A comma would be correct.

While I've read through the complaint once, I'm not ready to sign it.

What's wrong with the following sentences?

Since I'm late already; I won't stop for coffee.

When the car stopped suddenly; my son was restrained by a seat belt.

If the seller accepts our offer; we'll be in our new house by June 1st.

The answer to the question asked before the examples is that the first half of each sentence is introduced by a word (i.e., *since*, *when*, *if*) that makes the introductory clause incomplete; it can't stand alone, so the semicolon is incorrect. Insert commas instead.

Since I'm late already, I won't stop for coffee.

When the car stopped suddenly, my son was restrained by a seat belt.

If the seller accepts our offer, we'll be in our new house by June 1st.

Written Practice 5-1

Using the preceding information, decide whether each of the following sentences is correctly punctuated. Insert semicolons where necessary.

1. No one will ever forget those Olympics, so many records were shattered.
2. My heart was set on the American winning, my dream was shattered.
3. Although I was so disappointed that we had lost; I watched the award ceremony anyway.
4. Kate accepted our earlier invitation to stay for the weekend a week later she cancelled because of illness.
5. The purchase of Alaska in 1867 helped America take its first steps to power in the Asia-Pacific region meanwhile Russian efforts ceased to expand trade and settlements on the Pacific coast of North America.

AVOIDING CONFUSION WITH SEMICOLONS AND COMMAS

Using a semicolon sounds easy enough; for variety, just join two complete thoughts with a semicolon instead of a period. Or join two complete thoughts with a comma plus a connecting word such as *and*, *but*, *or*. However, if you do this, there is the potential for a problem. On occasion, two complete and related thoughts *already contain commas*. What can you do to avoid confusion?

I usually buy organic blueberries, strawberries, and grapes; but I don't buy them as often when the prices go up in the winter.

Normally, as noted earlier, two related thoughts can be connected by a comma when you use the word *but*:

I usually buy organic strawberries, but I don't buy them as often when the prices go up in the winter.

However, with all the commas in the original first clause (*blueberries, strawberries, and grapes*), you need to avoid the confusion that too many commas can cause. When this occurs, use a semicolon before the small connecting word:

Candy, my calico cat, is not very large; but even though she never wins, she tries to fight the local dogs.

Finally, use a semicolon between items in a series that contains internal punctuation. For example:

There are beautiful historic mansions in Newport, Rhode Island; Lake Geneva, Wisconsin; and Hudson Valley, New York.

Minna scored 2,837,770 points; Marcia, 2,312,760; and Joie, 1,714,450.

This is sometimes called a *serial semicolon*—for obvious reasons.

Written Practice 5-2

Correct the punctuation errors in the following sentences.

1. We packed lunch, put suitcases in the car, and filled the gas tank, so we ended up leaving late.
2. Our to-do list included addressing Christmas cards, taking clothes and shirts to the cleaners, and buying several last-minute gifts, but when our dog became ill, there was no time to do any of it.
3. Trucks, vans, and recreational vehicles are required to use the right lane, but cars can use three left lanes.

4. Early settlers prepared as carefully as possible for the journey, drove across the country, and used natural resources as they needed them, but they didn't practice renewal or replacement.

5. The secretary took our health insurance information, the nurse led us upstairs, and the laboratory technician drew blood, yet we were just getting started in what had to be accomplished.

USING SEMICOLONS WITH CONJUNCTIVE ADVERBS

The connecting words in the previous sentences were all short ones—*but, yet, so*. What if the connecting word you need is a long word? The following longer connecting words (conjunctive adverbs) are always preceded by a semicolon and followed by a comma when used to connect two complete thoughts.

however	therefore	nevertheless	inasmuch as
moreover	consequently	otherwise	

For example:

The realtor, an old friend of mine, prepared the sales agreement; however, we held up the signing until our financing was approved.

Marcello, my Italian friend, is a chef in Florence; nevertheless, he is currently in Boston taking classes and demonstrating his amazing skills.

Written Practice 5-3

Use the preceding two examples to help you correct the punctuation errors in the following sentences.

1. Supposedly, we've been on a low carbohydrate diet for a long time nevertheless we continue to eat bread at lunchtime and cookies at night.

2. Remove your shoes at the door otherwise you'll have to take the responsibility of cleaning the floor again.

3. The country has made its decision therefore we must move through the future with confidence and determination.

4. You may not have received exactly the position you expected however you still have to offer your best work.

5. Before you buy an expensive houseplant ask the grower how much light the plant needs moreover ask questions about watering and feeding the plant.

Written Practice 5-4

Punctuate the following sentences correctly according to the rules you have learned.

1. David and I went home after work; while Chico went to the game.
2. In 1772, Lord Mansfield's decision outlawed slavery only in England it did not apply to British colonies.
3. The painters plan to repaint the entire house however we will not be able to replace the roof at the same time.
4. The day is cloudy, we cannot take pictures.
5. When you are ready for dinner, please call me and I although still at work will meet you.
6. Although all the dress stores have sales now I can't go shopping.
7. If you have ever overspent your budget you know how I feel therefore no one will convince me to shop.
8. We brought an umbrella for each of us because it was raining heavily when we left home
9. The new school year is about to begin consequently we're busier than ever preparing for it.
10. For the longest time Julia worked at the counter in the kitchen or in a corner of her bedroom finally she had an attached porch finished and heated for her workspace.

Written Practice 5-5

This exercise is a review of many punctuation rules. You should be able to easily correct the punctuation errors. If you find it difficult to do so, review Chapter 4 and this chapter before you go further. Read the following paragraphs, and insert or delete punctuation marks wherever necessary.

Paragraph 1

I'm not a big eater however chocolate is my downfall. I know that dark chocolate is actually good for me but how much do I really need "for my health?" Each meal ends with an immediate desire for the dark chocolate that I love, (add almonds and it's even better.). Now I'm feeling the results of all that pleasure my waistline shows the results. I'm now willing to forget how good it is for me moreover I want to lose the new inches I've gained!

Paragraph 2

People who are concerned about the health of our planet go beyond warnings about plastic bottles and efficient lightbulbs they want us to become vegetarians. They believe that the growing, and killing of more than 60 billion animals worldwide each year is a large part of the devastation brought on by the farming industry. Experts say that while it takes 25 gallons of water to grow a pound of wheat; it takes 2,500 gallons of water to produce a pound of beef.

Quotation Marks

Quotation marks are used to set off the exact words said by someone. Notice the difference between a direct and an indirect quotation:

Direct quotation: My doctor said, "You should worry more about taking antibiotics you don't need than about not taking one at all."

Indirect quotation: My doctor said that I should worry more about taking an antibiotic I don't need than about not taking one at all.

In the second sentence, which small word tells you that this is an indirect quotation, that you don't need quotation marks? The word is *that. That* introduces the report of something said.

Look at the following examples:

Incorrect: My doctor continued many upper respiratory infections are viral, so antibiotics won't help.

Correct: My doctor continued, "Many upper respiratory infections are viral, so antibiotics won't help."

Incorrect: She explained that "bacteria almost immediately learn how to override our prescription."

Correct: She explained that bacteria almost immediately learn how to override our prescription.

No quotations marks are needed. The word *that* makes this sentence a report of what the doctor said, not a direct quote.

Incorrect: She advised, always ask three questions before you accept the prescription: Is it necessary, is there a less powerful drug, and can I wait a few days to see if I get better?

Correct: She advised, "Always ask three questions before you accept the prescription: Is it necessary, is there a less powerful drug, and can I wait a few days to see if I get better?"

Remember to capitalize the first word in the direct quotation.

HOW TO USE QUOTATION MARKS

1. Use quotation marks to set off the exact words of a speaker. Place a comma between the speaker and the quoted words. A period is placed inside a quotation. A semicolon is placed outside the closing quotation mark.

   Alex said, "I can design a desk that will be large enough for the two of you to work at."

   You said, "Plan a partner's desk for me"; so I planned one.

2. When a quotation is broken, use quotation marks to set off both parts. Capitalize the first word of the second part of the quotation only if it is the beginning of a new sentence.

   "Well, how could we have been on time," she asked, "when the traffic was bumper-to-bumper the entire way?"

   "Well, how could we have been on time?" he complained. "The traffic was bumper-to-bumper the entire way!"

3. Never use two forms of punctuation at the end of a quotation. When the entire sentence is a question, but the quotation is not, place the question mark after the closing quotation marks.

Did you hear Henry say, "Give your time to the charity if you don't have any money to spare"?

Was Mark's request, "Be in early tomorrow, people," the last thing you heard before you left?

When the quoted portion is a question, place the question mark inside the quotation marks.

Henry said, "Can you give some of your time to the charity instead of giving cash?"

Alicia responded, "Can you give me time off so that I can give that time to charity?"

Written Practice 5-6

Many punctuation errors occur when you add punctuation marks to quotations. Find the errors in the following quotations.

1. Did the delivery person say, "Please leave the garage door open for the delivery?"
2. The toddlers' parent said, "The children are already bored with their Christmas presents and added "we'll reintroduce them in a month or so."
3. The store associate said, "Please give me your credit card number".
4. "Is this your correct card number," the associate asked?
5. "Did you tell me you'd arrive home with a dinner guest tonight." my wife often asked?

MORE ON HOW TO USE QUOTATION MARKS

4. Rule 3 in the previous section applies to the exclamation mark as well: Place it outside the quotation marks if it refers to the entire sentence; place it inside the quotation marks if it refers to the quotation only.

"Please give! We're desperate for cash to carry on our important work!" the director pleaded.

I'm sure you heard how furious I was when he said, "We'll meet again tomorrow and the next day as well"!

5. Use quotation marks to enclose titles of poems, articles, chapters, or any part of a book or magazine.

> The third chapter of *The ABC's of Evaluation* is entitled, "Decision Making: Whom to Involve, How, and Why."

6. Use a single quotation mark for a quotation within a quotation.

> Jason asked, "Can you tell me if Marc said, 'I've already paid off the cost of the repairs' when you discussed his financial situation?"

Written Practice 5-7

Correct any punctuation errors in the following sentences.

1. My friend asked are you having trouble staying on your budget
2. Do you have a computer he asked. There are websites that can help you keep track of where your money is going he continued.
3. My banker, Meg Leary, said websites have been used more and more since people started banking online
4. If you're going to use your computer for shopping please check the site's security measures my wife cautioned
5. May I help you set up an account the teller asked
6. First, I want to read all the cautions about online banking I told him.
7. He said "that was a really good idea."
8. Let me first try this on my own I told my instructor then you can tell what I did wrong.
9. That's an excellent idea she said because that way we can skip the skills that you have already acquired.
10. "Did you know that Kathy entered the room laughing hysterically" Fred asked?

Colon

Both the colon and the semicolon can be used to build better, more interesting sentences. Good writers use these marks of punctuation to build memorable sentences. You know that you can use a semicolon to join two sentences to create a compound sentence when the two thoughts are closely related. On the other hand, you can use a colon when the first sentence creates an expectation in the reader that the second sentence will explain, illustrate, or fulfill the idea stated in the first sentence.

We've quoted John F. Kennedy; now fast-forward to Barack Obama's one line in his speech to the Democratic Convention, August 2008.

> *That's the true genius of America: America can change.* Our union can be perfected. What we've already achieved gives us hope for what we can and must achieve tomorrow.

What does the colon accomplish in the first sentence? It clearly helps fulfill the expectation set in the first half of the sentence. What is the true genius of America? The answer follows the colon.

Here is another example of building ideas with punctuation from Barack Obama's acceptance speech in Chicago:

> And for the sake of our economy, our security, and the future of our planet, I will set a clear goal as President: In ten years, we will finally end our dependence on oil from the Middle East.

What is the clear goal? The answer follows the colon.

After all the rules you've learned about various punctuation marks, you'll find the colon has very few. However, the colon offers the writer an opportunity for variety in sentence structure; consequently, it is a valuable addition to your writing power.

HOW TO USE THE COLON

1. Use a colon to introduce a list, as in the following sentence.

   Assemble these ingredients for the cake: flour, sugar, baking powder, eggs, and vanilla

2. Use a colon to introduce an explanation.

   I have a motto about getting distasteful chores done fast: Make a list of the chores, put a limit on the time you will devote to the work, and start with the one you dislike the most.

When you use the colon correctly, the information that comes before the colon should be able to stand alone as a complete thought. Otherwise, you should not use a colon.

Incorrect: I ordered: potatoes, sugar, flour, eggs, and coffee.

Also, if the information that comes after the colon is a complete sentence (as in the first example for Rule 2), use a capital letter, as you would normally do in the beginning of a sentence.

Look at another example:

> Children will take up activities if you supply some good ideas for play: Color and paint in an art center that you create, cut up used holiday cards and paste them as stickers, choose a costume from a costume box and create a play or dance routine.

NOTE: *In the preceding sentence, the words before the colon could stand alone as a sentence. What would happen if you added the words* which are *after* good ideas for play*?*

> Children will take up activities if you supply some good ideas for play which are: color and paint in an art center that you create, cut up used holiday cards to paste as stickers, choose a costume from a costume box and create a play or dance routine.

You now see a common colon error. To avoid it, do not use a verb before the colon—in this case the verb is the word are.

Written Practice 5-8

Correct the colon errors in the following sentences.

1. Expect to do the following as a part of your job open the office at 8:30 A.M., take messages from the answering machine, and distribute the mail.

2. Find these files before you leave Premium Plumbers, Apex Office Furniture, and ABC Business Management.

3. The board members' places at the table were covered with these pages of information, an agenda for the meeting, a schedule of meetings for the year, and the bylaws.

4. Although we had never met before, the young man gave me much-too-much information he was asking his girlfriend to marry him, he had just received a raise, and he was going to shop for a new car.

5. If you go to the store, buy these, hammer, nails, and bathroom tiles.

OTHER USES OF THE COLON

Use a colon after the salutation in a business letter:

Dear Dr. Murphy:

Dear Mrs. Light:

Use a colon between numbers to show the time:

1:45 P.M.

Written Practice 5-9

Correct the colon errors in the following sentences.

1. You should also take the following warm clothes, boots, and raincoat.

2. Kindergarten dismisses at 1145 A.M.

3. We know you'll need the following for our camping trip a tent, bug spray, a flashlight, and easily prepared foods.

4. Dear Professor Keene,

5. Dear Ms. Boxer,

   I'm applying for the job you advertised in the *Times Weekly*.

6. Dear Mom and Dad:

7. Call me anytime after 900 A.M. on the weekends.

8. We'll meet at 12: Noon.

9. Take my advice on the following prepare your home for Christmas early, shop all year for small gifts, and learn to relax with your family.

10. We gave everyone a choice we could eat out, order in, or let everyone just choose something for themselves.

Written Practice 5-10

Read the following paragraphs. Use all that you have learned about punctuation to correct the sentences. The sentences are numbered for clarity in the Answer Key.

Paragraph 1

1. High school students know all about the Hubble Space Telescope in fact they can't even remember a time when it wasn't there. 2. The Hubble was launched in 1990 and it has already outlived its expected 15-year life span in addition it has seen its fifth and final repair mission.

Paragraph 2

1. Hubble entered our lives in the 1990s its advent paralleled the enormous growth in access to the Internet as a result everyone's computer was capable of bringing the magnificent images of the universe up close. 2. However Hubble is much more than pretty pictures interestingly it has generated more research papers than any other scientific instrument. 3. Before Hubble astrophysicists could never agree on the age of the universe some had said it was 10 billion years old while others had said 20 billion. 4. Hubble did the correct calculations our universe was born 14 billion years ago. 5. Hubble accomplishments include the following measuring the age of the universe, discovering that the Milky Way has a massive black hole in its center, and uncovering the role of "dark energy" in an expanding universe.

Apostrophe

For a very small mark of punctuation, the apostrophe can cause a big problem. You need to use it correctly for clarity, and here are the rules you need to know.

HOW TO USE AN APOSTROPHE

Use an apostrophe to show the omission of a letter. In the following three examples, the *o*'s are omitted.

You weren't (were not) expected until noon.

My other friend isn't (is not) coming.

There aren't (are not) enough days in a New England summer.

NOTE: *Ain't* *is not a word and is* never *acceptable in written or spoken English.*

Use an apostrophe to show possession. Apostrophes are placed differently according to whether the word is singular or plural as well as the way a particular word forms its plural.

Singular: The *printer's* door is jammed. (Singular *printer*: Place the apostrophe before the *s*.)

Plural: The three *executives'* offices face the parking lot. (Plural *executives*: Place the apostrophe after the *s*.)

Singular: That *deer's* temperament is so tame it eats from my hand. (Singular *deer*: Place the apostrophe before the *s*.)

Plural: The two adult *deer's* eating habits don't change with the seasons. (Plural *deer*: The word *deer* is spelled the same whether singular or plural; therefore, the apostrophe is placed the same.)

Singular: A *man's* car was found at the scene of the crime. (Singular *man*: Place the apostrophe before the *s*.)

Plural: All the *men's* cars were brought to the car wash. (Plural: The plural of *man* [*men*] requires an internal spelling change from *a* to *e*. The apostrophe is still placed before the *s*.)

Singular: The *lady's* hat was huge. (Singular *lady*: Place the apostrophe before the s.)

Plural: The *ladies'* monthly book club meeting was rescheduled. (Plural *ladies*: The plural of *lady* requires a change in the ending from *y* to *ies*. The apostrophe is placed after the *s*.)

Exceptions: *Its* is the possessive form of *it*. However, *it's* means *it is*. *His* and *hers* are the possessive forms of *he* and *she*.

The dog puts *its* ears back when it is angry. (Possessive form of *it*.)

It's a perfect day for a picnic. (*It's* means *it is*.)

Hers is the new Apple computer. (*Hers* is the possessive form of *she*.)

He picked up *his* daughter. (*His* is the possessive form of *he*.)

Use an apostrophe to indicate the plural of letters in order to avoid confusion.

A's, *B*'s, *I*'s, *L*'s, *v*'s, *c*'s, *W*'s, *Z*'s

Written Practice 5-11

In each of the following sentences, insert or delete apostrophes where necessary.

1. Our homes front yard needs new plantings.
2. Deb wasnt expected for hours.
3. The dog vigorously shook it's wet coat when it went for its walk.
4. Did anyone ever instruct you to dot your *i* s and cross your *t* s?
5. Its a long journey, isnt it?

Dash and Hyphen

Take a look at the small, but important, differences in length between a hyphen, en-dash, and em-dash. Hyphens and dashes look slightly different, and, in fact, they are used for different purposes:

hyphen - en dash – (the width of a capital *n*) em dash — (the width of a capital *m*)

EM DASH

Use em dashes—one on each side of the interrupting thought—to emphasize an interruption within a sentence. Remember this one caution: Don't overuse them.
Here's an example:

Call me if you're going to be late—even 15 minutes—or I will worry about you.

The preceding sentence shows an example of an em dash. As you saw, the em dash signaled an abrupt, emphatic break in the sentence. If your word processor lacks this character, just type two hyphens, with no space on either side.
The em dash can also be used to amplify a thought or indicate a sudden break:

Her painting was reminiscent of the great painters—Monet, Manet, Bonnard—who preceded her.

That car—that is, my first car—was my favorite.

Will she—can she possibly—be here on time?

In addition, the em dash can be used with another form of punctuation, a question mark or exclamation point:

Suddenly, my son—was he out of his mind?—yelled at the police officer.

EN DASH

The en dash is used chiefly to connect numbers and sometimes words.

They lived in Italy from 1989–1993. (The en dash means *to*.)

For tomorrow's class, read chapters 1–5.

The Boston–New York train leaves at 9 A.M.

The Boston Red Sox beat the NY Yankees 7–2.

When an en dash is used with the birth year, it means that the person is still alive.

Professor Sandford Jamison (1978–) coauthored the book.

The professor was born in 1978 and is still living.

HYPHEN

You may want to think of hyphens as spelling devices. Their most common use is to join compound words. Look at the following examples:

brother-in-law

weight-bearing

Use a hyphen to join two or more words serving as a single adjective before a noun:

able-bodied men and women

one-way streets

out-of-date equipment

chocolate-covered cake

On the other hand, if the compound modifiers come after the noun, don't use a hyphen:

The cake was chocolate covered.

Use a hyphen with compound numbers:

fifty-three

seventy-two

Use a hyphen with the prefixes *ex-* (meaning "former"), *all-*, *self-*; between a prefix and a capitalized word; with the suffix *-elect*; and with figures or letters:

ex-wife

all-included

self-proclaimed

all-American

governor-elect

mid-1960s

Use a hyphen to avoid confusion regarding meaning or to avoid an awkward combination of letters:

re-sign your name (not *resign* [leave a job])

semi-independent (vs. *semicircular*)

Use a hyphen when you need to break a word at the end of a line. Break between syllables:

un-til

re-fer-ral

com-pre-hen-sive

Break between double consonants in words ending in -*ing*. Otherwise, hyphenate at the suffix:

run-ning

sun-ning

driv-ing

fall-ing

At the end of a line, divide already-hyphenated words at the hyphen:

self-induced

mass-produced

Parentheses and Brackets

Use parentheses for words not strictly necessary to the main thought of the sentence. The rule of thumb is this: When you read the sentence, you should be able to skip the words in parentheses and still have the sentence make sense. If it doesn't, the parentheses are used incorrectly.

Use heavy-weight (bright white) printing paper

In this sentence, the meaning and intention are clear without the additional information in the parentheses.

Do not use a capital letter or final punctuation (except the question mark) within parentheses. For example:

I left for Arizona on a Friday (or was it Saturday?) last year.

I completed (somehow or other) five forms in 20 minutes.

Use parentheses to enclose letters or numbers that mark items in a list:

The chapters include (1) Birth to Six Months Old, (2) Six to 18 Months Old, (3) etc.

Note that parentheses do not change the final punctuation in a sentence:

The movie was written by Harvey Allen (1934–1998).

Of course, when the parentheses hold a complete sentence, the punctuation goes inside the parentheses:

The movie was written by Harvey Allen. (He was born in 1934.)

Use brackets within parentheses and within a quotation for clarity. For example:

We traveled in Europe (Italy [Florence and Rome], Belgium, and England).

Arben said, "We read famous short stories aloud [Poe and O. Henry] just for the fun of it."

Written Practice 5-12

In each of the following sentences, insert or delete the dash, parentheses, or brackets as needed.

1. Winter has arrived can you feel it in your mood? and we really need to find a sunny place for our vacation.
2. We bought new clothes slacks, shirts, underwear, shoes when the airline lost our clothes.
3. Tracy told me, "Toby is on a buying trip for her store California, Washington, and Arizona and won't return until Monday."
4. Toby is on a buying trip for her store California, wines, Washington, apples, and Arizona, jicama and won't return until Monday.
5. Choose a restaurant you know what she likes and we'll take her out for dinner.

Written Practice 5-13

In each of the following sentences, insert or delete punctuation as needed.

1. Did the firemen shout, "Sound the alarm?"!

2. Her mother said I agree to finish your work however youll have to pay me for my time.

3. Its not too late to change your mind.

4. I spoke to him your dad and he agreed with me.

5. Its warmer than 32 degrees we can take the scouts camping in the woods.

6. Although Ive read through todays newspaper, Im not ready to throw it away.

7. Your term paper the one you just handed in shows great effort.

8. Three dates in history stick out in most peoples minds: December 7, 1941, April 30, 1975, and September 11, 2001.

9. The train stopped in Atlanta, Georgia, Newark, New Jersey, and New Paltz, New York.

10. We dreamed of buying shoes that were made in Europe (Italy Milan, France Paris, and Denmark Copenhagen).

QUIZ

Find and correct the punctuation errors in the following sentences.

1. Recent surveys of teens show some unexpected results teens feel positive about themselves.

2. The mechanic at the garage said you need to leave this car for two to three days.

3. These two sentences are closely related thoughts use a semicolon to combine them.

4. James Monroe, John Quincy Adams, Andrew Jackson, and Martin Van Buren are the faces on the newest $1 coins and they will join George Washington in the collection.

5. A spokesman for the mint said, we want these coins to be used in all transactions and he added they will be given out as change as well.

6. I couldn't believe that a cardboard sun shield had this printed on it do not drive with sun shield in place.

7. John McKee, author of *Career Wisdom—101 Proven Strategies to Ensure Career Success*, says that "really successful ople are clear about what they want."

8. There are some surprising ways you can boost your mental functioning socializing helps, exercising is also beneficial.

9. By the time I read the second chapter, entitled, exercise and the mind, I was bored.

10. You will not believe the activity level of American adults just three of every ten get enough physical activity.

CHAPTER 6

Capitalization

In this chapter you will learn:

Brief History of the Alphabet and Capitalization

Modern Rules of Capitalization

Brief History of the Alphabet and Capitalization

In Chapter 4 you experienced what it would have been like many, many years ago to read a sentence without any spacing or punctuation, and with capitals or lowercase letters used at will. The Romans might also have written it in the following way, using capitals as the first letter of every word. Neither way makes the meaning of the sentence accessible to the reader.

GoBackManyYearsToTheGreeksAndRomansThisIsWhatYouMightHaveRead

Now we can look at the importance of capital letters for clarity.

But first, here's a bit of history about the alphabet. Thousands of years ago, people used drawings to tell their life stories. For example, early drawings, or hieroglyphs, were drawn to show that people fought and were brave in war. Other drawings showed the hunting they did. But drawing couldn't express everything.

For example, these early communicators could easily draw a picture of an animal, a spear, a fish, or a cave. But they couldn't draw pictures of concepts such as love, hate, or loyalty. Eventually, they couldn't remember all the pictures. There were just too many of them.

Then about 3,500 years ago, the root of the alphabet was first conceived of by the Semites, who invented twenty-two sound symbols for their language, ancestor of both Hebrew and Arabic. Before long, the Phoenicians also began to use the same symbols. Because they were sea merchants who sailed to many parts of the world, the Phoenicians spread this writing system to people of other nations. The Greeks added two more letters, and the Romans used the twenty-four alphabet letters.

By the time the Roman Empire reached its peak, the alphabet was established in the following way. Notice the missing letters:

ABCDEFGHIKLMNOPQRSTVXYZ

Romans dominated Europe, so it was logical that the Roman alphabet would become the standard alphabet throughout Western Europe and eventually throughout the Western world.

The Romans also changed the alphabet a bit and brought it to England. Since then, people in many countries have used the English alphabet of twenty-six letters. In fact, from the seventeenth century on, the English alphabet has contained the same twenty-six letters we use now. This was such a huge accomplishment that many consider the alphabet to be one of the most important inventions in the history of the world.

Lowercase letters were introduced in manuscript writing in the Middle Ages. This change from all capital letters to small letters was influenced by the nature of the writing material—the difficulty of writing the large, angular letters with a pen on expensive papyrus, parchment, and later paper. Manuscript writers loved lowercase letters because they could be written faster. From the reader's standpoint, it was much easier to read.

Today, the languages that use the Latin alphabet generally use capital letters to begin sentences and to indicate proper nouns. The rules for capitalization have changed significantly over time, and different languages have varied the rules of capitalization. Old English, for example, was rarely written with even proper nouns capitalized; whereas Modern English of the eighteenth century frequently capitalized all nouns:

Old English: my aunt jane takes the kids by bus to toy outlet to choose some treats.

Eighteenth-century Modern English: My Aunt Jane takes the Kids by Bus to Toy Outlet to choose some Treats.

Twenty-first-century English: My Aunt Jane takes the kids by bus to Toy Outlet to choose some treats.

Modern Rules of Capitalization

Capitalization custom varies among languages. The full rules of capitalization for English are complicated, but they have changed over time, generally to capitalize fewer terms. To the modern reader, an eighteenth-century document seems to use initial capitals excessively. Compared with Old English and English used in the eighteenth century, current capitalization strives to clarify the text. For example, a capital letter signals the beginning of a new thought. Capitals also clarify by distinguishing between common nouns and proper names . . . and those are just two among many rules! Here are capitalization rules you need to master.

RULES OF CAPITALIZATION

1. Capitalize the first letter of the first word in a sentence.

   Books make a great gift.

2. Capitalize the pronoun *I* and the interjection *O* or *Oh.*

   I decided to stay home for dinner.

   And Oh! that even now the gust were swelling ("Dejection," a poem
       by Samuel Taylor Coleridge)

3. Capitalize the first letter of the first word in each new line of poetry if the poet has capitalized it.

   What is so rare as a day in June?

4. Capitalize the deity, place names, street names, persons' names and initials, organization names, languages, and specific course names.

God in His Universe, Allah, Columbia River, New York City, New York, Main Street, John T. McMasters, American Red Cross, Spanish I, Algebra, Modern European History

5. Capitalize *Mother*, *Dad*, and other titles if you can insert the person's name, and titles like *Grandma* and *Major* when they appear with a formal name. If you can replace the "*mother/mom*" or "*father/dad*" with the person's formal name, "*Mother/Mom*" or "*Father/Dad*" should be capitalized.

Mother is really my best friend.

Donna is really my best friend.

If you cannot replace the "*mother/mom*" or "*father/dad*" with the person's formal name, then "*mother/mom*" or "*father/dad*" should not be capitalized.

My father is really tall.

Fred is really tall.

Written Practice 6-1

In each of the following sentences, insert capital letters wherever they are needed.

1. When we arrived in chicago, we quickly found out why it was named the windy city.
2. My friend, a 5′1″ girl, yelled, "oh, wait! I can't walk any faster in this wind!"
3. I received a call from mother the minute we landed in chicago.
4. I'm taking french and world history 101 at the university.
5. i'm volunteering for four hours a week at a local grammar school.

MORE RULES OF CAPITALIZATION

6. Capitalize days, months, holidays, and special days.

Monday, May, Christmas, New Year's Day, Martin Luther King Day

7. Capitalize historical events, documents, periods, or movements but not the small words that surround them.

World War II (not In World War II); Declaration of Independence
(not Declaration Of Independence); Magna Carta, Middle Ages,
Romantic Movement

8. Capitalize names of organizations, businesses, and institutions.

   The American Red Cross, American Airlines, Providence County
   Mental Health

9. Capitalize specific places, structures, or geographic locations. Carefully
   consider the names of places. Capitalize directions that are *names* (North,
   South, East, and West when used as sections of the country, but not as
   compass directions). We capitalize the *Middle East* and *Southeast Asia*,
   because these regions have their own distinctive identity; however, we write
   central Europe and *southeast Rome*, because these regions are not thought
   of as having the same kind of identity. Note, too, the difference between
   South Africa (the name of a particular country) and southern Africa (a
   vaguely defined region).

   The Ku's have moved to the Southwest.

   Mac's house is two miles north of Providence.

   Turn south at the next corner.

   Other examples include:

   the Lake District; Newport, RI; Radio City Music Hall; the
   Northeast; the Midwest

10. Capitalize the names of languages, races, and nationalities.

    English, Native American, Portuguese

11. Capitalize religions and their followers.

    Christianity, Christian; Islam, Muslim; Judaism, Orthodox Jew

12. Capitalize religious terms for sacred persons and things.

    Christ, Allah, Buddha, the Bible, and the Koran

13. Capitalize the Roman numerals and the letters of the first major topics in
    an outline.

    I, II, III, A, B, C,

Written Practice 6-2

In each of the following sentences, insert capital letters wherever they are needed.

1. I would like to travel to seattle in the northwest on my next vacation.
2. My friend just visited the eiffel tower in paris.
3. Not too many people can tell you about the war of the roses, a civil war that took place in england from 1455–1487.
4. I asked if he, a baptist, was really considering studying buddhism as i had heard.
5. He said he didn't think it mattered by which name he referred to the supreme deity—christ, allah, or buddha.

MORE RULES OF CAPITALIZATION

14. Capitalize the first word of a direct quotation.

    My son asked, "Will you buy me a guitar for my birthday?"

15. In a broken quotation, capitalize the first word in the second part of the quotation only if it starts a new sentence.

    "I'll start the meeting," she said, "if you will finish it after lunch."

    "I'll start the meeting," she said. "You can finish it after lunch." (*You* starts a new sentence.)

16. Do not capitalize the *report* of something said.

    My son asked if I would buy him a guitar for his birthday.

Written Practice 6-3

In each of the following sentences, insert capitals where they are needed.

1. We think that representative stephanie brown will hold a very high office in the administration.
2. i heard the policeman say, "may I see your license, please?"

3. As he started to say, "where is your registration," I interrupted with, "you'll want this too, officer."

4. I knew that officer kent would say that he needed to see my registration.

5. i didn't hear him say, "you may drive on now" and add, "but don't speed anymore."

EVEN MORE RULES OF CAPITALIZATION

17. Capitalize brand names but not products.

    Dodge, Xerox, Kleenex tissue

18. Capitalize titles when they precede proper names, but not when they follow proper names or are used alone.

    Principal Walters, Superintendent Konner

    Example: Mr. Walters, principal; Mr. Konner, superintendent

19. Capitalize the titles of books, plays, and films. Do not capitalize the small, unimportant words in those titles.

    Example: *The Secret Life of Bees*, *Romeo and Juliet*

Written Practice 6-4

In the following sentences, insert capitals where they are needed.

1. corporal marylou ryan said, "i bought a ford convertible, and i'm so excited about driving it!"

2. captain and mrs. talbott led the parade on memorial day.

3. be sure to see *gone with the wind* if the movie returns to your town.

4. we took jack's principal to Mama Mia, an italian restaurant, saturday night for dinner.

5. he came from the southwest, but he lives in maine now.

Written Practice 6-5

In each of the following sentences, insert or delete capital letters wherever necessary.

1. each year our community celebrates the fourth of july with a parade and fireworks. we hire a Professional Fireworks Company, and they never disappoint us. the displays are brilliant and loud! my son, matt, cried through the first performance we took him to.

2. this year, matt is driving in from Chicago for the holiday with his son, alex. we're curious to see if alex stays for the whole performance. His father didn't.

3. we've decided to go to new york for a long weekend in september. Believe it or not, i've never been to the top of the empire state building. that is first on my Agenda. we'll stay at a Hotel, but I don't know which one yet.

4. i subscribe to the *reader's digest*. if I had my wish, the Publisher would serialize one of the Harry Potter books.

5. in modern american history II, we'll study world war II and the atomic age.

6. jeff worked for ford motor company until the plant in our town was closed.

7. Our town has launched a refurbishing effort in center city.

8. americans have always been proud of the declaration of independence.

9. my children—as young as they are—are already learning chinese and spanish in school.

10. "i don't take you for granted," he yelled. "you're just not forceful enough in our discussions!"

11. we saw claire mcCaskill, senator from missouri, on the steps of the Senate Building.

12. mr. reed, senator from ri, has worked hard on behalf of his state and the nation.

13. "oh, you scared me!" she cried.

14. the american red cross has been challenged to meet many disasters in recent years.

15. the jamestown bridge was totally replaced.

Written Practice 6-6

For each of the following sentences, choose the word in the parentheses that is written correctly.

1. We're moving our company to Las Vegas, Nevada in the (spring/Spring) of 2010.
2. Send our proposal to the (department/Department) of Transportation in Washington.
3. We'll leave San Francisco and then travel in the (orient/Orient) for three weeks.
4. I just finished an inspiring book of poems by Linda Eve Diamond called *The Human* (*experience/Experience*).
5. You're expected for dinner on (friday/Friday).

Written Practice 6-7

Insert or delete capitalization as needed in the following paragraph. The sentences are numbered for clarity in the Answer Key.

Paragraph 1

1. the terms *greenhouse effect* and *global warming* have been used in scientific history for many, many years. 2. discussions of global warming first appeared when a swedish scientist, svante arrhenius (1859–1927), claimed in 1896 that burning Fossil fuel might eventually increase global warming. 3. he further proposed that a relationship existed between carbon dioxide in the atmosphere and Temperature gains. 4. arrhenius noted that because of the absorption of water and carbon dioxide, the Average Surface Temperature of the earth is about 15 degrees Celsius. 5. this is what we call the natural greenhouse effect. 6. however, arrhenius then suggested that doubling carbon dioxide would result in a 5 degrees Celsius temperature increase.

Paragraph 2

1. arrhenius and his colleague, thomas chamberlin, made another calculation: human activities could warm the earth by adding carbon dioxide to the atmosphere. 2. years passed before this was actually verified in 1987. 3. then the topic was forgotten because

scientists thought that human influences were minute compared to Natural Forces such as solar activity and ocean circulation. 4. in fact, a popular theory was that the oceans acted as huge carbon sinks that automatically cancelled out pollution.

Paragraph 3

1. this is a new one. 2. eco-anxiety is taking hold of many, many well-meaning consumers. 3. "what is it?" you ask.

QUIZ

Correct the capitalization error(s) in each of the following sentences.

1. My dentist's office is on elmgrove avenue, East of wayland avenue.
2. Did you hear him say, "all lights should be turned off"?
3. to catch up on weekly events, I buy *time magazine* and a sunday newspaper.
4. I love the paintings of john singer sargent.
5. My friend's aunt polly met us at the train.
6. We bought all our supplies at forest camping supplies, inc., in boston.
7. Leave your car in the garage; i'll drive.
8. Robert t. Masters, President of the division, gave a welcoming speech.
9. She cried, "oh no! I was supposed to turn at that corner."
10. In 2008, many people read and were inspired by Randy Paush's book, *the last lecture*.

PART TWO TEST

Circle the letter of the word, phrase, or sentence that best completes or corrects each sentence.

1. Although we live in Akron, ohio, we frequently travel to new york city.
   (a) Although we live in Akron ohio, we frequently travel to new York city.
   (b) Although we live in Akron, Ohio, we frequently travel to new york city.
   (c) Although we live in Akron, ohio, we frequently travel to New York city.
   (d) Although we live in Akron, Ohio, we frequently travel to New York City.

2. They gave us good advice, don't always insert yourselves into your children's arguments.
   (a) They gave us good advice. don't always insert yourselves into your children's arguments.
   (b) They gave us good advice, Don't always insert yourselves into your children's arguments.
   (c) They gave us good advice; don't always insert yourselves into your children's arguments.
   (d) They gave us good advice don't always insert yourselves into your children's arguments.

3. The American red cross is an organization that has been represented at many major tragedies.
   (a) The American red cross is an Organization that has been represented at many major tragedies.
   (b) The american Red cross is an organization that has been represented at many major tragedies.
   (c) The American red Cross is an organization that has been represented at many Major Tragedies.
   (d) The American Red Cross is an organization that has been represented at many major tragedies.

4. I told mother that I had decided not to take that job.
   (a) I told Mother that I had decided not to take that job.
   (b) I told mother that i had decided not to take that job.

(c) I told Mother that i had decided not to take that job.

(d) i told mother that i had decided not to take that job.

5. This is the year that I've decided to study great historical documents, from the Magna Carta to the U.S. constitution.

   (a) This is the year that I've decided to study great historical documents: from the Magna Carta to the U.S. constitution.

   (b) This is the year that I've decided to study great historical documents, from the Magna Carta to the U.S. Constitution.

   (c) This is the year that I've decided to study Great Historical Documents, from the Magna Carta to the U.S. constitution.

   (d) This is the year that i've decided to study great historical documents, from the Magna Carta to the U.S. constitution.

6. Did you hear me say, "dinner is at 7 P.M."?

   (a) Did you hear me say, "Dinner is at 7 P.M."?

   (b) Did you hear me say, "Dinner is at 7 P.M."

   (c) Did you hear me say, "dinner is at 7 P.M.?"

   (d) Did you hear me say; "dinner is at 7 P.M."?

7. You always tell me that you're not hungry, then you ask what time we're having dinner.

   (a) You always tell me that you're not hungry. then you ask what time we're having dinner.

   (b) You always tell me that you're not hungry, Then you ask what time we're having dinner.

   (c) You always tell me that you're not hungry; then you ask what time we're having dinner.

   (d) You always tell me that you'r not hungry, then you ask what time we're having dinner.

8. While I'm eager to work with you; you understand that we have to be on the same schedule.

   (a) While I'm eager to work with you, you understand that we have to be on the same schedule.

   (b) While I'm eager to work with you: you understand that we have to be on the same schedule.

   (c) (While I'm eager to work with you); you understand that we have to be on the same schedule.

   (d) While I'm eager to work with you. You understand that we have to be on the same schedule.

9. I'll never forget that Broadway show, I've wanted to repeat that experience each year.

   (a) I'll never forget that Broadway show, I've wanted to repeat that experience each year.

   (b) I'll never forget that Broadway show I've wanted to repeat that experience each year.

   (c) I'll never forget that Broadway show? I've wanted to repeat that experience each year.

   (d) I'll never forget that Broadway show; I've wanted to repeat that experience each year.

10. I usually play softball, bowl with a team, and swim competitively, but I don't have that much time this year.

   (a) I usually play softball bowl with a team and swim competitively, but I don't have that much time this year.

   (b) I usually play soft-ball, bowl with a team, and swim competitively, but I don't have that much time this year.

   (c) I usually play softball, bowl, with a team, and swim competitively, but I don't have that much time this year.

   (d) I usually play softball, bowl with a team, and swim competitively; but I don't have that much time this year.

11. Narragansett, Rhode Island, Cape Cod, Massachusetts, and Stowe, Vermont are well-known vacation areas.

    (a) Narragansett Rhode Island, Cape Cod Massachusetts, and Stowe Vermont are well-known vacation areas.

    (b) Narragansett, RI, Cape Cod, MA, and Stowe, VT are well-known vacation areas.

    (c) Narragansett, ri, Cape Cod, ma, and Stowe, vt are well-known vacation areas.

    (d) Narragansett, Rhode Island; Cape Cod, Massachusetts; and Stowe, Vermont are well-known vacation areas.

12. Semicolons are very useful in building sentences, moreover, they help writers to bring variety to their writing.

    (a) Semicolons are very useful in building sentences; Moreover, they help writers to bring variety to their writing.

    (b) Semicolons are very useful in building sentences; moreover, they help writers to bring variety to their writing.

    (c) Semicolons are very useful in building sentences. moreover, they help writers to bring variety to their writing.

    (d) Semicolons are very useful in building. sentences, moreover, they help writers to bring variety to their writing.

13. Emanuelle said, "If I join that club, please come with me".

    (a) Emanuelle said, "If I join that club, please come with me."

    (b) Emanuelle said, "If I join that club, please come with me"!

    (c) Emanuelle said, "If I join that club, please come with me"?

    (d) Emanuelle said, "If I join that club: please come with me".

14. Sgt and Mrs Alvarez are stationed in Texas.

    (a) Sgt and Mrs. Alvarez are stationed in Texas.

    (b) Sargeant and Mrs Alvarez are stationed in Texas

    (c) Sgt. and Mrs. Alvarez are stationed in Texas.

    (d) Sgt. and Mrs Alvarez are stationed, in Texas.

15. Did you hear Leon say, "I'm leaving for vacation at the end of work today?"

   (a) Did you hear Leon, say, "I'm leaving for vacation at the end of work today?"

   (b) Did you hear Leon say, "I'm leaving for vacation at the end of work today"?

   (c) Did you hear Leon say, "I'm leaving for vacation at the end of work today!"

   (d) Did you hear Leon say, "I'm leaving for vacation at the end, of work today?"

16. My great aunt wondered if I would ever have children?

   (a) My great aunt wondered, "if I would ever have children."

   (b) My great aunt wondered if I would ever have children.

   (c) My great aunt wondered: if I would ever have children?

   (d) My great aunt wondered; if I would ever have children.

17. Have you started carrying cloth bags to the supermarket yet.

   (a) Have you started carrying cloth bags to the supermarket yet?

   (b) Have you started carrying cloth bags to the supermarket, yet.

   (c) Have you started carrying cloth, bags to the supermarket yet.

   (d) Have you started carrying? Cloth bags to the supermarket yet.

18. The inspector in charge yelled, "Don't touch the crime scene"!

   (a) The inspector in charge, yelled, "Don't touch the crime scene"

   (b) The inspector in charge yelled! "Don't touch the crime scene"!

   (c) The inspector in charge yelled, "Don't touch the crime scene!"

   (d) The inspector in charge yelled; "Don't touch the crime scene"!

19. Oh, You scared me.

   (a) Oh; You scared me.

   (b) Oh? You scared me.

   (c) Oh: . . . You scared me.

   (d) Oh! You scared me.

20. If we don't meet at the Copley St entrance, I'll see you at home.

    (a) If we don't meet at the Copley St entrance; I'll see you at home.

    (b) If we don't meet at the Copley St. entrance, I'll see you at home.

    (c) If we don't meet at the Copley St entrance: I'll see you at home.

    (d) If we don't meet at the Copley St entrance. I'll see you at home.

21. Plant the bulbs, rake the leaves and paint the railing by the time I get home.

    (a) Plant the bulbs, rake the leaves. and paint the railing by the time I get home.

    (b) Plant the bulbs; rake the leaves and paint the railing by the time I get home.

    (c) Plant the bulbs, rake the leaves, and paint the railing by the time I get home.

    (d) Plant the bulbs, (rake the leaves) and paint the railing by the time I get home.

22. In the meantime however we'll use the only available room.

    (a) In the meantime, however, we'll use the only available room.

    (b) In the meantime however; we'll use the only available room.

    (c) In the meantime, however we'll use the only available room.

    (d) In the meantime however we'll, use the only available room.

23. Roderigo wore a new stylish sport coat for his date.

    (a) Roderigo wore a new stylish sport coat, for his date.

    (b) Roderigo wore a new, stylish sport coat for his date.

    (c) Roderigo wore, a new stylish sport coat for his date.

    (d) Roderigo, wore a new stylish sport coat for his date.

24. After all we prepared for our guests they cancelled.

    (a) After all we prepared for our guests they cancelled?

    (b) "After all we prepared for our guests they cancelled."

    (c) After all we prepared; for our guests they cancelled.

    (d) After all we prepared for our guests, they cancelled.

25. I had done all the baking yet Kim took the credit for it.

    (a) I had done all the baking yet, Kim took the credit for it.

    (b) I had done all the baking! yet Kim took the credit for it.

    (c) I had done all the baking: yet Kim took the credit for it.

    (d) I had done all the baking, yet Kim took the credit for it.

26. "Had you asked her for help" Martha inquired.

    (a) "Had you asked her for help!" Martha inquired.

    (b) "Had you asked her for help" Martha inquired!

    (c) "Had you asked her for help" Martha inquired?

    (d) "Had you asked her for help?" Martha inquired.

27. I never ask for help, unless I really need it.

    (a) I never ask for help! unless I really need it.

    (b) I never ask for help; unless I really need it.

    (c) I never ask for help unless I really need it.

    (d) I never, ask for help unless, I really need it.

28. I will become a citizen on July 4 2010.

    (a) I will become a citizen on July 4! 2010.

    (b) I will become a citizen on July 4, 2010.

    (c) I will become a citizen on July 4. 2010.

    (d) I will become a citizen on July 4; 2010.

29. Dear Dr Issacs

    I will be happy to report for work on Monday December 16th as you asked

    (a) Dear Dr. Issacs:

        I will be happy to report for work on Monday, December 16, as you asked.

    (b) Dear Dr Issacs

        I will be happy to report for work on Monday December 16th as you asked

(c) Dear Dr Issacs—

I will be happy to report for work on Monday. December 16th as you asked?

(d) Dear Dr Issacs

I will be happy to report for work on Monday, December 16th as you asked!

30. My indoor plants always include a Christmas cactus, an amaryllis, and an orchid indoor conditions however are not always perfect for these plants.

(a) and an orchid, indoor conditions however are not always perfect for these plants.

(b) and an orchid. indoor conditions however are not always perfect for these plants.

(c) and an orchid; Indoor conditions however are not always perfect for these plants.

(d) and an orchid; indoor conditions, however, are not always perfect for these plants.

31. Coronary heart disease doesn't discriminate against women, it's the number one killer of women over twenty-five years old.

(a) women, it's the number

(b) women. it's the number

(c) women; it's the number

(d) women! it's the number

32. Even those women who exercise regularly and eat exceptionally well need to be checked for heart disease otherwise a fatal event may take them by surprise.

(a) disease, otherwise a fatal event

(b) disease; otherwise, a fatal event

(c) disease: otherwise a fatal event

(d) disease otherwise; a fatal event

33. A woman dies of heart disease every minute in the United States. but only 13 percent of women consider the statistic a threat.

    (a) in the United States, but only 13 percent

    (b) in the United States! but only 13 percent

    (c) in the United States? but only 13 percent

    (d) in the United States: but only 13 percent

34. We arrived in phoenix, az, on February 26th and quickly decided it was a good place for a winter vacation.

    (a) We arrived in Phoenix, AZ, on February 26th

    (b) We arrived in phoenix, Az, on February 26th

    (c) We arrived in Phoenix, az, on February 26th

    (d) We arrived in Phoenix, AZ, on february 26th

35. On December 24th, I'm still not finished shopping for christmas!

    (a) On December twenty-fourth, I'm still not finished shopping for christmas!

    (b) On December 24th, I'm still not finished shopping for the christmas holiday!

    (c) On december 24th, I'm still not finished shopping for Christmas!

    (d) On December 24th, I'm still not finished shopping for Christmas!

36. Her husband speaks french, portuguese, german, and his native english.

    (a) Her husband speaks French, portuguese, german, as well as his native English.

    (b) Her husband speaks French, Portuguese, German, and his native English.

    (c) Her husband speaks French, Portuguese, German, and his native english.

    (d) Her husband speaks french, and portuguese, and german, and his native english.

37. I would like to travel to Boston in the northeast for a week.

    (a) I would like to travel to Boston; it's in the northeast for a week.

    (b) I would like to travel to Boston in the Northeast for a week.

    (c) I would like to travel to Boston which is in the northeast for a week.

    (d) I would like to travel north to Boston in the northeast for a week.

38. The ad said, "We don't inflate our prices we simply offer a great product."

    (a) The ad said, "We don't inflate our prices! we simply offer a great product."

    (b) The ad said, "We don't inflate our prices we simply offer a great product."!

    (c) The ad said, "We don't inflate our prices. We simply offer a great product."

    (d) The ad said, "We don't inflate our prices we simply offer a great Product."

39. My son insists that I see the movie, *The matrix*.

    (a) My son insists that I see the movie, *The Matrix*.

    (b) My son insists that I see the Movie, *The matrix*.

    (c) My son insists that I see the movie, *the matrix*.

    (d) My son insists that I see the movie? *The matrix*.

40. dr. henry ryan says we parents should be stricter with four-year-old tyrants.

    (a) Dr. Henry Ryan says we parents should be stricter with four-year-old tyrants.

    (b) dr. henry Ryan says we parents should "be stricter with four-year-old tyrants."

    (c) Dr. henry Ryan says we Parents should be stricter with four-year-old tyrants.

    (d) dr. henry ryan says we parents' should be stricter with four-year-old tyrants.

41. His theory—though never published is that parents simply talk too much to misbehaving children.

    (a) His theory—though never published—is that parents simply talk too much to misbehaving children.

    (b) His theory—though never published is that, parents, simply talk too much to misbehaving children.

    (c) His theory—though never published; is that parents simply talk too much to misbehaving children.

    (d) His theory—though never published are that parents simply talk too much to misbehaving children.

42. My personal to do list includes learning to give my children directions without giving a lengthy speech.

    (a) My personal to do list includes learning to give my children direction's without giving a lengthy speech.

    (b) My personal to do list include's learning to give my children directions without giving a lengthy speech.

    (c) My personal to-do list includes learning to give my children directions without giving a lengthy speech.

    (d) My personal, to do list includes learning to give my children directions without giving a lengthy speech.

43. A very important concept in todays world is that you learn new skills and polish the old ones before youre unemployed!

    (a) A very important concept in todays world is that you learn new skills and then you should polish the old ones before you're unemployed!

    (b) A very important concept in todays world is: that you learn new skills and polish the old ones before youre unemployed?

    (c) A very important concept in today's world is that you learn new skills and polish the old ones before you're unemployed!

    (d) A very important concept, really, in todays world is that you learn new skills and polish the old ones before youre unemployed!

44. While I was shoveling the snow, I saw three deer a field mouse, and a rabbit they were all looking for food.

  (a) While I was shoveling the snow, I saw three, deer a field mouse, and a rabbit they were all looking for food.

  (b) While I was shoveling the snow, I saw three deer, a field mouse, and then I saw rabbit they were all looking for food.

  (c) While I was shoveling the snow, I saw three deer a field mouse, and a rabbit they were all looking for food.

  (d) While I was shoveling the snow, I saw three deer, a field mouse, and a rabbit; they were all looking for food.

45. Although I think it's wrong for a five-year-old to carry a blanket outside of the house; I'm unwilling to set that rule.

  (a) Although, I think it's wrong for a five-year-old to carry a blanket outside of the house; I'm unwilling to set that rule.

  (b) Although I think it's wrong for a five-year-old to carry a blanket outside of the house, I'm unwilling to set that rule.

  (c) Although I think it's wrong—for a five-year-old to carry a blanket outside of the house; I'm unwilling to set that rule.

  (d) Although I think it's wrong for a five-year-old to carry a blanket outside of the house: I'm unwilling to set that rule.

46. In addition to creating your own budget, there are many new websites— Mint.com, Geezeo.com, Quicken Online, Mvelopes.com—that will help track your money, but always protect yourself with antispyware programs.

  (a) In addition to creating your own budget, there are many new websites— Mint.com, Geezeo.com, Quicken Online, Mvelopes.com—that will help track your money; but always protect yourself with antispyware programs.

  (b) In addition to creating your own budget, there are many new websites— Mint.com; Geezeo.com; Quicken Online; Mvelopes.com—that will help track your money, but always protect yourself with antispyware programs.

(c) In addition to creating your own budget: there are many new websites—
Mint.com, Geezeo.com, Quicken Online, Mvelopes.com—that will
help track your money, but always protect yourself with antispyware
programs.

(d) In addition to creating your own budget, there are many new websites—
Mint.com, Geezeo.com, Quicken Online, Mvelopes.com—that will
help track your money, But always protect yourself with antispyware
programs.

47. How late do you wait to shop for Christmas?" she asked. "do you still wait
until the last day"?

   (a) How late do you wait to shop for Christmas" she asked?. "do you still
   wait until the last day"?

   (b) How late do you wait to shop for christmas?" she asked. "do you still
   wait until the last day"?

   (c) "How late do you wait to shop for Christmas?" she asked. "Do you still
   wait until the last day?"

   (d) How late do you wait to shop for Christmas"! she asked. "do you still
   wait until the last day"?

48. An intelligent well-behaved curious child is such a pleasure to teach.

   (a) An intelligent, well-behaved curious child is such a pleasure to teach.

   (b) An intelligent well-behaved curious child; is such a pleasure to teach.

   (c) An intelligent, well-behaved, curious child is such a pleasure to teach.

   (d) An intelligent; well-behaved; curious child is such a pleasure to teach.

49. I returned to the store, before it was even open.

   (a) I returned to the store; before it was even open.

   (b) I returned to the store! before it was even open.

   (c) I returned to the store. before it was even open.

   (d) I returned to the store before it was even open.

50. A long complicated contract arrived in the mail.

    (a) A long complicated contract, arrived in the mail.

    (b) A long complicated contract; arrived in the mail.

    (c) A long complicated contract arrived, in the mail.

    (d) A long, complicated contract arrived in the mail.

PART THREE

MASTERING GOOD SENTENCE STRUCTURE

CHAPTER 7

Building Better Sentences

In this chapter you will learn:

Building Balanced Sentences
Creating Well-Connected Sentences
Trimming Unnecessary Words from Sentences

Building Balanced Sentences

At this point, you have reviewed the essentials of grammar and you can identify parts of speech and their functions. You also recognize common errors in grammar. Now you are ready to make sure the words you use function correctly in sentences.

For example, you know how to recognize describing words and phrases. However, do you know how to use them to create *balanced* sentences?

Balanced sentences are ones in which related descriptions, actions, or ideas are written in the same form. Grammarians call this *parallel construction*. There is power in parallel construction. In fact, some very famous examples of parallel construction exist in history:

> **Julius Caesar:** I came; I saw; I conquered.

How does this sentence exemplify parallel construction? There are three verbs—*came*, *saw*, and *conquered*—all expressed in the past tense and all preceded by *I*.

> **Abraham Lincoln:** But in a larger sense, we cannot dedicate—we cannot consecrate—we cannot hallow—this ground.

Again we read three verbs, *dedicate*, *consecrate*, and *hallow*, all in the present tense and all preceded by *we cannot*.

> **Sir Winston Churchill:** I have nothing to offer but blood, toil, tears, and sweat.

In Churchill's sentence, the parallel is accomplished by using four words, all the same part of speech, that is, nouns.

> **John F. Kennedy:** Ask not what your country can do for you; ask what you can do for your country.

This is actually a quote from Marcus Tullius Cicero, a first-century Roman statesman. President Kennedy considered it memorable enough to use in his 1961 inaugural address. In it, the repetition of *ask not what* and *can do* provide a parallel structure for the sentence. The two halves of the sentence start with the command form of the verb, *ask*.

Examples of not-so-famous *unbalanced* sentences follow. Where did the writer go wrong? What part of speech or related idea was not carried forward in a consistent way?

> **Incorrect:** Cari is attractive and has good sense.

If you say this sentence aloud, you will probably agree that it sounds unbalanced. Why? If you analyze the sentence, you see that Cari is the subject and *is* is the

linking verb. You recall that a linking verb brings together or links the subject to a descriptive word or a word that stands for the subject. In this sentence, Cari is being described. What two elements describe her? *Attractive* and *has good sense* are the elements. How can you change the second element, *has good sense,* to match the first, *attractive*? *Attractive* is an adjective describing Cari. Convert *has good sense* into an adjective, a single word, to match *attractive*. This is the result:

Correct: Cari is *attractive* and *sensible.*

Now the sentence is balanced.
   Try this sentence:

Incorrect: Chess is mentally challenging and makes me tired.

The sentence describes chess. What two phrases follow the linking verb *is* and describe *chess*? They are *mentally challenging* and *makes me tired.* The second phrase contains a verb, *makes.* The first descriptive phrase does not contain a verb. Immediately, you know that the description is unbalanced. With what simple change can you balance this sentence? Take a clue from the *-ing* ending on *challenging.* Place an *-ing* ending on one word of the second phrase—*tiring*—and you can eliminate the words *makes me.* You've created a balanced sentence:

   Chess is mentally challenging and tiring.

You can see that a balanced sentence tends to eliminate unnecessary words, and that's a good thing. In the sentence about chess, the correction eliminated the awkward phrase, *makes me.*
   How can you tighten and balance the following sentence?

Incorrect: The deer we saw was tall, alert, and he was obviously hungry.

Because it is unbalanced, this sentence actually carries an extra sentence within it. The deer is described in the sentence. The linking verb *was* is followed by the adjectives *tall* and *alert* but then ends, not with another adjective, with a complete thought—*he was obviously hungry.* How can you correct the sentence?

Correct: The deer we saw was tall, alert, and obviously hungry.

The complete thought was changed to a simple adjective, *hungry*. The adverb, *obviously*, adds more meaning by describing *hungry*.

Written Practice 7-1

Balance each of the following sentences.

1. The coffee here is delicious, hot, and it's also inexpensive.

_____

2. The lawyer asked his client to tell the truth and if he could provide evidence.

_____

3. The rain splashes on the roof and always is soaking the porch.

_____

4. Soda is filling, full of calories, and eventually it's fattening.

_____

5. My cooking skills are new, limited to simple dishes, and I think sometimes my choices are boring.

_____

6. Teaching physicians have several jobs, including doing research, reducing pain and suffering, and they teach other physicians.

_____

7. Their decision was to expand the space, buy all new equipment, and then they would install a new security system.

_____

8. Add the dry ingredients, the eggs should be whipped, and preheat the oven.

_____

9. Whoever leaves the house last should lower the heat, turning off the lights, and check the stove.

_____

10. David played classical guitar, jazz guitar, and then he tried rhythm and blues.

_____

CREATING BALANCE WITH PARALLEL VERB FORMS

Look at a different kind of balancing error:

Incorrect: For exercise, I like dancing and to in-line skate.

In this sentence there is an action verb, *like*, followed by words that express what exercises this person likes. Are they expressed in the same form? No, the first, *dancing*, ends in *-ing* while the second, *in-line skate,* is introduced by *to*. Choose either form but never both:

Correct: I like *to dance* and *to in-line skate.*

Correct: I like *dancing* and in-line skating.

How would you correct the following sentence?

Incorrect: I gave my old car to my nephew, my water skis to my father, and my tennis racket I gave away to a charity.

At the beginning of the sentence, you see two parallel constructions: *my old car to my nephew* and *my water skis to my father.* How can you change the wording of the last gift—*the tennis racket*—to the same form? Just revert to the form already used: *car to my nephew, skis to my father*, and *tennis racket to a charity.*

Correct: I gave my old car to my nephew, my water skis to my father, and my tennis racket to a charity.

Often, balancing errors occur when verbs are expressed in different forms:

Incorrect: I enjoy writing poetry, reading biographies, and stamp collection is a favorite of mine.

There are three actions in the sentence, *writing, reading,* and *collecting.* They need to be expressed in the same way. If you start with *writing*, an *-ing* ending verb, continue with that form. Notice that *collection* is a noun, but, as you know, English words can do more than one job. In this case, change the noun, *collection,* into an action word:

Correct: I enjoy writing poetry, reading biographies, and collecting stamps.

Written Practice 7-2

Balance the following sentences.

1. Every day, I walk the trails with my dog, cleaning the car, and go to work.

   _____

2. Jim loves painting the house, planting shrubs, and he loves to plan to add another room.

   _____

3. Elias looked for a toy, grabbed it, and he was throwing it across the room.

   _____

4. My friend eats dinner first, lunch second, and then he is eating breakfast last.

   _____

5. Spring is warm, flower-filled, and it rains a lot.

   _____

6. At the Center, Betsy did the accounting, made sure the preschoolers were safe, and then she also would take care of her own household as well.

   _____

7. My new printer is quieter, faster, and prints with higher resolution.

   _____

8. I'll know my son's work habits are improving when he arrives at school on time, corrects his own homework, and staying out of fights.

   _____

9. The chairman thanked everyone for their dedication, loyalty, and because they attended every meeting.

   _____

10. The only way we can leave on time is if I prepare the snacks, you fill up the gas tank, and if the children will get up on time.

   _____

CREATING BALANCE WITH CORRELATIVE CONJUNCTIONS

Another form of balancing a sentence involves correlative conjunctions. In Chapter 2, you learned that correlative conjunctions come in pairs that relate to one another.

Examples are *either/or, neither/nor, both/and, not only/but also*. These conjunction pairs need to be used correctly so that sentences are balanced:

Incorrect: Nadia is *not only* a *fine doctor* but an *accomplished artist also*.

In this sentence, Nadia is two things—a *fine doctor* and an *accomplished artist*. Two phrases link *doctor* to *artist*. What are they? They are *not only* and *but*. However, you need to add the word *also*, which just happens to be misplaced. The corrected sentence follows:

Correct: Nadia is not only a fine doctor but also an accomplished artist.

In the same way that *not only* comes before *a fine doctor*, *but also* must be placed before an *accomplished artist*.

Written Practice 7-3

The following sentences lack balance. Find and correct the errors to restore balance.

1. The longtime employee was not only energetic and liked to be punctual also.

   _____

2. We insisted that our son write his application truthfully and he should show some humility.

   _____

3. My two-year-old not only likes to walk in the puddles and is always jumping in the leaves.

   _____

4. Your new outfit is neither colorful and it isn't well fitting either.

   _____

5. This summer I will either plant a bed of flowers, or maybe I'll build a deck.

   _____

6. Debbie is neither prepared for parenthood nor is her career willing to be sacrificed.

   _____

7. Chocolate is not only delicious but it is energizing also.

   _____

8. Either you take the late shift and then I'll be leaving the house before you return.

   _____

9. Last summer, my vacation was not only busy but full of bad weather also.

   _____

10. We'll know we've succeeded when we see the children following our family's rules and then they should do well in school, too.

   _____

Creating Well-Connected Sentences

Writers add meaning and emphasis to sentences by using connecting words. In Chapter 2, you learned about connecting words, called conjunctions. Now you will see how you use conjunctions to connect sentences or parts of sentences to each other. The conjunction you choose depends upon the relationship of the parts to each other.

For example, how would you combine these two *equally important* statements to make one stronger sentence?

> Our children are very good at sports. We've decided to send them to a sports day camp this summer.

First look at this list of coordinating conjunctions:

also	and	besides	but	consequently
for	further	furthermore	however	moreover
nor	or	so	then	therefore
thus	yet			

A simple way to coordinate or connect these two equal thoughts would be to use the word *so*:

> Our children are unusually good at sports, *so* we've decided to send them to a sports day camp this summer.

Notice that a comma is inserted before *so*.

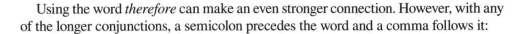
Using the word *therefore* can make an even stronger connection. However, with any of the longer conjunctions, a semicolon precedes the word and a comma follows it:

Our children are unusually good at sports; *therefore*, we've decided to send them to a sports day camp this summer.

Later you will learn much more about the role of punctuation in combining sentences. Now look for a connection between the following two thoughts:

Eden gave us too many alternatives. It confused us.

If you simply add the word *and*, you successfully bring the two thoughts together.

Eden gave us too many alternatives, and it confused us.

NOTE: *Whenever you've written a sentence that begins with it (e.g., It confused us.), look again. That sentence can undoubtedly join the previous one.*

One more example:

I paid for the car. Jan does nothing but complain about it.

Choose a conjunction that shows a contrast between the generosity of the person in the first sentence and the lack of appreciation of the person in the second sentence.

I paid for the car, *yet* Jan does nothing but complain about it.

Written Practice 7-4

For each of the following items, choose a coordinating conjunction from the previous list to connect the sentences.

1. We want to buy shoes on sale. The sale will last just this week.

   _____

2. The homebuilder hoped to attract buyers from the area. He advertised the new homes in the local paper.

   _____

3. We could walk anywhere on the grounds. We couldn't disturb the workers.

_____

4. When you bake, first turn on the oven to the temperature stated. Gather all the ingredients you'll need.

_____

5. She asked her husband to take the trash to the recycling depot. He quickly left for work.

_____

6. I had promised to arrive at 1 P.M. Heavy traffic delayed me.

_____

7. Take some sandwiches with you. Stop at a restaurant and spend a great deal of money.

_____

8. I've spent two weeks' pay. I'll be eating very meagerly for a while.

_____

9. Lend me $50. I'll pay you next month.

_____

10. I've studied and studied for the test. I feel unsure of myself.

_____

USING CONJUNCTIONS TO CONNECT IDEAS THAT ARE NOT EQUAL

Obviously, good writers use the appropriate words to bring ideas together. However, the writer also has to make decisions about the relative importance of the ideas in a sentence. For example, in the following sentence, which of the two clauses seems to be the less important one?

If we train diligently, our team can win the title.

You might begin by reading the first clause (all of the words before the comma). Do you think that clause can stand alone as a sentence? The answer, of course, is no. The word *If* makes the clause dependent, that is, dependent upon the rest of the sentence to complete the thought.

If we train diligently . . .

You read about such a clause in Chapter 1; it is a fragment. After reading it, you want to ask, "Then what?" The answer to the question is in the rest of the sentence (after the comma), rightfully named the independent clause. *Our team can win the title* is independent because it can stand alone as a sentence. The writer added the *if clause* to stress one idea over another.

Now look for a connection between the following two thoughts:

Although he likes to walk in the woods and photograph flowers, David loves to rest in an open field.

What did the writer want to emphasize in this sentence? The word *although* signals the dependent clause, the part of the sentence that cannot stand alone. It tells you that the writer wanted to emphasize the second (or independent) half of the sentence. The first part of the sentence is subordinated to the second half by the word *although*.

Look at another example:

Although you have driven for many more years than I have, I have experience in cross-country driving.

What is this sentence stressing, the years of driving or the cross-country driving experience? The latter is the stressed idea and the independent clause. How do you know? The clause can stand alone. The clause starting with *although* would be a fragment if it stood alone. What one word makes it a dependent clause? The word *although* does that.

To connect ideas that are *not* equal, choose from the following list of conjunctions:

after	although	as	because
if	since	though	unless
when	whenever	where	whereas

Written Practice 7-5

To complete each of the following sentences, choose a conjunction from the previous list.

1. _____ you babysit for us, I don't worry about the children.

2. _____ you hear otherwise, I'll pick you up at 5 P.M.

3. I have been taller than you _____ the sixth grade.

4. _____ the game, we tailgated.

5. You bought me a very expensive gift _____ I asked you not to.

6. _____ you agree with me, vote yes on that issue.

7. You're expected to arrive _____ I leave.

8. _____ a storm is expected, we still think we can drive to the lake.

9. You're the one to break a promise _____ we have an agreement.

10. _____ both children are sick, I have to miss work.

USING CONJUNCTIVE ADVERBS TO SHOW RELATIONSHIP OF IDEAS

Another kind of sentence-building conjunction shows a particular relationship between independent clauses. Grammarians call these conjunctive adverbs. Conjunctive adverbs are adverbs that act as a transition between complete ideas. They normally show comparison, contrast, cause-effect, sequence, or other relationships. They usually occur between independent clauses or sentences. Because they are transition words, conjunctive adverbs can occur at the beginning, in the middle, or at the end of either the second of the two clauses in a compound sentence or in the second of two related sentences. For example:

You haven't shown any interest in the project; *therefore*, I will lead it.
(*Therefore* = the logical conclusion.)

Notice that the conjunction *therefore* is preceded by a semicolon and followed by a comma.

Look at more examples:

My nephew is not a very good Ping-Pong player; *nevertheless*, he loves the game. (*Nevertheless* = a not-so-logical conclusion)

We were experiencing the hottest day of the year; consequently, we kept the children in the baby pool for as long as possible. (*Consequently* = as a direct result.)

Following is a more complete list of conjunctions that are used to connect and show the relationship between two independent clauses. Conjunctive adverbs express time, contrast, result, condition, and addition. The list organizes the conjunctions according to these categories.

Conjunctive Adverbs That Express Time

then	meanwhile	at one moment . . . at the next
afterward	later	sometimes . . . sometimes
henceforth	soon	now . . . then

Conjunctive Adverbs That Express Addition

likewise	moreover	in addition
furthermore	besides	partly . . . partly
then too	also	for one thing . . . for another (thing)

Conjunctive Adverbs That Express Contrast

however	nevertheless	still
on the contrary	instead	rather
exactly the opposite	on (the) one hand . . . on the other hand	

Conjunctive Adverbs That Express Result

consequently	hence	then	therefore
thus	accordingly	as a result	

Conjunctive Adverb That Expresses Condition

otherwise (= if not)

Written Practice 7-6

Choose a conjunction from the following list to complete each of the sentences.

however	instead	meanwhile	on the contrary	incidentally
in fact	next	as a result	otherwise	still

1. We thought we'd be able to save money this month; _____ , we're spending more!

2. My new car performed very well this winter; _____ , it surpassed all expectations.

3. I've picked up all our mail; _____ , one package has not been delivered.

4. We installed a new deck; _____ , we can see that the lumber was not cut correctly.

5. I've already called the designer and the carpenter; _____ , I'll call the lumberyard.

6. They will need to come up with a simple solution; _____ , the deck will have to be removed.

7. You may think that is what I want; _____ , I am really hoping to avoid that result.

8. You change the beds and dust the rooms; _____ , I'll start the laundry.

9. I hurt my back using the weight machine; _____ , I won't be exercising for a long time.

10. I picked up the concert tickets; _____ , they were $18 each.

NOTE: *A conjunctive adverb can be used in another position in a sentence. In that case, it is set off by commas and does* not *connect two complete thoughts. For example:*

Senator Blakeley, *however*, did not vote for the amendment.

Nonetheless, the Senate hopes to pass the bill.

Written Practice 7-7

For each of the following sentences, choose a conjunction from the previous categorized list. The categories are noted before the sentence.

1. (Time) We'll be at Stephanie's school this morning; _____ , we'll visit Matthew's school this afternoon.

2. (Contrast) I thought the weather was improving; _____ , our basement was flooded by three inches of rain.

3. (Result) To make this change, we'll need a substantial loan; _____ , I will call our bank.

4. (Addition) Our motivation for this growth is to provide more services to our customers; _____ , we'll be able to speed the results of our testing.

5. (Condition) Some populations are difficult to survey; _____ , our work would be easier.

6. (Time) I'll make dinner; _____ , you set the table.

7. (Contrast) We started our day very early so that we could relax in the afternoon; _____ , we hadn't accounted for the volume of customers.

8. (Result) Half of my staff was sick; _____ , I called in temporary employees.

9. (Addition) We'll pack our files and computers; _____ , we'll take the desks and chairs.

10. (Time) Sometimes we're fully staffed; _____ we're not.

Trimming Unnecessary Words from Sentences

Many of the sentences that we write groan under the weight of unnecessary words:

Wordy: We were searching for a painter who had experience.

Corrected: We were searching for an experienced painter.

The second sentence represents a very small, but important, change. The correction eliminates a clause, *who had experience*, and replaces it with one word—an adjective, *experienced*. Let's look at another example:

Wordy: Record these names in a place to which all of us have access.

Corrected: Record these names in a place accessible to all of us.

Corrected: Record these names in an accessible place.

A common error is the use of *my reason for . . . was that*:

My reason for shopping on Thursday was that I knew the vegetables would be fresh.

How much simpler would it be to say, *I shopped on Thursday because I knew the vegetables would be fresh.*

Repetition of ideas is another common error:

Wordy: Here is a picture of the new Mac desktop that they just introduced.

Corrected: Here is a picture of the newly introduced Mac desktop.

Wordy: George Washington, he was most notably painted by Gilbert Stuart

Corrected: George Washington was most notably painted by Gilbert Stuart.

One last but very important rule: Substitute strong verbs for boring noun phrases.

Wordy: If you *have an objection* to the menu, please let me know.

Corrected: If you *object* to the menu, please let me know.

Wordy: Please make *a recommendation* for chairperson.

Corrected: Please *recommend* a chairperson.

Written Practice 7-8

Simplify each of the following sentences.

1. The tour on the buggy tour of Charleston was enlightening.

   _____

2. Our reason for leaving the party early was because we knew how heavy the traffic would be.

   _____

3. Here is an example of the new hybrid vehicle just introduced at the automobile exposition.

   _____

4. This is a report about an analysis of our town water.

   _____

5. I have a suspicion that the meeting will end in an argument.

   _____

6. We were looking for a house painter who was skilled.

_____

7. While we were waiting for the train to arrive, we decided on a restaurant for lunch.

_____

8. We sent in all the paperwork that was demanded by the manufacturer.

_____

9. Hire only qualified welders who are certified in the skill.

_____

10. Store these foods in a place to which we all have access.

_____

QUIZ

Correct each of the following sentences.

1. Either I will start college or I may be going to work.

_____

2. The winner's demeanor was joyous and she was not without tears.

_____

3. English, reading and to study history were always my favorites.

_____

4. Though John shared my concern for the environment.

_____

5. Style guides for writing papers discuss not only researching the subject but footnoting sources also.

_____

6. Since you've eaten here before, please make a suggestion from this menu.

_____

7. Hillary Clinton, she was the first woman to run for the presidency.

_____

8. Our town was interviewing for a new town manager who would take over the job.

_____

9. Both options they are expensive, but we have to choose one.

_____

10. We looked at a 1,000 sq. ft. space. It was too small.

_____

CHAPTER 8

Punctuation Builds Sentences

In this chapter, you will learn

Punctuation in Sentence Building

As you read earlier, sentence building has everything to do with punctuation. Punctuation is not the only issue, but it is an important one. For example, with the help of punctuation, simple sentences can be combined to produce compound, complex, and compound-complex ones. For example:

Doreen could finish the task. Lily knew she wouldn't.

When you read the two preceding simple sentences, you can easily understand what they mean. The question, however, is this: How can you express this idea using an interesting style that clarifies the idea even more? The answer is to add a small word that allows you to bring the two sentences together to form a compound one:

Doreen could finish the task, yet Lily knew she wouldn't.

The small connecting word *yet* establishes a contrast between what Doreen *could* do and what Lily, by contrast, *knows* Doreen will do. Clearly, a connecting word can pack a meaningful wallop!

By the time you finish studying this chapter, you will know the differences among the four types of sentences covered: simple, compound, complex, and compound-complex. Obviously, sentence variety will make your writing more interesting. For example, read the following paragraph containing five simple sentences. No variety there! You will learn how to use combining words and punctuation to add variety to this paragraph and to your writing.

A solitary mouse lived in the Timothy house. He crept about late at night. He looked for food. His enemy was always waiting for him. His enemy was the family cat.

Sentence building begins by reviewing the different kinds of English sentences.

Simple Sentences

A simple sentence is an independent clause containing a subject, a verb, and a complete thought. For example:

Visualization prepares athletes for success.

No punctuation, other than a period, is necessary in this simple sentence. You can even add a compound subject, and the sentence remains a simple one:

Visualization and practice prepare athletes for success.

In the second sentence, two nouns, *visualization and practice*, form the subject, but no comma is used to separate the two.

Visualization and practice prepare athletes for peak performance and success.

In the preceding sentence, not only is there a compound subject but also a compound object of the preposition *for*.

Visualization and practice prepare athletes for peak *performance and success*.

Still, no comma is necessary to separate the compound elements of this simple sentence.

Written Practice 8-1

In each of the following simple sentences, label the subject (S), the verb (V), and the object(s) (O). The first one is done for you.

      S   S V   O   O (of preposition)

1. Matthew and I found our seats in the theater.

2. Late arrivals caused a stir.

3. On the stage, the main character, Bess, looked fleetingly at the audience.

4. She continued her dialogue.

5. The audience members regained their composure.

Compound Sentences

Move on now to compound sentences, and you need to add punctuation. A compound sentence is composed of two independent clauses brought together by a comma and conjunction or just a semicolon.

USING COORDINATING CONJUNCTIONS

As you will learn, there are two ways to connect these complete thoughts, but *a comma alone is not one of them*. Do you remember studying these coordinating conjunctions in Chapter 2?

for, and, nor, but, or, yet, so

You can easily remember these coordinating conjunctions by using the acronym *FANBOYS*. The letters are the first letter of each conjunction.

FANBOYS

Conjunction	Definition and Example Sentence
for	means "because" and shows logical consequences
	Example: No tulips grew that spring, *for* I had forgotten to plant them the previous fall.
and	means "along with, in addition"
	Example: I took an antibiotic, *and* I went to bed for the entire day.
nor	indicates a negative point
	Example: There was no heat in the house, *nor* was there any electric power.
but	means "except, however, on the other hand" and shows contrast
	Example: Many people have studied Stonehenge, *but* no one knows for sure why it was built.
or	indicates a choice
	Example: Should the electoral college decide a presidential election, *or* should it be decided by the popular vote?
yet	shows contrast
	Example: I thought that Dana was talented enough to make the team, *yet* the coach judged his performance inadequate.
so	means "therefore" or "as a result" and indicates logical consequences
	Example: I bought all the holiday gifts, *so* why don't you plan on wrapping them?

COMMON ERRORS

An important reminder: Complete thoughts *cannot* be strung together with commas. Doing so creates a serious error called a *comma fault* or a run-on sentence.

Incorrect: Visualization prepares athletes for success, consistent practice is a must.
Correct: Visualization prepares athletes for success; consistent practice is a must.
Correct: Visualization prepares athletes for success. Consistent practice is a must.

With the use of a comma, coordinating conjunctions join *independent clauses* to one another, and they add meaning:

(Coord. Conj.)

[Independent Clause] ↓ [Independent Clause]
↓ ↓

[Visualization prepares athletes for success], (but) [practice is a must].

[Independent Clause] (Coord. Conj.) [Independent Clause]
↓ ↓ ↓

[My cat likes kibble], (but) [my dog eats table food only].

[Independent Clause] (Coor. Conj.) [Independent Clause]
↓ ↓ ↓

[Lenny ate all the pizza], (so) [Phil finished the salad].

Written Practice 8-2

Correct each of the following sentences by adding a conjunction.

1. I use only unscented products, all my friends use scented detergents.
2. Meet me at 6 P.M., we'll have dinner together.

3. We've been recycling plastic, glass, and newspapers, our town says we need to do more.

4. I have to work at home tomorrow, my office is being painted.

5. I'm trying to save energy at home, we've lowered the thermostat and switched to energy-saving lightbulbs.

USING CONJUNCTIVE ADVERBS

Other conjunctions such as *however, therefore, furthermore,* and *nevertheless* also join independent clauses to one another and express relationships between them. Notice that these longer conjunctions, also called transitional words or conjunctive adverbs, are preceded by a semicolon and followed by a comma:

> Sunday was the hottest day of the summer; consequently, we decided to go to the beach.

What relationship does *consequently* express in this sentence? Clearly, the second clause is a result of the first clause.

Here is a more complete list of transitional words:

after all	also	as a result
besides	consequently	finally
for example	furthermore	hence
however	in addition	incidentally
indeed	in fact	in other words
instead	likewise	meanwhile
moreover	nevertheless	next
nonetheless	on the contrary	on the other hand
otherwise	still	then
therefore	thus	

Written Practice 8-3

Choose any five transitional words from the preceding list, and write sentences that join independent clauses.

1. _____

_____

_____

2. _____

_____

_____

3. _____

_____

_____

4. _____

_____

_____

5. _____

_____

_____

To summarize, you've learned three different ways to join independent clauses:

I like Cape Cod, but Marcel likes Nantucket.

(independent clause, comma, coordinating conjunction, independent clause)

I like Cape Cod; Marcel likes Nantucket

(independent clause, semicolon, independent clause)

I like Cape Cod; however, Marcel likes Nantucket.

(independent clause, semicolon, transition word, comma, independent clause)

Written Practice 8-4

Correct the punctuation errors in the following sentences.

1. Luke reads the *Times*, his friend reads *USA Today*.
2. We will travel to Massachusetts or we'll stop in Connecticut.
3. The car's radiator overheated therefore we called a service mechanic.
4. Traffic was bumper-to-bumper, nevertheless we stayed on the road until we reached our destination.
5. I babysit twice a week, my friend babysits every day.

USING CONJUNCTIONS TO ADD MEANING TO SENTENCES

Coordinating conjunctions are commonly used to connect sentences, and that's fine. However, they can be overused. The word *and*, for example, is one such conjunction since it simply adds one sentence to another and doesn't really indicate what kind of relationship you wish to establish. On the other hand, the word *although* conveys a much more specific relationship than *and* does. For example:

1. We have done little to effect change, and greenhouse gases continue to soar.

2. We have done little to effect change; consequently, greenhouse gases continue to soar.

The first sentence simply adds one sentence to another. With the addition of *consequently*, the second sentence indicates an opinion or indictment on the part of the writer. It says that *despite* or *notwithstanding* what's happening regarding greenhouse gases, we have done little, and there is a consequence.

Here's an opportunity for you to use transitional words to add meaning to sentences. In each of the following sentences, how would you add meaning by replacing *and* with a more meaning-filled transitional word? Look back to the list of transitional words for ideas.

1. I will make dinner, *and* you need to pick up Amelia after school.

   _____

2. Tillie was always late for work, *and* she received a cut in pay.

   _____

3. We started by clearing the attic, *and* we emptied the garage.

   _____

When you looked at the list of transitional words, you probably found several possibilities for each sentence. Here are some:

Sentence 1

I will make dinner; meanwhile, you need to pick up Amelia after school.

I will make dinner; on the other hand, you need to pick up Amelia after school.

I will make dinner; consequently, you need to pick up Amelia after school.

Sentence 2

Tillie was always late for work; consequently, she received a cut in pay.

Tillie was always late for work; finally, she received a cut in pay.

Tillie was always late for work; as a result, she received a cut in pay.

Sentence 3

We started by clearing the attic; next, we emptied the garage.

We started by clearing the attic; finally, we emptied the garage.

We started by clearing the attic; in addition, we emptied the garage.

You probably noticed that the revised sentences convey so much more of the writer's meaning and attitude.

This brings us to the more specific relationships established through the use of *complex* sentences.

Complex Sentences

As you learned earlier, a comma plus a coordinating conjunction, or a semicolon alone, join compound sentences and equalize the two thoughts. What if you want to make one idea less important than the other—not equal? In that case, you need to construct a *complex* sentence.

A complex sentence joins an independent clause (a complete thought) and a dependent clause (an incomplete thought). It uses a subordinating conjunction to join a dependent (subordinate) clause to an independent or main clause and express the relationship between the dependent and independent clauses. Common subordinating conjunctions are:

after	although	as	as if
because	before	how	in that
in so far as	if	once	since
so that	than	that	though
until	when	whenever	why
where	whether	while	

For example:

When we have time, we read and enjoy fiction.

Which part of the sentence can stand on its own? The answer, of course, is the part that follows the comma:

We read and enjoy fiction.

The first part of the sentence is a fragment. *When we have time* leaves you with the question, "Then what?"

The complex sentence gives you a powerful tool, that is, the ability to subordinate a less important idea to the more important one, the dependent clause to the independent clause. Another power it gives is variety in the length of your sentences.

How can you subordinate one idea to another with the following sentences?

Tom works in Phoenix. Elliot still works in Los Angeles.

Examples:

Dependent Clause   Independent Clause
        ↓   ↓

(Although Tom works in Phoenix), (Elliot still works in Los Angeles).

Elliot still works in Los Angeles although Tom works in Phoenix.

NOTE: *Notice that when the dependent clause follows the independent clause, no comma is needed.*

Independent Clause   Dependent Clause

↓   ↓

(Elliot still works in Los Angeles) (although Tom works in Phoenix).

In addition, if you find that you frequently start sentences with the word *it*, you can overcome that poor word choice by combining two short independent clauses into a complex sentence. For example:

It is sunny today.

We don't have raincoats in the car.

An obvious causal relationship exists between these two statements. Why not express it? Of course, you will have to decide which idea is the more important one for your purposes. The following may be your choice:

[Dependent Clause] (Comma)   [Independent Clause]

↓   ↓   ↓

Because it is sunny today, we don't have raincoats in the car.

In this case, the first clause is dependent, emphasizing the second clause.
Writing strong sentences requires placing emphasis on the most important idea. You can usually achieve that emphasis by placing the key idea at the end of the sentence.

Losing weight and building strength are the clear goals of our new health and fitness program, although other activities will be included.

Which clause holds the more important idea?

Independent: Losing weight and building strength are the clear goals of our new health and fitness program

Dependent: although other activities will be included

We can assume that the independent clause holds the more important idea. If that is the case and considering the earlier note regarding emphasis on the key idea, how should we put this sentence together? Look at the following examples:

[Dependent Clause]   (Comma) [Independent Clause]
        ↓   ↓   ↓

Although other activities will be included, losing weight and building strength are the clear goals of our new health and fitness program.

The end of the sentence now contains and emphasizes the important idea.

Written Practice 8-5

Create complex sentences by combining each of the following sets of dependent and independent clauses, using commas where necessary. Decide which clause is more important, and place it at the end of the sentence.

1. Because of my excellent advice

    Marla and Darren had a great trip.

    _____

2. We read the book and saw the movie

    Although many people advised against it

    _____

3. When you arrive

    We'll have dinner

    _____

4. If Daria arrives on time

    We'll have time to get to the late movie

    _____

5. The traffic began to flow

    After we passed the construction site.

    _____

Written Practice 8-6

Read the following paragraphs. Eliminate the choppy sentences by creating compound or complex sentences. Insert a comma plus conjunction or just a semicolon where necessary.

1. We have always bought our baby educational toys. Manufacturers of those toys make extravagant claims about verbal skill building. Researchers have studied the toys. They concluded that the toys did not increase vocabulary. We buy expensive toys. We expect them to live up to their advertising.

   _____

   _____

   _____

   _____

2. Back problems are common. It's a result of our walking upright. It's also because of degenerative changes in the spine. That's because walking upright places a great deal of weight on the lower spine. In middle age, some changes can occur. Arthritis and other changes affect the disks.

   _____

   _____

   _____

   _____

Compound-Complex Sentences

You will understand why compound-complex sentences require punctuation after you read some examples. Begin by noting that compound-complex sentences contain at least two independent clauses and one or more dependent clauses. For example:

Though Rachel usually prefers watching tennis on TV, she watched the World Series, and she enjoyed it very much.

According to the previous definition, you should be able to find two independent clauses in the sentence:

1. she watched the World Series (independent clause)

2. she enjoyed it very much (independent clause)

You also should find at least one dependent clause.

Though Rachel usually prefers watching tennis on TV (dependent clause)

Now, what about the punctuation? The introductory, dependent clause requires a comma. As you know, a compound sentence formed by combining two independent clauses with a conjunction also requires a comma. So this compound-complex sentence required two commas. Look at another example:

I had planned to drive to work on good weather days, but I couldn't drive on any day, because my car was in the repair shop for so long.

In this case, the word *because* follows a negative verb phrase, *couldn't drive*. The *because* clause explains why the event didn't occur. The comma before *because* clarifies that *because* refers to *couldn't* and not to *drive*.
Find the two independent clauses:

1. I had planned to drive to work on good weather days

2. I couldn't drive on any day

Find the dependent clause.

because my car was in the repair shop for so long

Mike, who walks to the corner each morning for his newspaper, rarely has his newspaper delivered; however, on very rainy days, he regrets that good habit.
Find the two independent clauses.

1. Mike rarely has his newspaper delivered

2. on very rainy days, he regrets that good habit

Find the dependent clause.

who walks to the corner each morning for his newspaper

Why did the original sentence require a semicolon? Recall that when two independent clauses are joined by a longer, transitional word, called a conjunctive adverb, you use a semicolon before the conjunction and a comma after it.

> Road building in the West was dangerous; consequently, when construction began in the nineteenth century, many construction workers died in climbing accidents.

Find the two independent clauses.

> 1. Road building in the West was dangerous
>
> 2. consequently, many construction workers died in climbing accidents

Find the dependent clause.

> when construction began in the nineteenth century

Written Practice 8-7

Clarify each of the following sentences by inserting punctuation where needed.

1. Ani who plays the piano rarely listens to any other kind of music however Mal plays no instrument and listens to all kinds of music.

2. We knew the prize was hidden in the house somewhere nevertheless even with that knowledge we couldn't find it.

3. Jake and Leela never told us they were not coming so even though we had planned so carefully we had much too much food.

4. Halloween never ceases to amaze me for although it appears year after year both children and their parents exhibit unrelenting enthusiasm.

5. By the time he was fourteen he had begun a professional career from the Atlantic City Boardwalk to touring in vaudeville he rose by force of his extraordinary ability to star billing as W.C. Fields Tramp Juggler.

6. While Stephen Douglas maintained a popular sovereignty stance, Lincoln stated that the United States could not survive as half-slave and half-free states consequently the Lincoln–Douglas debates drew the attention of the entire nation.

7. Because of the delays we've experienced we are no longer using the U.S. mails hence you will receive our new catalog via e-mail.

8. When the contaminated water had finally drained out of the pool the special cleaning crew climbed in and began to scrub all surfaces.

9. As I've told you before I'm not perfect nevertheless I never turn down an opportunity to try something new even if I think I might not succeed.

10. Eighteenth-century cities were not models of cleanliness furthermore crime and poverty were rampant while public sanitation was clearly non-existent.

QUIZ

Insert or delete punctuation where necessary.

1. The 100-acre Busch Gardens in Williamsburg, VA, is open to the public; from March to the end of October.

2. Whenever he professed his love for her she blushed.

3. I planted the flowering perennial plant; that you gave me.

4. Even though I said I wanted to be alone Jimmy insisted on joining me consequently I hated the movie.

5. Her husband because he is the opposite of a chauvinist cares deeply about her career therefore he even writes her résumé for her.

6. I wore my new black suit, and coat to the interview.

7. Itemize all the food in your refrigerator you'll be amazed at the quantity and variety of things.

8. Except for the pots and pans I've itemized my entire kitchen.

9. Although he had been walked and fed the dog barked loudly for a long time until finally we realized that he was afraid of the dark.

10. My teenage son should have been studying for exams instead he was outside playing basketball with his friends.

CHAPTER 9

Style and Clarity

In this chapter, you will learn about:

Writing Clearer Sentences

Have something to say, and say it as clearly as you can.
That is the only secret of style.
—Matthew Arnold

This quotation from the mid-nineteenth-century English poet and critic states the main idea of this chapter very well. You may write sentences that are correct; yet they may still lack style and clarity. Once you have the mechanics of English under control (e.g., the punctuation, spelling, and grammar rules you've learned), you need to concern yourself with clarity. That means making your writing accessible to the reader—unambiguous and impossible to be misread.

What common pitfalls block style and clarity? Look at the upcoming list in the next section, and get ready to learn how you can avoid the pitfalls.

Using Active Verbs

Too many passive (nonactive) verbs definitely block clarity. Passive verbs always contain a form of *to be* such as *is*, *was*, *were*, and *been*. For example:

> **Muddled:** A survey was taken of all board members by the governance committee.

In the preceding sentence, the nonactive or passive verb *was* buries the subject, *governance committee*. Why not start the sentence with the subject, the *governance committee*, and follow that with the active verb *took*? The passive verb *was* is a form of *to be*—delete it. *What* did they take? They took a *survey* (object).

> **Clearer:** The governance committee took a survey of all board members.

> **Even clearer:** The governance committee surveyed all the board members.

Let's look at another example:

> **Muddled:** A free book program is offered by the bookstore.

Why not give credit where it is due? Find the buried subject. Who offers the program? The bookstore. What is the action form of the verb? *Offers*. Notice the pas-

sive verb *is*—a form of *to be*. What does the bookstore offer? A free book program.

> **Clearer:** The bookstore offers a free book program.

> **Muddled:** A survey was taken of the townspeople by the town council.

Again, what is the buried subject? The town council. What is the action form of the verb *was taken*? *Took*. What did the town council take? A survey.

If for some reason the writer does *not* want to emphasize the subject in the reader's mind, then a passive or nonactive verb works very well. In the following sentence, no one takes the blame for *tabling the vote* because *the bill* is the subject. Notice the verb *was*, a form of *to be*:

> The bill was tabled by a 3-to-1 vote.

If you reread the previous improved sentences, you'll see that eliminating passive or nonactive verbs uncovers the subject and clarifies the sentences.

Written Practice 9-1

Rewrite the each of the following sentences by using active verbs. The first one is done for you.

1. This was the first year that a profit was realized by us.

   This year we realized a profit for the first time.

2. Their approach was to play their strongest people at the beginning of the game.

   _____

3. It is necessary to take a shopping list with you.

   _____

4. Building your speed on the treadmill is the next step.

   _____

5. The electric pen should be used to sign the documents.

   _____

As you read earlier, you may have a reason to use nonactive or passive verbs on occasion. If, however, you write ten sentences, all with passive verbs, you can probably change seven or eight to active verbs. Why should you take the time to do that? The answer is clear: Passive verbs contribute to the fog in anyone's writing. They also contribute to the following:

Passive verbs add unnecessary words to sentences.

Passive verbs make sentences harder to understand.

Passive verbs hide subjects.

We can prove all of these assertions.

1. Read the following sentence. Change the passive verb to an active verb, and remove two words.

   In the next chapter, the family dynamics are explained.

   _____

2. In the next sentence, find the hidden subject and change the passive verb to an active verb.

   It has been determined that we will bid on that job.

   _____

3. In the last sentence, find the buried subject and select an active verb.

   It was argued strongly that making cars more efficient was the committee's first concern.

   _____

Did you change the sentences in the following ways? Answers may vary.

1. The next chapter explains the family dynamics.
2. We have decided to bid on that job.
3. As a first concern, the committee argued strongly for more efficient cars.

Written Practice 9-2

Rewrite each of the following sentences, using active verbs.

1. The price of gas was raised for the second time this week by that gas station.

   _____

2. A litter of puppies was born recently from which Amelia can choose a pet.

   _____

3. The spring flowers are blooming that I planted last month.

   _____

4. It is believed by many people that global warming will eventually affect everyone.

   _____

5. Weaknesses were detected by the new automotive equipment.

   _____

6. A favorite Christmas movie is seen by our family every year.

   _____

7. Many dogs and cats are offered for adoption by that agency.

   _____

8. A tall fence will be placed between the Corbett and Balise properties.

   _____

9. Radar is used by meteorologists to forecast weather.

   _____

10. New sheets and blankets are needed for all the beds in the house.

Placing Important Information Last

Placing important information last also promotes clarity. You probably recall learning this in Chapter 8. Here's another way to think about introducing important ideas in sentences: Start with what your reader already knows, and then add the new information.

> Each year, the growing season ends [old information], and I'm left with barrels and barrels of tomatoes [new information]. These red, ripe beauties [old information] are luscious to behold, but how many pots of tomato sauce can I cook and store [new]? As it is, jars of tomato sauce [old] threaten to take over all my freezer space [new].

Written Practice 9-3

Rewrite each of the following sentences. In each sentence, place the important idea at the end.

1. How can I prepare for the future in a depressed economic climate?

   _____

2. Before the banks close, let's make a deposit.

   _____

3. You should file a police report if you are in a collision.

   _____

4. Improving style and clarity in your sentences is something you need to look at.

   _____

5. Sit down and reread your essay after you take time to think about other things for a while.

   _____

6. While your creativity is flowing, the first draft is an opportunity to put your words on paper.

   _____

7. Each department should review our joint goals after the first of the year.

   _____

8. The likelihood of growing food locally remains the important topic of the day.

   _____

9. The need for better art supplies in the middle school exists.

_____

10. We have stopped using that truck company because of the delays we experienced.

_____

Using Verbs Instead of Nouns

Clear sentences avoid "smothered verbs." Smothered verbs occur when we string noun phrases through our writing. Often the phrases start with the word *have* or the word *make*. You're sure to recognize these phrases:

make a recommendation

make a suggestion

have knowledge

have an objection

Find the buried verb in each of the following sentences:

1. I will make a recommendation that we skip our vacation this year.
2. I have no knowledge of his skills.
3. The judges have an objection to your uniform.

Let's look at how to change the noun *recommendation* into a verb:

1. I *recommend* that we skip our vacation this year.

In the next two sentences, change *knowledge* to *know* and *objection* to *object*.

2. I don't *know* about his skills.
3. The judges *object* to your uniform.

These simple changes bring your verbs into the open and make your sentences so much clearer.

Smothered verbs appear in many other ways. Hundreds of other expressions exist that use *do*, *reach*, *give*, and many others. For example:

do an inspection

hold a meeting

furnish an explanation

reach an agreement

Written Practice 9-4

Rewrite each of the following sentences by uncovering the smothered verbs. The first one is done for you.

1. I will send an invitation to all your friends.

   I will invite all your friends.

2. When you reach a decision, let me be the first to know.

   _____

3. Do I always have to give a justification for my actions?

   _____

4. A long time ago, I reached a conclusion that I can't please everyone all the time.

   _____

5. We can do an inspection of the house before we move in.

   _____

6. We shouldn't move on until we form a plan for the future.

   _____

7. Don't give an answer unless you are absolutely sure how you feel.

   _____

8. I give an apology anytime I offend someone.

   _____

9. Your father holds the opinion that you shouldn't drive unless your grades improve. (Note: Find a different word for *opinion*.)

_____

10. I'll help you clean up when you reach the end of the project.

_____

Written Practice 9-5

Read the following paragraph. Rewrite any sentences that seem cumbersome. Change passive verbs to active verbs, reveal hidden subjects and hidden verbs, and place important information last in sentences.

This advancement in science is hard to believe unless you see it in action. Thanks to the new Brain Computer Interface, people who are completely paralyzed due to illness or trauma will get help in the future. By connecting patients' brains to a computer, scientists can help these patients make a communication with others and even use their paralyzed limbs. Scientists have done an experiment with several people. It can be done but teaching a patient to move a cursor with his or her mind is neither fast nor fluid.

_____

_____

_____

_____

_____

_____

_____

Avoiding Unclear Pronoun References

Unclear pronoun reference leads directly to lost clarity. Every pronoun needs an antecedent, which is a noun or noun phrase it can point to. For example:

Muddled: Bob told the service representative *his* phone was not working.

Whose phone was not working? The sentence does not answer that question. We're trained to assign the pronoun (*his*) to the closest logical noun—*representative* in this case—but that's not necessarily what the writer meant. Instead, the phone might belong to the subject, *Bob.*

Clearer: Bob told the service representative that his, Bob's, phone was not working.

Sometimes rewriting the sentence is the better, clearer thing to do. That may entail dropping the pronoun in favor of a noun. For example:

Muddled: Jen dropped the laptop computer on the glass-top desk and broke it.

What broke, the computer or the glass-top desk? What does *it* refer to?

Clearer: Jen dropped the laptop computer on the glass-top desk and broke the glass.
Clearer: When Jen dropped the laptop computer on the glass-top desk, the glass broke.

Written Practice 9-6

Rewrite the sentences to correct the pronoun reference errors. The first one is done for you.

1. Don't give new uniforms to employees until they have name tags.

   Don't give new uniforms to employees until the uniforms have name tags.

2. Myrna told Jodi she had a terrible cold and shouldn't go to the PTA meeting.

   _____

3. Our new water tank holds 20 percent less than our old one. It cost 30 percent more, though.

   _____

4. My daughter wrote a report and studied for a spelling test. It was a long one.

_____

5. The chart at the end of the magazine article was included in its original form.

_____

Written Practice 9-7

Make the pronoun references clear in the following sentences.

1. My neighbor frequently buys my family food because they are so kind.

_____

2. I hammered the nail into the picture hook, and now it is crooked.

_____

3. Both Gloria and Priscilla played with her children.

_____

4. The turkey platter was empty, but we were tired of eating it anyway.

_____

5. The principal was speaking to Jason, and he looked unhappy.

_____

6. Although Robin likes working at the cake shop, she never eats them herself.

_____

7. Although the car smashed into the tree, it was not damaged.

_____

8. After interviewing several teachers, I realized that it was not for me.

_____

9. I went to see my father and my grandfather, who told me his latest health problem.

_____

10. White and Smith made his presentation.

_____

Placing Descriptive Words Correctly

If at all possible, place a descriptive word or phrase next to the word it describes. Misplacement of descriptive words and phrases results in confused meaning. For example:

Muddled: The elderly man relaxed after years of hard work on his porch.

Did the man really do all those years of hard work *on his porch*? Probably not, but that's what the sentence states. Undoubtedly, the sentence meant to state that the man *relaxed on his porch* after years of hard work. *On his porch* describes *relaxed*, telling where the man relaxed.

Corrected: The elderly man relaxed on his porch after years of hard work.

Let's look at another example:

Muddled: Established employees who talk about the past constantly overawe new employees.

Did the employees talk constantly about the past? The correction comes when you move the descriptive word, *constantly*, next to the word it describes, that is, *talk*.

Corrected: Established employees who talk *constantly* about the past overawe *new employees.*

Look at another example:

Muddled: I wrote my evaluation of the new product on the provided lines.

Is there a new product *on the lines provided*? Most likely, there is not.

Clearer: I wrote on the provided lines my evaluation of the new product.
Clearer: Using the provided lines, I wrote my evaluation of the new product.

Written Practice 9-8

Clarify the following sentences by placing descriptive phrases where they belong.

1. The man in his desk found his glasses.

   _____

2. The student hung on the wall of her room a picture of a favorite music group.

   _____

3. The horse belongs to that rider with the brown spots.

   _____

4. The teacher posted the notes for the students covered in class.

   _____

5. My old car has driven 100,000 miles in the driveway.

   _____

Written Practice 9-9

Read the paragraph. Correct any unclear pronoun references, and place the descriptive words correctly. One sentence is correct as written.

When you take your child to the doctor because he is coughing and sneezing, with asthma type symptoms, do you really know what's wrong? Up to now, doctors have depended upon physical exams, symptoms, and the child's history to explain the illness in the office visit. Doctors prescribe antibiotics using their best judgments, but often they don't cure the child because the ailment as far as the cause of it is concerned cannot be pinpointed. Now, however, there is a new test, which gives hope of understanding viruses associated with asthma attacks using the Virochip. A new study has found an unexpected number of viruses and viral subtypes led by University of California–San Francisco scientists in patients with respiratory tract infections (RTIs). The technique used in the study may help identify new viruses associated with human diseases and lead to specific strategies for treatment and prevention.

Deleting Unnecessary Words

How many times have you heard or read this classic example of repetition in a sentence:

> My friend, he eats a huge lunch and then an even larger dinner.

Which word do you need to delete? Of course, the answer is *he*. The pronoun just repeats the subject, *friend*, and for no reason.

Here is another frequent error:

> My reason for ordering in dinner is that I thought we would have more time to talk.

My reason . . . is that is the unnecessarily wordy version of the following:

> I ordered in dinner so that we would have more time to talk.

In addition, when your aim is clarity in writing, you need to weed out vague, overwritten phrases.

> We need a course in *effective communications*.

Did you mean *clear writing*? Then say it! We need a course in *clear writing*.

> In some offices, there are *equipment malfunctions*. In my office, there are only *clogged printers*.

Other vague, overused phrases include:

financial resources for *money*

inclement weather conditions for *rain, sleet, snow*

human resource development for *training*

banking facility for *bank*

retail facility for *store*

In addition, vagueness in writing persists because we insist on overqualifying terms. If something is clear, is *perfectly clear* clearer? No. Why not just drop the overqualification *perfectly*?

Here are more examples of imprecise overqualifications. How would you simplify them?

1. He utterly rejected my proposal.
2. The route drawing was quite precise.
3. My computer is radically new.
4. We thought their solution was quite imaginative.
5. My dog is completely devoted to the children.

You probably realize that the overqualifications—*utterly*, *quite*, *radically*, and *completely*—add little meaning. Delete them!

Another obstacle to clarity is using wordy expressions instead of a single word. What one word can you substitute for these phrases?

as of this time	at this time
at the present time	at present
our current belief is	at this point
after further consideration	at this point in time
upon further reflection	

By the time you finished reading this list, it probably occurred to you that all the expressions referred to *now*. Any one of these expressions might be avoided by using the simple word *now*:

Wordy: *At this time*, we're not hiring.

Clearer: We're not hiring *now*.

Look at the other wordy expressions that substitute for the word *then*:

during the past	at that date
up until that time	at that time
at that point	in that period
at that point in time	during the past
as of that time	

Did you realize that using the word *then* could substitute for any of the expressions?

Wordy: In that period, we read all the child-rearing books we could find.

Clearer: Then we read all the child-rearing books we could find.

Wordy: As of that time, we started toilet training children at a year old.

Clearer: We started toilet training children at a year old then.

My favorite unnecessary words are listed in the following practice.

Written Practice 9-10

On the lines provided, write a matching expression that eliminates the extra words from the original expression. The first one is done for you.

1. repeat again *repeat*
2. refer back _____
3. true facts _____
4. active consideration _____
5. present status _____
6. entirely complete _____
7. past history _____
8. midway between _____
9. in ten years from now _____
10. at that time _____

Written Practice 9-11

Simplify each of the following sentences by eliminating unnecessary words.

1. Juana's mother she agreed to bake for her granddaughter's birthday party.

_____

2. Mickey thought the staging of that play was quite imaginative.

_____

3. At this point in time, we need to consider a significant budget cut.

_____

4. My reason for looking for a job is that I heard the company I work for is downsizing.

_____

5. The department head she said, "We're not giving any bonuses at this time."

_____

Written Practice 9-12

Delete repetitions and overqualifications in the following sentences.

1. Your schedule is completely full, so you won't be going out for lunch.

_____

2. My reason for not returning the book to the library is that I hadn't finished it.

_____

3. We were perfectly happy not to leave the house on a rainy day.

_____

4. Upon further reflection, I've decided to adopt a kitten from the local animal shelter.

_____

5. At this point in time, a vacation is out of the question.

_____

6. As of that time, we still had our out-of-date computers.

_____

7. Midway between my house and yours there's a beautiful park.

_____

8. My car it has 80,000 miles on its odometer.

_____

9. Before you offer your opinion, at least get the true facts.

10. We're looking for a new retail facility.

Correcting Illogical Statements

Check the logic of the following sentence:

Most of the days of our vacation were cloudy, but we went boating or swimming.

Logic would dictate that you went swimming despite the clouds! How can you say that?

Most of the days of our vacation were cloudy; yet, we went boating or swimming.

Written Practice 9-13

In each of the following sentences, look for unnecessary words and illogical statements. Make changes as necessary.

1. The carriage tour on the carriage around Charleston was fascinating.

2. The reason I enjoyed the ride was because I love historical architecture.

3. The carriage driver, he was full of intriguing stories.

4. The highlight of the tour was when we saw the outdoor crafts market.

5. Despite the wonderful tour, I signed up for another one for next year.

Written Practice 9-14

In each of the following sentences, find misplaced words and descriptive phrases, unnecessary words, and illogical statements, and correct the errors.

1. At the end of the season, the team, it gave a party for its supporters.

   _____

2. The reason I bought this TV was because it was on sale.

   _____

3. At that point in time, I couldn't afford one.

   _____

4. All of the new graduates who graduated from the citizenship class met at the school for an awards ceremony.

   _____

5. Since I despise that band's kind of music, I attend their concerts frequently.

   _____

6. My favorite part of the afternoon was when we went through the bead museum.

   _____

7. After signing the bill, the pen was given to one of the senators.

   _____

8. Complicated computer problems are solved by quite precise corrections.

   _____

9. The voters on the desk completed registration forms.

   _____

10. The applicant's present status is perfect for our needs.

   _____

Written Practice 9-15

Read the following paragraph. Look for and correct unnecessary words, illogical statements, and unbalanced sentences in the first four sentences.

The Presidential Medal of Freedom it is awarded each year by the President. Even though it is important, it is the highest civilian award in the United States. People who served in WWII were honored first in 1945 by Harry Truman and John F. Kennedy was reviving the medal in 1963 on or near July Fourth when it became a yearly tradition to give it. There were two doctors, one congressman, a retired general, a university chancellor, and a judge were honored in 2008 by President George W. Bush.

Writing Balanced Sentences—a Reminder

Chapter 7 explained balanced sentences, and they deserve a second look under the topic of style and clarity. A balanced sentence contributes to clarity because related ideas, actions, and descriptions take the same form. When a sentence flows smoothly from beginning to end, it is balanced.

Remember that clarity relates to accessibility. When a sentence lacks balance, it is clearly not as accessible to the reader. At the least, unparallel sentences almost always force a reader to reread the sentence. How accessible are the ideas in the following sentences?

> The candidate thanked them for their loyalty, dedication, and because they were willing to work overtime.

In this sentence, you read the two nouns, *loyalty* and *dedication* (objects of the preposition *for*), and you rightfully expected a third one. But it's not there. Instead, the writer switched to a clause, *because they were willing to work overtime.* How can you take the idea of that clause and change it to a noun? Try this:

> The candidate thanked them for their *loyalty*, *dedication*, and *willingness* to work overtime.

As you can see, changing the verb *were willing* to the noun *willingness* restored parallel form to the sentence.

Now turn from nouns to adjectives, and see how they are written in parallel form.

Incorrect: My new computer is faster, more powerful, and it's more flexible.

Correct: My new computer is faster, more powerful, and more flexible.

Changing the clause, *and it's more flexible,* to a one-word adjective, *flexible,* restores parallel form to this sentence.

Find the errors in the following sentences:

1. The website said that the program taught tennis, swimming, and how to row a canoe.

   _____

2. This week the family will wash the windows, rake the leaves, and they'll take the time to clean the garage.

   _____

3. Today I have a parent-teacher conference, a planning meeting at work, and I will cook dinner for company.

   _____

4. Ellen thought the movie was boring, childish, and was too long.

   _____

5. I kneaded the dough, prepared the wet ingredients, and then I remembered to turn on the oven.

   _____

Your answers should have included these words (or similar parallel choices):

1. and rowing
2. and clean the garage
3. and a dinner to cook for company
4. and too long
5. remembered to turn on the oven

To sum up, when you list ideas, items, or actions, the list elements must be all nouns, all infinitives, all prepositional phrases, all gerunds, or all clauses.

Using Prepositions Correctly in a Series

Finally, prepositions also need to introduce words in a series correctly. When prepositions are used incorrectly, a lack of parallelism results. For example:

There are meals in the morning and noon.

The way it is written, this sentence actually says that there are meals *in* the morning and *in* the noon. The preposition is *in*. Is this the correct word for each item? No, it should be *in* the morning and *at* noon.

Some words and verbs use prepositions as well. Look at this example:

The cancer researcher is interested and excited about the new advances in medical technology.

What are the words in the parallel structure? They are *interested and excited*. The researcher is excited *about* the advances. This use of the preposition *about* is correct. What about *interested*? Does *about* go with *interested*? Test the phrases:

excited *about* the advances . . . ? Correct.

interested *about* the advances . . . ? Incorrect.

The correct preposition to use with *interested* is *in*. Therefore, the earlier sentence is incorrect. The correct preposition must be used with each item of a parallel structure. The following is correct:

The cancer researcher is interested *in* and excited *about* the new advances in medical technology.

When you are in doubt about which preposition to use, consult the following list:

Common Verbs and Adjectives with Prepositions*

agree with	apologize for	apply for	apply to
approve of	argue for	argue with	arrive at
arrive in	be	be absent from	be accused of
be accustomed to	be acquainted with	be addicted to	be afraid of
be angry at	be angry with	be annoyed at	be annoyed with
be associated with	be aware of	be capable of	be cluttered with

---

*Used by permission of http://www.MyEnglishTeacher.net, http://www.myenglishteacher .net, 2009. All rights reserved.

be committed to	be composed of	be concerned about	be connected to
be content with	be convinced of	be coordinated with	be covered with
be crowded with	be devoted to	be disappointed in	be disappointed with
be discriminated against	be divorced from	be done with	be dressed in
be engaged to	be envious of	be equipped with	be excited about
be exhausted from	be exposed to	be faithful to	be familiar with
be filled with	be finished with	be fond of	be frightened of
be friendly to	be friendly with	be frightened by	be furnished with
be gone from	be grateful for	be grateful to	be guilty of
be innocent of	be interested in	be involved with	be jealous of
be known for	be limited to	be located in	be located to
be made from	be made of	be married to	be opposed to
be pleased with	be polite with	be prepared for	be prepared to
be proud of	be qualified for	be related to	be relevant to
be responsible for	be satisfied with	be terrified of	be tired of
be upset with	be used to	be worried about	believe in
blame (someone) for	compare to	compare with	complain about
complain of	consist of	contribute to	count on
count upon	decide on	decide upon	depend on
distinguish from	dream about	dream of	escape from
excel at	excel in	excuse for	feel for
fight for	forgive (someone) for	have a reason for	have an excuse for
hide from	hope for	insist on	introduce to
keep (someone) from (doing something)	look forward to	object to	participate in
pray for	prevent (someone) from (doing something)	prohibit (someone) from (doing something)	recover from
rescue from	respond to	stop (someone) from (doing something)	succeed in
take advantage of	take care of	talk about	talk of
thank someone for	think about	think of	

Written Practice 9-16

For each of the following sentences, correct any errors in parallel structure.

1. The astronauts will launch from the space center, capture the telescope, service it, and repairing it is the plan.

   _____

2. They will service the Hubble Telescope, upgrade its parts, and replacing broken parts is an option.

   _____

3. The Hubble was launched in 1990 and is outliving its 15-year life expectancy already.

   _____

4. Hubble gives us colorful, crisp, and in detail images of the cosmos.

   _____

5. Our drama teacher taught us how to stand, project our voices, and then there's moving on stage.

   _____

6. My son learned how to play the guitar, the trumpet, and the drum was a part of his lessons, too.

   _____

7. This new car is faster, sleeker, and it seems to use less gas.

   _____

8. We'll know our new program is working when staff arrive on time, keep their equipment in good repair, and used fewer sick days.

   _____

9. The leaves are greener, the grass is more lush, and the flowers they're growing taller than ever.

   _____

10. Angie is pleasant and has intelligence.

   _____

QUIZ

Correct the following sentences.

1. A rest period was taken by the preschoolers.

_____

2. My friend, she left before I did.

_____

3. Mr. Bacari made a recommendation that the company hire me.

_____

4. The visitors gave the animals peanuts and they continued to play.

_____

5. Your travel directions were quite precise.

_____

6. The building was old and dilapidated, so the city planner decided to use it for students.

_____

7. The reason I took the bus was because I had no money for gas.

_____

8. I'm acquainted and devoted to that charity.

_____

9. The store was closed by the creditors.

_____

10. It is believed by the police that Wally drove the car.

_____

PART THREE TEST

Circle the letter of the word, phrase, or sentence that *best* completes or corrects each sentence.

1. This was the first summer a cross-country trip was made by our family.
   - (a) This was the first cross-country summer trip that was made by our family.
   - (b) A first summer cross-country trip was made by our family.
   - (c) Our family made a cross-country trip for the first time this summer.
   - (d) Did you know that this was the first summer cross-country trip that was made by our family.

2. It has been determined that our council will elect a new president.
   - (a) Our council has decided to elect a new president.
   - (b) It has been determined that our council needs to elect a new president.
   - (c) Our council it will elect a new president.
   - (d) It has been determined that our council will elect a new president and we'll do it soon.

3. Before the product is no longer offered, let's consider ordering one.
   - (a) Before the product is no longer offered, you order one.
   - (b) Before the product is no longer offered, let's order one.
   - (c) Before that product is no longer offered, let's just try to order one.
   - (d) Let's order that product before it's no longer offered.

4. I have no knowledge of the benefits of vitamins.
   - (a) I have no benefits from the knowledge of vitamins.
   - (b) I don't know about the benefits of vitamins.
   - (c) Nobody gave me no knowledge of vitamins.
   - (d) I have no knowledge or any benefits either from vitamins.

5. Limiting calories, and walking daily are the most effective ways to lose weight.

   (a) Limiting calories and walking daily are the most effective ways to lose weight.

   (b) For me, limiting calories, and walking daily are the most effective ways to lose weight.

   (c) Walking daily and calories, are the most effective ways to lose weight.

   (d) Limiting calories, and walking daily, they are the most effective ways to lose weight.

6. We're trying to limit the miles we drive, do all our errands at once, and using less gasoline.

   (a) We're trying to limit the miles we drive, do all our errands at once, and using less gasoline is also a choice.

   (b) We're trying to limit the miles we drive, do all our errands at once, and use less gasoline.

   (c) We're trying to limit the miles we drive do all our errands at once and using less gasoline.

   (d) We're trying to limit the miles we drive, do all our errands at once, and then we're using less gasoline.

7. A free food program is offered by our town.

   (a) A free food program is offered by our town and others also.

   (b) A free food program is offered our town.

   (c) Also, our town it offers a free food program.

   (d) Our town offers a free food program.

8. In the last chapter, we then finally meet the killer.

   (a) In the last chapter, finally the killer.

   (b) In the last chapter, we then finally in the end meet the killer.

   (c) In the last chapter, it is then we finally meet the killer.

   (d) We finally meet the killer in the last chapter.

9. A litter of kittens was born at the animal shelter from which we'll choose our next pet.

   (a) A litter of kittens was born at the animal shelter; from which we'll choose our next pet.

   (b) We'll choose our next pet from the litter of kittens born at the animal shelter.

   (c) A litter of kittens are at the animal shelter from which we'll choose our next pet.

   (d) A litter of kittens, born at the animal shelter; we'll choose our next pet.

10. The snow and ice storm lasted for hours yet our power stayed on!

    (a) The snow and ice storm lasted for hours; yet we never lost power!

    (b) The snow and ice storm lasted for hours: yet our power stayed on!

    (c) The snow and ice storm lasted for hours, yet we never lost power!

    (d) The snow and ice storm lasted for hours Yet our power stayed on!

11. Should I serve a lot of hors d'oeuvres or should I concentrate on making a larger dinner?

    (a) Should I serve a lot of hors d'oeuvres or should I concentrate on making a larger dinner!

    (b) Should I serve a lot of hors d'oeuvres, or should I concentrate on making a larger dinner?

    (c) Should I serve a lot of hors d'oeuvres. or should I concentrate on making a larger dinner?

    (d) Should I serve a lot of hors d'oeuvres or do you think I should concentrate on making a larger dinner?

12. There was no dinner served at the Wood's party nor was there any wine or beer neither.

    (a) There was no dinner at the Wood's party nor was there any wine or beer for anyone neither.

    (b) There was no dinner at the Wood's party: nor was there any wine or beer.

    (c) There was no dinner at the Wood's party, nor was there any wine or beer.

    (d) There was no dinner at the Wood's party; nor was there any wine or beer.

13. One business owner thought her salespeople quit because they were on the road too much on the contrary they were simply the wrong fit for the job.

    (a) One business owner thought her salespeople quit because they were on the road too much; on the contrary, they were simply the wrong fit for the job.

    (b) One business owner thought her salespeople quit because they were on the road too much. On the contrary they were simply the wrong fit for the job.

    (c) One business owner thought her salespeople quit because they were on the road too much, on the contrary, they were simply the wrong fit for the job.

    (d) One business owner thought her salespeople quit because they were on the road too much on the contrary, they were simply the wrong fit for the job.

14. This particular employer put congeniality at the top of her list of important employee characteristics, however she soon learned that other features were more important.

    (a) This particular employer put congeniality at the top of her list of important employee characteristics—however she soon learned that other features were more important.

    (b) This particular employer put congeniality at the top of her list of important employee characteristics; however she soon learned that other features were more important.

    (c) This particular employer put congeniality at the top of her list of important employee characteristics, however, she soon learned that other features were more important.

    (d) This particular employer put congeniality at the top of her list of important employee characteristics; however, she soon learned that other features were more important.

15. Some employers think that they are at fault if a new employee starts work
    and then; instead leaves immediately.

    (a) Some employers think that they are at fault if a new employee starts
        work but then leaves immediately.

    (b) Some employers think that they are at fault. If a new employee starts
        work and then instead leaves immediately.

    (c) Some employers think that they are at fault, if a new employee starts
        work and then; instead leaves immediately.

    (d) Some employers think that they are at fault if a new employee starts
        work and then; instead leaves immediately.

16. Hernando was always early for work but he received a raise in pay.

    (a) Hernando was always early for work; but he received a raise in pay.

    (b) Hernando was always early for work, but he received a raise in pay.

    (c) Hernando was always early for work; as a result, he received a raise
        in pay.

    (d) Although Hernando was always late for work he received a raise
        in pay.

17. Randi who loves raising both annual and perennial flowers always does his
    own gardening, however on very hot days he regrets not having help.

    (a) Randi who loves raising both annual and perennial flowers always does
        his own gardening, however; on very hot days he regrets not having
        help.

    (b) Randi, who loves raising both annual and perennial flowers always
        does his own gardening, however on very hot days he regrets not
        having help.

    (c) Randi, who loves raising both annual and perennial flowers, always
        does his own gardening; however, on very hot days he regrets not
        having help.

    (d) Randi he loves raising both annual and perennial flowers always does
        his own gardening, however on very hot days he regrets not having help.

18. My son has an objection to the school's dress code.

   (a) My son has an objection to the school's dress code.

   (b) My son he has an objection to the schools' dress code.

   (c) My son's dress code is objected to by the school.

   (d) My son objects to the school's dress code.

19. A free membership is offered by the health club each January.

   (a) In January, a free membership is offered by the health club.

   (b) The health club offers a free membership each January.

   (c) A free membership each January is offered by the health club.

   (d) Each January is when a free membership is offered by the health club.

20. Their plan was to offer the best people more hours.

   (a) They offered the best people more hours.

   (b) They were offering the best people more hours as a part of their plan.

   (c) Their plan for the best people was to offer more hours to them.

   (d) There plan was offering more hours to the best people.

21. It has been determined that we need to increase revenues or risk going out of business.

   (a) We have been determining that we need to increase revenues or risk going out of business.

   (b) We have determined that we need to increase revenues or risk going out of business.

   (c) Going out of business has been determined.

   (d) It has been determined that we need to increase revenues or risk going out of business or just wait another year.

22. The need for music and art programs in public schools exists.

   (a) The need for music and art programs in public schools, doesn't it exists.

   (b) Public schools they think they need music and art programs.

   (c) The need for at least music and art programs in public schools exists.

   (d) Public schools need music and art programs.

23. Will you allow me to make a suggestion regarding the names of babysitters?

    (a) Will you allow me to suggest the names of babysitters?

    (b) Will you allow me to give you a suggestion regarding the names of babysitters?

    (c) You should allow me to make a suggestion regarding the names of babysitters?

    (d) When will you allow me to make a suggestion regarding the names of babysitters?

24. Mack, and Melia enjoyed a day away from work.

    (a) Mack, and Melia, enjoyed a day away from work.

    (b) Mack, and Melia they enjoyed a day away from work.

    (c) Mack and Melia enjoyed a day away from work.

    (d) Mack, and Melia enjoyed a day, away from work.

25. My children have joined me in an effort to save energy, we're also saving money.

    (a) My children they have joined me in an effort to save energy, we're also saving money.

    (b) My children have joined me in an effort to save energy; as a result, we're also saving money.

    (c) My children have joined me in an effort to save energy; We're also saving money.

    (d) My children have joined me in an effort to save energy: we're also saving money.

26. When the temperature drops below 32 degrees I prefer to sit home and read.

    (a) When the temperature it drops below 32 degrees I prefer to sit home and read.

    (b) I prefer to sit home and read, when the temperature drops below 32 degrees.

    (c) When and if the temperature drops below 32 degrees I prefer to sit home and read.

    (d) When the temperature drops below 32 degrees, I prefer to sit home and read.

27. A delicious dessert was offered by the chef.

    (a) A delicious dessert was offered immediately by the chef.

    (b) A delicious dessert was also offered by the chef.

    (c) When the chef offered a delicious dessert.

    (d) The chef offered a delicious dessert.

28. Albie runs a marathon at least once a year and while it takes rigorous training he enjoys it very much.

    (a) Albie runs a marathon at least once a year; and while it takes rigorous training he enjoys it very much.

    (b) Albie runs a marathon at least once a year; and while it takes rigorous training, he enjoys it very much?

    (c) Albie runs a marathon at least once a year, and, while it takes rigorous training, he enjoys it very much.

    (d) Albie runs a marathon at least once a year: and while it takes rigorous training he enjoys it very much.

29. When the new president finally took office the moving trucks appeared and the transition from one household to another was finally complete.

    (a) When the new president finally took office; the moving trucks appeared and the transition from one household to another was finally complete.

    (b) When the new president finally took office; the moving trucks appeared, and the transition from one household to another was finally complete.

    (c) When the new president, finally took office, the moving trucks appeared, and the transition from one household to another it was finally complete.

    (d) When the new president finally took office, the moving trucks appeared, and the transition from one household to another was finally complete.

30. Each year I'm left with a huge amount of studying and exams are looming.

    (a) Each year I'm left with a huge amount of studying and exams they are looming.

    (b) Each year I'm left with a huge amount of studying and many exams looming.

    (c) Each year, I'm left, with a huge amount of studying; and exams are looming.

    (d) Each year I'm left with a huge amount of studying and exams are looming.

31. A book club and monthly discussions are offered by our neighborhood bookstore.

    (a) A book club, and monthly discussions are offered by our neighborhood bookstore.

    (b) Our neighborhood bookstore is offering a book club.

    (c) Our neighborhood bookstore offers a book club and monthly discussions.

    (d) A monthly discussions and book club are offered by our neighborhood bookstore.

32. Both Lynn and Kascia sewed party dresses for her children.

    (a) Both Lynn and Kascia sewed party dresses for Lynn's children.

    (b) Both Lynn and Kascia they sewed party dresses for her children.

    (c) Both Lynn and Kascia sewed party dresses for her children.

    (d) Both Kascia and Lynn sewed party dresses for her children.

33. Aidan and Elias ran, and jumped in every room in the house.

    (a) Aidan and Elias ran and jumped, in every room in the house.

    (b) Aidan and Elias ran and jumped in every room in the house.

    (c) Aidan and Elias, they ran and jumped in every room in the house.

    (d) Aidan and Elias; they ran and jumped in every room in the house.

34. I will be leaving in a few minutes.

    (a) I will leave in a few minutes.

    (b) I will be leaving for sure in a few minutes.

    (c) I will have been leaving in a few minutes.

    (d) I had been leaving in a few minutes.

35. My stamp collection has increased in value; and I still enjoy working on it.

    (a) My stamp collection has increased in value; but I still enjoy working on it.

    (b) My stamp collection has increased in value, and I still enjoy working on it.

    (c) My stamp collection has increased in value: and I still enjoy working on it.

    (d) My stamp collection, it has increased in value; and I still enjoy working on it.

36. The bride and groom left the reception, as they waved to their guests.

    (a) As the bride and groom left the reception, they waved to their guests.

    (b) The bride and groom left the reception, as they waved to their guests.

    (c) The bride and groom left the reception, and waved to their guests.

    (d) The bride and groom left the reception; as they waved to their guests.

37. The mayor made a declaration that the roadwork would go forward.

    (a) The mayor made a declaration today that the roadwork would go forward.

    (b) The mayor, he made a declaration that the roadwork would go forward.

    (c) The mayor declared that the roadwork would go forward.

    (d) The mayor made a declaration that the roadwork would go forward.

38. The large truck braked suddenly and was swerving into the left lane.

    (a) Although the large truck braked suddenly and was swerving into the left lane.

    (b) The large truck braked suddenly and it was swerving into the left lane.

(c) The large truck braked suddenly (and was swerving into the left lane).

(d) The large truck braked suddenly and swerved into the left lane.

39. Although we were warned to stay off the slick roads we drove to work anyway.

   (a) Although we were warned to stay off the slick roads, we drove to work anyway.

   (b) Although, we were warned to stay off the slick roads we drove to work anyway.

   (c) Although we were warned to stay off the slick roads; we drove to work anyway.

   (d) Although we were warned to stay off the slick roads we drove to work anyway.

40. Because of the warning to stay off the slick roads, we drove to work.

   (a) Because of the warning to stay off the slick roads—we drove to work.

   (b) Because, of the warning to stay off the slick roads, we drove to work.

   (c) Because of the warning to stay off the slick roads: we drove to work.

   (d) Despite the warning to stay off the slick roads, we drove to work.

41. My friends and I went out for lunch, and she paid the bill.

   (a) My friends and I went out for lunch, and she was paying the bill.

   (b) Me and my friends went out for lunch, and she paid the bill.

   (c) My friends and me went out for lunch, and she paid the bill.

   (d) My friends and I went out for lunch, and Elyn paid the bill.

42. His woodcarvings that were made of mahogany wood had a large audience of eager buyers.

   (a) His carvings that were wood and made of mahogany wood had a large audience of eager buyers.

   (b) His mahogany woodcarvings had a large audience of eager buyers.

   (c) His woodcarvings that he made of mahogany wood had a large audience of eager buyers.

   (d) His woodcarvings that were made of wood that was mahogany had a large audience of eager buyers.

43. Our first-grader had a very successful year and a slow start in kindergarten.

    (a) Our first-grader had a very successful year. He had a slow start in kindergarten.

    (b) Although he had a slow start in kindergarten, our son had a very successful year in first grade.

    (c) Our first-grader, he had a very successful year. He had a slow start in kindergarten.

    (d) Our first-grader had a very successful year: He had a slow start in kindergarten.

44. We took Route 9, the Palisades Parkway, and the Connecticut Turnpike, finally we reached Bridgeport.

    (a) We took Route 9 the Palisades Parkway and the Connecticut Turnpike, finally we reached Bridgeport.

    (b) We took Route 9, the Palisades Parkway, and the Connecticut Turnpike; finally, we reached Bridgeport.

    (c) Finally we took Route 9, the Palisades Parkway, and the Connecticut Turnpike, then we reached Bridgeport.

    (d) We took Route 9, the Palisades Parkway, and the Connecticut Turnpike, finally we reached bridgeport.

45. The small lunch truck advertised bottled water, sandwiches, and four different cakes, still people asked for hot dogs.

    (a) The small lunch truck advertised bottled water, sandwiches, and four different cakes; still people asked for hot dogs.

    (b) The small lunch truck advertised bottled water sandwiches and four different cakes, still people asked for hot dogs.

    (c) The lunch truck which was small advertised bottled water, sandwiches, and four different cakes, still people asked for hot dogs.

    (d) The small lunch truck advertised bottled water, sandwiches, and four different cakes! still people asked for hot dogs.

46. If you make a demand, you may receive good service.

    (a) If you demand good service, you may receive it.

    (b) If you make a demand, you may receive good service on your second request.

(c) If you make a demand, you may eventually receive good service.

(d) If you do it and you make a demand, you may receive good service.

47. *Cars, Trucks, and Power Boats* was the title of the book.

   (a) *Cars, Trucks, and Power Boats* were the title of the book.

   (b) *Car, Truck, and Power Boat* was the title of the book.

   (c) The book's title was *Cars, Trucks, and Power Boats.*

   (d) *Cars, Trucks, and Power Boats,* that was the title of the book.

48. They told me in the space provided to write my answer.

   (a) They told me in the space provided was where I should write my answer.

   (b) I heard them tell me in the space provided to write my answer.

   (c) Did I hear them tell me in the space provided was where I should write my answer?

   (d) They told me to write my answer in the space provided.

49. The museum on the only blank wall hung a famous painting by Monet.

   (a) The famous museum on the only blank wall hung a painting by Monet.

   (b) The museum on the only blank wall, hung a famous painting by Monet.

   (c) The museum hung a famous painting by Monet on the only blank wall.

   (d) The museum on the only blank wall hung a famous painting that was by Monet.

50. The division chief posted the work rules for the employees listed in the manual.

   (a) The division chief posted the work rules for the employees recently listed in the manual.

   (b) The division chief posted the work rules listed in the manual for the employees.

   (c) The division chief posted the work rules for the employees listed in the manual and the hours as well.

   (d) The division chief posted the work rules at least for the employees listed in the manual.

PART FOUR

SPELLING AND WORD USAGE SKILLS

CHAPTER 10

Proven Techniques to Improve Spelling

In this chapter you will learn:

Who Needs Help with Spelling?
Techniques for Improving Spelling Skills
Helpful Spelling Rules—or Not
Becoming a Better Speller

Who Needs Help with Spelling?

Many people need help with spelling. Adults don't necessarily like to talk about it, but they fear spelling and spelling errors as much as children do. And they have good reason. Some are natural spellers, learning to spell and retaining the spellings very easily. For others, spelling is a lifelong problem. If you have spelling problems, however, having a plan of attack really helps.

If you can't rely on yourself to spell words correctly at least 98 percent of the time, spelling is a concern that may cause you considerable worry. Your readers notice the errors immediately. If you are submitting writing to teachers, test examiners, or employers—even friends—poor spelling creates a bad impression. Interestingly, these people may place undue emphasis on spelling, ignoring the brilliant argument, the correct answer, or the dazzling description. Your only choice is to improve your spelling.

Interesting, too, is that even though people use word processors equipped with a spell-checker, there are still times when people need to write. Consequently, although many adults can read well at work, they do all they can to avoid writing because of their fear of and embarrassment over their spelling.

If there is any comfort in it, you should know that poor spellers are not alone. Some very famous, successful people have had significant problems with spelling. One of the more surprising examples is Alfred Mosher Butts, the inventor of the game Scrabble who said to a reporter, "I'm really a terrible speller." Perhaps developing the game was his way of tackling the problem. Other famous people on the poor-spellers list may surprise you. Note that most had learning disabilities that if noticed today would probably be treatable. Many on the list were or are dyslexic (having a disability that makes understanding written language and actually writing language very difficult), which would account for serious spelling problems. Some notable poor spellers include Albert Einstein, Norman Rockwell, Winston Churchill, Agatha Christie, Thomas Edison, General George Patton, and Charles Schwab.*

This is only a partial list of famous people who had trouble reading and writing. Each one attacked the problem in a different way, but the way was always difficult. Undoubtedly, your spelling problem, if you have one, is not as serious as those you just read about; however, whatever your need—from a simple review to a serious spelling makeover—try the following suggestions and practices to improve your spelling. And by the way, please don't ever send an e-mail or other electronic message without first using the spell-checker!

---

*Most of these quotes were originally published on Susan Barton's "Bright Solutions for Dyslexia" website. They are reprinted with written permission of Susan Barton. Fuller descriptions were added by Steve Miller. To learn more about dyslexia, go to: www.BrightSolutions.US.

Techniques for Improving Spelling Skills

If spelling is a problem for you, try a more organized approach to learning. First, learning to spell correctly takes time and patience. Never try to learn to spell a whole list of words at one time. Instead, take your time and do a small amount of studying at any one time. Review on a regular basis. The following constitutes just the beginning of a new plan:

1. Keep a small notebook handy to record words that you have spelled incorrectly or those that are new to you.

2. When you enter a word into the notebook, divide it into syllables. For example, the word *constitute* would be listed in the spelling book in syllables first, then with pronunciation help, a definition, and the part of speech:

   con-sti-tute (kon-stə-toot), comprise, make up (v.)

   Make sure you are spelling and pronouncing the word correctly. Check with a dictionary or use the spelling or dictionary tool on your computer. Use an audible dictionary to hear the correct pronunciation.

3. Read the word. Say it in syllables.

4. Try to connect the word to a common spelling rule. For example, niece, *i* before *e* except after *c*.

5. Close your eyes, and picture the word.

6. Write the word. Check it. Write it again if necessary.

7. Review a word until you are sure you know how to spell it.

IDENTIFYING WHAT KIND OF LEARNER YOU ARE

Second, have you ever considered what *type of learner* you are? Knowing *how* you learn may help you a great deal as you try to improve your spelling. Consider the following:

- Are you a visual learner? You learn primarily through the written word. You read explanations or texts and then take copious notes. You like visuals, graphics, and flip charts. You prefer a written response to a verbal one. You are frequently the recorder in a group. You should continue to read as much as possible. Avid readers find learning to spell a bit easier.

• Are you an auditory learner? You learn primarily through listening. You are a focused listener. You may like to talk rather than write; therefore, discussing what you've learned is always more fun than either writing or reading.

• Are you a kinesthetic learner? You learn primarily by doing. Underlining and highlighting key words or ideas work for you. You need to practice what you've learned, so whatever you're learning, it's hands-on for you. The computer keyboard, an instrument, ice-skating, skiing—learning is all in the doing.

How does this apply to improving your spelling? You should think about how you prefer to learn *when you study words*. Do you prefer to move around (kinesthetic) as you study? Do it! Have your list handy, perhaps on 3-by-5 cards, and spell the words out loud as you walk. Then write, correct, and rewrite if necessary. If you learn better by listening, dictate the words into a recorder and then listen to the way the words are spelled. In every case, and no matter what kind of learner you are, make writing one of the steps in the learning process. For some, the writing simply may not be the first step.

WHAT YOU HAVE TO KNOW

To improve your spelling, you need to know the following: English has forty-five distinct sounds, called phonemes, but only twenty-six letters. This makes spelling all the more difficult. Specifically, there are vowels, *a, e, i, o, u*, and sometimes *y*, and consonants, which are the rest of the alphabet. Letters are put together in syllables, or small units of sound. Any word that contains more than one syllable has an accent on one of those syllables.

Example: bi-'O-gra-phy.

This word is made of four syllables. Say it out loud. Can you hear the accented or stressed syllable? The second syllable is stressed; therefore, an accent mark appears before it.

There are reasons for English spelling being as peculiar as it is. English is made of words from many different languages and has inherited spellings from all of them. Until about three hundred years ago, there were no set spellings and there were no dictionaries in English. That is no longer a problem; there are many excellent dictionaries—some with clear guidance on pronunciation.

Another peculiarity: We use some letters illogically. The most famous example is *gh*. *Gh* stands in for many different sounds. Look at the following list of words in which *ough* is sounded in seven different ways:

bou*gh*	cou*gh*	sou*gh*t	thorou*gh*
thou*gh*	tou*gh*	throu*gh*	

That leads us to the old riddle: What does *ghoti* spell? The answer is *fish*, as in rou*gh*, w*o*men, na*ti*on: gh-o-ti = fish.

To complicate the problem further, many English words are spelled the same but have different meanings depending on their use. Chapter 11 explores this thoroughly, but here are just a few examples:

The *wind* was too strong for us to *wind* the kite's string. (noun, verb)

The special parking permit was *invalid* for the *invalid*. (adjective, noun)

Our neighbors use the community farm to *produce produce*. (verb, noun)

Written Practice 10-1

Say each of the following words. Put an accent mark over the syllable you hear is stressed. The first one is done for you.

1. Span-ish   'Spa-nish
2. tel-e-phone
3. to-day
4. yes-ter-day
5. pre-sent (a gift)
6. con-ta-gious

Helpful Spelling Rules—or Not

Not everyone learns to spell by memorizing spelling rules. Some people prefer to use spelling resources such as print dictionaries or electronic dictionaries. If, however, your spelling problem is severe, you may spell what you hear, and normally that doesn't work with a print dictionary. For example, you hear *praktis*, *anser*, and *stor* when you mean *practice*, *answer*, and *store*. How will you find any of these words in the dictionary? The answer for you may be a dictionary that lists the common misspelling, followed by the correct spelling. Look for a book called, *How to Spell It*, by Harriet Wittels and Joan Greisman. In it, you'll find many misspellings, each followed by the correct spelling in red.

If you use a computer, your word-processing program has a spell-checking function that will find incorrectly spelled words and highlight them or even correct them as you type. One caution, however: Although spell-checkers recognize when a word is spelled incorrectly, they won't always tell you if you're using a word in the *wrong context*. For example:

Don't you think its to hot for baseball? (Correct: It's, too)

We chose there uniforms. (Correct: their)

The city counsel made a decision regarding the new school. (Correct: council)

On the other hand, if you find rules extremely helpful and not too hard to remember, you may choose that route to better spelling. One caution: Don't try to learn too many rules at one time. Sometimes, however, a series of rules naturally go together. One such rule has to do with adding prefixes and suffixes to words: Prefixes are added to the beginning of a word; suffixes are added to the end.

RULE 1: ADDING A PREFIX

In most cases, you can add a prefix to a word without changing the spelling of that word.

Example: Add prefix *un-* to *necessary* and you have *unnecessary*.

Prefix	Meaning	Root Word	New Word
ir-	not	responsible	irresponsible
un-	not	necessary	unnecessary
pre-	before	fix	prefix

Written Practice 10-2

Use the following negative prefixes to make a new word from each of the following words.

ir-   il-   im-   un-

1. _____ possible
2. _____ logical
3. _____ replaceable
4. _____ complicated
5. _____ necessary

RULE 2: ADDING A SUFFIX THAT BEGINS WITH A CONSONANT

When you add a suffix that begins with a consonant, the spelling of the root word does not change (with few exceptions).

Word	Suffix	New Word
bare	-ly	barely
careful	-ly	carefully
careless	-ness	carelessness
economic	-al	economical

Exceptions

true	-ly	truly
due	-ly	duly

RULE 3: ADDING A SUFFIX THAT BEGINS WITH A VOWEL

When you add a suffix that begins with a vowel to a word that ends in *e*, drop the *e* before you add the suffix.

Word	Suffix	New Word
continue	-ous	continuous
fame	-ous	famous

Exceptions

Words that end in *ge* or *ce* must keep the final *e* to retain the soft sound of *g* or *c*.

Word	Suffix	New Word
notice	able	noticeable

Another exception is the word *dye*: dye + -ing = dyeing

RULE 4: SUFFIXES THAT CHANGE THE SPELLING OF WORDS THAT END IN *-Y*

Suffixes change the spelling of words that end in *-y*.

Word	Suffix	New Word
hearty	-ily	heartily
necessary	-ily	necessarily
happy	-ness	happiness

Written Practice 10-3

Circle the incorrectly spelled word in each of the following sentences.

1. Carlessness is not an option in a doctor's office.
2. She was noticably less productive.
3. Happyness means different things to different people.
4. I am truely committed to losing weight.
5. The movie was not fameous for his exceptional acting.

RULE 5: DOUBLING THE FINAL CONSONANT IN A ONE-SYLLABLE WORD

When a one-syllable action word ends in a consonant preceded by a vowel (e.g., *run*), double the final consonant before you change the form of the word.

run	runner
plan	planned
thin	thinner

RULE 6: DOUBLING THE FINAL CONSONANT IN A TWO-SYLLABLE WORD

When a two-syllable word ends in a consonant preceded by a vowel and is accented on the second syllable (e.g., *occur*), change its form by doubling the final consonant (e.g., *occurred*).

refer   referred

occur   occurrence

RULE 7: NOT DOUBLING A FINAL CONSONANT BASED ON ACCENT CHANGES

In a two- or three-syllable word, if the accent changes from the final syllable to a preceding one when a suffix is added (e.g., *refer/reference*), do not double the final consonant.

prefer   preference

confer   conference

Written Practice 10-4

Circle the incorrectly spelled word in each set of words.

1. unanimous   nominate   confer   spoting

2. occurred   painter   carelesness   satisfactory

3. developped   prefer   funny   wonderful

4. preferrence   reference   refined   misspell

5. except   occurred   baddly   stun

Written Practice 10-5

For each of the following sentences, correct any misspelled words. If there is no error, leave the space blank.

1. It ocured to me to check the weather report before I left. _____

2. John was refered to me as a possible candidate for the job. _____

3. Your bad attitude has never deterred me. _____

4. I consider myself a runer, not just a fast walker. _____

5. Suning yourself day after day is not a healthful thing to do. _____

RULE 8: *I* BEFORE *E* EXCEPT AFTER *C*

believe   relief

receive   niece

Exceptions to this rule occur when *e* comes before *i* in words that have a long *a* sound:

neighbor   weigh

Other exceptions include:

weird   leisure   neither   seize

Written Practice 10-6

Choose the correctly spelled word in each of the following sentences.

1. I will feel great (relief/releif) once I have finished my report.
2. Does your (neice/niece) come to stay with you every summer?
3. "(Sieze/Seize) the day," is a famous saying.
4. Once she (deceived/decieved) me, I couldn't be her friend.
5. We'll have more (liesure/leisure) time next month.

RULE 9: RULES FOR FORMING PLURALS

Add an *s* to most words.

rug   rugs

shoe   shoes

Add *es* to words ending in *-o* preceded by a consonant.

hero   heroes

tomato   tomatoes

Add only an *s* to words that end in *-o* preceded by a consonant and refer to music.

alto   altos

piano   pianos

Add *es* to words ending in *-s*, *-sh*, *-ch*, and *-x*.

boss	bosses
crush	crushes
church	churches
sex	sexes

Change *y* to *i*, and add *es* in words that end in *-y* preceded by a consonant.

fly	flies
story	stories

Written Practice 10-7

Choose the correctly spelled word to complete each sentence.

1. It seems that our children always need new (shos/shoes).
2. At least once a year, a car (crashs/crashes) into that telephone pole.
3. My son loves to play with (trains/traines).
4. Who are the (heros/heroes) in that story?
5. How many (stories/story's) have you read?

RULE 10: MORE RULES FOR FORMING PLURALS

Words ending in *-ful* form their plurals by adding *s* to the end of the word.

mouthfuls   spoonfuls

A compound word forms its plural by adding *s* to the main word.

mother-in-law	mothers-in-law
court-martial	courts-martial

Numbers and letters form plurals by adding *'s*.

7	7's
m	*m*'s

Some words keep the same spelling for singular and plural forms.

sheep	deer
Chinese	trout

Some words form their plurals by irregular changes.

child	children
leaf	leaves
tooth	teeth
crisis	crises
thief	thieves
knife	knives
woman	women
louse	lice
alumnus	alumni
appendix	appendices

Written Practice 10-8

For each of the following lines, circle the plural noun that is spelled incorrectly and spell it correctly.

1. holiday   bulletin   knifes   teeth   _____
2. father-in-laws   chairs   bows   towels   _____
3. lice   childs   deer   bunches   _____
4. gestures   occurrences   bulletin   radioes   _____
5. trays   handsful   clients   women   _____

RULE 11: WORDS SPELLED WITH A -*CEED* ENDING

Only three words are spelled with a -*ceed* ending:

exceed	proceed	succeed

Only one word is spelled with an *sede* ending: *supersede*. All other words of this type are spelled with a *-cede* ending.

Written Practice 10-9

Choose the correctly spelled word in each sentence.

1. This manual (superceeds/supersedes) the first one we received.
2. (Procede/Proceed) to the corner and turn right.
3. At the meeting, Manuel (preseeded/preceded) me on the program.
4. Have you read about the states that wanted to (secede/seceed) from the union?
5. Your praise (exceeds/excedes) what I expected.

Becoming a Better Speller

Here are some more tips on improving your spelling skills:

- Develop an interest in words.
- Feel safe about trying new words and not just words you're sure about.
- Learn about:
  - the way words are built up using syllables
  - basic spelling patterns of English
  - memorizing strategies
  - the meanings of words
  - prefixes and suffixes
  - writing for your own enjoyment, without the fear that you will be criticized

Read for pleasure! It's the best way to improve your spelling and increase your vocabulary.

QUIZ

Choose the correctly spelled word in each sentence.

1. Your actions were (iresponsible/irresponsible).
2. That's a common (misspelling/mispelling).
3. They're so lucky; they own two (pianos/pianoes).
4. To help with the (planting/plannting), we bought a new shovel.
5. I've read two (biographys/biographies) of John Adams.
6. (Referring/refering) to her in that way is very insulting.
7. (Mother-in-laws/Mothers-in-law) are the object of some really bad jokes.
8. Two (thiefs/thieves) were caught as they left the bank.
9. Be sure to use a paint (thinner/thiner) in that can.
10. I'm (truely/truly) sorry for that mistake.

CHAPTER 11

Correct Word Usage

In this chapter you will learn about:

Easily Confused Words: Homonyms, Homophones, and Homographs

Incorrectly Used Words and Phrases

Words That Sound Almost *Alike but Have Different Meanings*

Easily Confused Words: Homonyms, Homophones, and Homographs

As the preceding chapter subtitles indicate, a distinction is made between easily confused words and the incorrect use of a word or phrase. The English language is

full of words that are easy to confuse. However, knowing the histories of homonyms, homophones, and homographs may help you remember them. The three words originate from the Greek language:

- **Homonym:** *homos* (same) + *nym* (name); means "same name for two different definitions" (e.g., *lead* and *lead*)

- **Homophone:** *homos* (same) + *phone* (sound); means "same sound" for two different definitions (e.g., *compliment, complement*)

- **Homograph:** *homos* (same) + *graph* (spelling); means "same spelling" for two different definitions (e.g., *bow* of a ship, *bow* in her hair)

HOMONYMS

From the preceding introduction, you know that homonyms are words that are spelled alike but have different meanings.

Look at the following examples:

pitch (throw a ball)   pitch (a black mineral)
bank (a business offering   bank (land alongside or sloping down
financial services)   to a river or lake)

In the following list, each homonym is followed by two definitions. Familiarize yourself with both definitions before you complete Written Practice 11-1.

bark: hard covering of a tree or plant; a dog's sound
bat: heavy stick or club, used in sports; only mammal that can fly
bear: large mammal; to tolerate or support
dear: regard with deep affection; expensive
down: toward a lower place; soft fine feathers of a young bird
exact: precise or accurate; inflict (revenge) on someone
fair: entertainment exhibition; reasonable
fawn: baby deer; a color; to be servile
fine: of very high quality; sum of money exacted as a penalty
grave: hole dug in ground to receive a coffin; giving cause for alarm
just: morally right and fair; barely or simply
kind: considerate and generous; class or type of things having similar
characteristics

left: opposite of *right*; departed
mead: a drink made from honey; meadow
order: arrangement of things to a particular sequence or method; authoritative
   command or directive, instruction to provide something
peak: pointed top of a mountain; stiff brim at front of a cap
pile: a heap; the nap of velvet
pole: ends of the axis of rotation; fishing rod; long piece of metal or wood
trip: to stumble or fall; journey or excursion
wave: motion with hand in greeting; ridge of water curling into shore

Written Practice 11-1

Choose a homonym from the preceding list to complete each sentence.

1. We saw the _____ run out of the wooded area.

2. Our troops were in _____ danger.

3. _____ is used to stuff some pillows.

4. The court delivered a _____ decision.

5. Scientists finally realized that _____ was very dangerous to the
   health of small children.

6. When its _____ began to peel off, we knew the tree was in
   danger of dying.

7. If you drive drunk, the law will _____ punishment.

8. I love your daughter; she's very _____ to me.

9. Above the hat's _____ is the name of my favorite team.

10. The teenager cried, "I can't _____ another disappointment!"

11. Let me know when you're taking your next _____ to New
    England; I'll join you.

12. My job was to _____ more supplies before we ran out of them.

13. An attic full of _____ is always an unpleasant surprise.

14. We didn't even know they had _____ until we saw them turning
    _____ at the corner.

15. Our children always _____ to us as they back out of the driveway.

HOMOPHONES

As you read earlier, homophones are pronounced the same way but differ in spelling and meaning. Look at the following examples:

Everyone likes a *compliment* on something well done.

These two colors *complement* each other.

In the first sentence, *compliment* means an "admiring comment"; in the second sentence, *complement* means "balance or go together." Although the two words are pronounced alike, their distinction is important and should be learned.

Written Practice 11-2

The following columns contain homophones. Read through them carefully before you complete the exercise. Then choose a homophone to complete each sentence in the exercise. Use your dictionary to find the meaning of any unknown word.

aisle	bases	carat	does	palate	sew	their	yore
I'll	basis	caret	dough's	pallet	so	there	you're
isle	basses	carrot	doze	palette	sol	they're	your
		karat			sow		

1. As she walked down the _____ , the bride was a vision in white.
2. The orchestra had a large section of _____ .
3. The two _____ , female deer, graze in my garden.
4. What a beautiful _____ of colors.
5. A _____ is a measure of weight for precious stones.
6. The farmer _____s corn at the end of April.
7. I heard from everyone; _____ expected to arrive before noon.
8. As for you, _____ expected an hour later.
9. The heavy machinery was delivered on a _____ .
10. I marked the missing word with a _____ .

COMMON ERRORS

Here are examples of some of the most common mistakes:

Incorrect: The Portuguese water dog is known for *it's* ability to swim.
Correct: The Portuguese water dog is known for *its* ability to swim.

Incorrect: It's *to* cold for swimming.
Correct: It's *too* cold for swimming.

Incorrect: We arrived at our friends' party and realized we had forgotten *there* gift.
Correct: We arrived at our friends' party and realized we had forgotten *their* gift.

Written Practice 11-3

Circle the correct homophone in each sentence. If you need help, consult the extended list of homophones that follows this exercise.

1. I always remembered the spelling of (principle, principal) after one teacher told me to think of him or her as a "pal."
2. Please (pair, pare) the (pear, pare), and I will eat it.
3. If something stays in place, it's (stationary, stationery).
4. (Its, It's) another rainy day!
5. I don't know many people who eat (currants, currents), do you?
6. The (plain, plane) was in its (ascent, assent) when the problem occurred.
7. The (capital, capitol) building in Providence, Rhode Island, has one of the few unsupported domes.
8. (To, Too, Two) many children eat empty calories instead of fruits and vegetables.
9. (Peace, Piece) seems like a thing of the (past, passed).
10. I depend on Jeffrey to (council, counsel) me.

Study the following words a few at a time. They are defined for you. Whenever you are not sure which homophone to use, consult a dictionary.

ad (advertisement), add (combine things)

allowed (permitted), aloud (audibly)

ant (insect), aunt (father or mother's sister)

ascent (upward movement), assent (agreement)

ate (past tense of *eat*), eight (8, the number that follows 7)

ball (round thing, sphere), bawl (cry noisily)

band (group, musicians playing together), banned (barred, excluded)

bear (endure; mammal with large stocky body), bare (naked)

be (exist), bee (honey-making insect)

beach (seashore), beech (deciduous tree)

billed (owed), build (construct)

blew (past tense of *blow*), blue (color; depressed)

board (plank), bored (uninterested)

bolder (more daring), boulder (large rock)

born (brought into life), borne (stand)

boy (young man), buoy (marker; keep afloat)

brake (a device that stops or slows a machine), break (fracture, shatter)

bread (food made from flour and water), bred (brought up)

by (a preposition expressing a spatial relationship), bye (good-bye), buy (pay money for, purchase)

capital (assets; seat of government), capitol (U.S. congress building)

caret (mark to show missing text), carrot (vegetable), carat (weight used for gems), karat (measure of gold content)

cell (basic unit of living things; range of mobile phone transmitter; a small room), sell (exchange for money)

cent (common currency subunit), scent (fragrance), sent (past tense of *send*)

census (poll; survey), senses (physical faculty, intelligence)

cereal (grain; breakfast food), serial (sequential; in series)

chews (grinds up food before swallowing), choose (select)

choral (performed by a choir), coral (hard marine deposit)

chute (shaft, tube), shoot (fire a weapon)

cite (quote), sight (view, vision), site (location)

coarse (rough), course (route)

council (board), counsel (advise)

currant (small dried grape), current (existing now)

dear (beloved, prized), deer (animal with antlers)

dew (water droplets), do (act, see to), due (owing)

die (stop living), dye (coloring)

disc (in computer science, another spelling of *disk*, or recording), disk (part between bones of the spine)

discreet (tactful), discrete (completely separate)

discussed (talked over), disgust (revulsion)

doe (deer), dough (mixture of flour and water; money)

ewe (female sheep), you (person being addressed)

feat (achievement), feet (part of the legs)

find (discover something), fined (punished by imposing a payment)

fir (evergreen), fur (animal hair)

flea (bug), flee (run away)

flew (past tense of *fly*), flu (influenza), flue (smoke or heat outlet)

for (preposition meaning "in favor of"), four (4), fore (front)

foul (unclean, unpleasant), fowl (chicken)

knew (past tense of *know*), new (recently made, recently discovered)

grate (bars in front of fire; make into small pieces), great (large in number; important)

heal (make well), heel (back of foot), he'll (he will)

heard (past tense of *hear*), herd (a large group of animals)

higher (above something else), hire (give somebody work)

hoarse (harsh, grating voice), horse (four-legged animal)

hole (opening, cavity), whole (undivided, complete)

hour (60 minutes), our (belonging to us)

idle (not working or in use), idol (object of worship)

incite (provoke), insight (clear perception)

its (indicating possession), *it's* (contraction for *it is*)

jeans (pants), *genes* (basic units of heredity)

knead (work dough until smooth), *need* (require something essential)

knows (familiar with), *nose* (organ of smell), *no's* (more than one objection)

lead (chemical element), *led* (guided)

leased (rented), *least* (smallest amount possible)

lessen (reduce), *lesson* (instruction)

lie (deliberately say something untrue; recline), *lye* (strong chemical cleaner)

links (associations), *lynx* (short-tailed wildcat)

load (something carried or transported), *lode* (deposit of ore; abundant supply), *lowed* (mooing sound of a cow)

loan (money lent), *lone* (only)

loot (stolen goods; steal), *lute* (musical instrument)

maize (corn), *maze* (confusing network of paths)

manor (noble's house and land), *manner* (way something is done)

meet (get together), *meat* (edible animal flesh)

mince (cut up), *mints* (pieces of mint-flavored candy)

miner (mine worker), *minor* (small; describes musical scale)

missed (did not hit target), *mist* (thin fog)

morning (early part of day), *mourning* (period of sadness)

no (indicating the negative), *know* (comprehend something)

not (indicating "opposite"), *knot* (object made by tying)

or (otherwise), *oar* (pole used to propel a boat), *ore* (mineral from which metal is extracted)

overdo (exceed), *overdue* (late)

paced (set the speed), *paste* (adhesive mixture)

pail (bucket), *pale* (light)

pain (ache; feeling of discomfort), *pane* (piece of glass in window)

pair (two of a kind), *pare* (remove outer layer), *pear* (fruit)

passed (move past; approved), *past* (what went before)

patience (endurance), *patients* (people given medical treatment)

peace (freedom from war; calm), *piece* (a portion)

peal (ring), peel (remove outer layer)

pedal (foot-operated lever), peddle (sell)

peer (gaze, stare), pier (dock)

plain (simple), plane (airplane)

plum (fruit), plumb (weight attached to line)

praise (admire), prays (speaks to God), preys (hunts someone or something)

presence (attendance; being there), presents (gifts)

principal (school administrator; main), principle (belief)

quarts (one-quarter of a gallon), quartz (crystalline mineral)

rain (precipitation), reign (period in office), rein (horse's bridle)

raise (lift), rays (narrow beams of light), raze (demolish)

rap (tap; music genre), wrap (cover something)

read (interpret written material), reed (tall water plant)

real (genuine), reel (spool)

rest (relax), wrest (gain control)

review (look at something critically), revue (variety show)

ring (chime; encircle), wring (squeeze)

role (position; task), roll (turn over and over)

root (underground base of plant), route (course)

rote (repetition), wrote (past tense of *write*)

rye (cereal grain), wry (amusing and ironic)

sail (travel by water), sale (opportunity to buy goods at discount)

scene (sight; view), seen (past participle of *see*)

seam (place where pieces join), seem (look as if)

seas (salt waters of Earth), sees (perceive with eyes), seize (take hold of something)

serge (strong cloth), surge (rush forward)

sew (stitch), so (as a result), sow (plant seed or an idea)

side (perimeter of figure), sighed (made exhaling sound)

slay (kill), sleigh (horse-drawn carriage for in the snow)

soar (fly), sore (painful)

sole (only; bottom of foot), soul (spirit; essence)

some (a number of), sum (total; money)

spade (shovel), spayed (neutered an animal)

staid (sedate, serious), stayed (remained)

stair (step), stare (long, concentrated look)

stake (thin, pointed post in ground; bet), steak (cut of beef)

stationary (not moving), stationery (writing paper)

steal (take something unlawfully), steel (alloy of iron and carbon)

straight (not curved), strait (channel joining large bodies of water)

suede (leather with soft surface), swayed (swing; influence somebody)

summary (short version), summery (warm)

tail (rear part of animal's body or aircraft), tale (story)

taut (tight), taught (educated)

tents (collapsible shelters), tense (anxious, stressed)

there (an adverb used to indicate place), their (belonging to them), they're (contraction for *they are*)

threw (past tense of *throw*), through (movement from one side of something to or past the other)

throne (monarch's chair), thrown (past participle of *throw*)

thyme (herb), time (duration; method of measuring intervals)

tide (rise and fall of the ocean or other large body of water), tied (joined)

two (2), to (preposition indicating direction), too (also)

toad (amphibian similar to frog), towed (pull something along)

told (past tense of *tell*), tolled (rang slowly)

tracked (followed), tract (area of land or water)

trussed (supported), trust (have faith in)

vein (vessel carrying blood to the heart), vane (rotating blade)

vial (small glass bottle), vile (evil, despicable)

vice (immoral habit), vise (tool for keeping things immobile)

wade (walk in water), weighed (measured by weight)

wail (howl, cry), whale (large ocean mammal)

waist (body area between ribs and hips), waste (squander)

wait (stay), weight (heaviness)

waive (surrender claim), wave (ocean ripple; to motion with the hand)

war (armed fighting between groups), wore (past tense of *wear*)

ware (ceramics), wear (have something on body), where (adverb used to question place)

warn (caution), worn (showing effects of wear)

wax (polish), whacks (sharp blows)

way (method; route), weigh (find the weight of something; consider), whey (watery byproduct of the cheesemaking process)

weather (climate), whether (introduces alternatives)

we'll (contraction for *we will*), wheel (rotating round part)

weak (frail), week (7-day period)

which (asks a question), witch (somebody with alleged magic powers)

whine (high-pitched sound), wine (alcohol from grapes)

who's (contraction for *who is*), whose (belonging to someone)

yoke (animal harness, burden), yolk (yellow of egg)

your (belonging to the person spoken to), you're (contraction for *you are*), yore (in the distant past)

Written Practice 11-4

Choose the correct homophone to complete each of these sentences.

1. A laundry (shoot/chute) is extremely useful.
2. I was (fined/find) for driving through a yellow light.
3. You'll find that (needing/kneading) dough is great exercise
4. The recipe says you should (mints/mince) the garlic.
5. Did you know there was a (sail/sale) on children's shoes?
6. With any luck, we can look forward to an era of (peace/piece).
7. After the accident, the motorists created an ugly (scene/seen).
8. That movie stirred me to the bottom of my (sole/soul).
9. If I send a payment immediately, they'll (wave/waive) the fee.
10. When you (wine/whine) and cry, it doesn't help.

HOMOGRAPHS

Just to be clear, there is yet another group of words to mention: homographs. Homographs are words spelled alike but have a different pronunciation or meaning (e.g., the *bow* [*bou*] of a ship, a *bow* [*b*] that decorates something.

We walked to the *bow* of the ship.

Wrap that gift with a *bow*.

Changing pronunciation affects meaning. To show the differences in meaning, transliteration (loosely defined) is used to show pronunciation in the list that follows. The sounds of the letters are written in more easily recognizable form. Capital letters indicate the accented or stressed syllables. Then the homographs are used in sentences to clarify meaning.

Affect: 1. ehFEKT—to change; 2. AFFekt—a person's feelings or emotion
1. My budget definitely affects how much I go out to dinner each month.
2. Following the tragedy, her affect was distinctly subdued.

Alternate: 1. ALternit—the next choice; 2. ALternait—switch back and forth
1. Carl is running as an alternate in the race.
2. In this recipe, alternate the addition of the flour and the eggs.

Bass: 1. BASE—a string instrument; 2. BASS (rhymes with *mass*)—a fish
1. We wondered how a child could play the bass, such a large instrument.
2. Bass seems to be a favorite fish choice in restaurants.

Close: 1. CLOZE—to shut; 2. CLOS—near
1. Close the door, please!
2. Our children are playing close by.

Desert: 1. dihZURT—to leave; 2. DEZert—arid region
1. Please don't desert me when I need your help.
2. The Arizona desert is a beautiful place when the cacti bloom.

Dove: 1. DUV—a bird; 2. DOEV—jumped off
1. The dove has become the symbol of peace and love.
2. A foolish child dove off the high bridge.

Excuse: 1. EKskyooz—to let someone off; 2. ekSKYOOS—a reason or explanation

1. The judge said, "I'll excuse your speeding this time, but don't let it happen again!"

2. He continued, "No excuse will be acceptable."

House: 1. HOWS—a building that serves as living quarters; 2. HOWZ—to provide with living quarters

1. Our house is more than a hundred years old.

2. We can't house any more pets.

Invalid: 1. inVALid—not valid; 2. INvahlid—an ill person

1. You haven't paid your bill, so your membership is invalid as of today.

2. He became an invalid after a massive stroke.

Lead: 1. LEED—to guide; 2. LED—a metallic element

1. I will lead you to the exit.

2. We found lead in the old paint.

Minute: 1. MINNit—sixty seconds; 2. myNOOT—tiny

1. It takes one minute to drive from Exit 10 to Exit 9.

2. Your contribution to this class has been minute.

Perfect: 1. PERfekt—exactly correct; 2. perFEKT—to make correct

1. My spelling is not always perfect.

2. I'm trying hard to perfect it.

Produce: 1. PROdoos—vegetables; 2. proDOOS—bring forth

1. My favorite place in the market is the produce aisle.

2. My friend's son produces CDs.

Record: 1. RECKord—a list; 2. RECKORD—best yet; 3. reKORD—to write down

1. I've kept a record of all my lunch and snack expenses for six months.

2. We made the trip in record time.

3. Record your voice for me.

Row: 1. ROH—a line; 2. ROUW—a fight

1. I planted a row of annual flowers.

2. What a row they had! Finally the police came to break up the fight.

Separate: 1. SEPerATE—to divide into groups; 2. SEPret—not joined together

1. SEPerATE the cotton and the wool socks into two piles.

2. The dark socks were kept SEPret from the white ones.

Tier: 1. TEER—layer; 2. TYER—a person who ties

1. The first tier of the cake was pure chocolate.

2. Can you imagine being known as the best tier of bows?

Tear: 1. TARE—to rip; 2. TEER—fluid in eye; flow fluid from eye

1. If you tear the package at the perforation, it's much easier to open.

2. The pollution made my eyes tear.

Wind: 1. WHINEd—to coil up; 2. WINd—the blowing air

1. I dislike having to wind the kite string.

2. The wind lifted the kite high into the sky.

Wound: 1. WOOND—to injure; 2. WOWND—coiled up

1. Tim didn't mean to wound the animal with the BB gun.

2. A bandage was wound around the dog's leg.

Written Practice 11-5

Choose the correct homograph to complete each sentence. Use the transliteration to show the correct form. The first one is done for you.

1. A healthful diet and increased exercise will ehFEKT how you feel.

2. Our rooms were _____ but on the same floor.

3. The athlete's win did not place him on the team, but it did make him an _____ to the Olympic Games.

4. His choice made only the tiniest, most _____ difference in the end.

5. Fortunately, the soldier's injuries did not make her an _____ for life.

6. That chore was done in _____ time!

7. The nurse _____ a bandage around the _____ .

8. After the hurricane, one of the main tasks was to _____ the victims.

9. Today, workers are judged on how much work they _____ .

10. If I try hard enough, I can always find an _____ for my lateness.

Incorrectly Used Words and Phrases

We all know of words or phrases that are frequently misused. For example, consider the use of *anxious* and *eager*. These two words are misused on a regular basis.

Incorrect: I'm *anxious* to meet your family.

Do you mean that you are *nervous, worried,* or *uneasy* about meeting the family? If you do, then use the word *anxious*—think *anxiety*. If not, choose a more precise word.

Correct: I'm *eager* to meet your family.

Are you *excited, ready,* or *enthusiastic* to meet the family? That's what *eager* means.

COMMON ERRORS

The following word is misused so much that it may—someday, but not yet—find it's way into accepted usage. Until it is fully accepted, use the correct form—*regardless*. Think of *irregardless*—the incorrect form—as containing a double negative: *ir* means "not" and *less* means "without." You don't need that many negatives to express the thought.

Incorrect: I'm going *irregardless* of the weather. (. . . not without regard to the weather?)
Correct: I'm going *regardless* of the weather.

On the other hand, misused words and phrases present an additional challenge. There is no single list of words and phrases to study; there are *books* of them. How can you learn more about these frequently misused words? People are usually unaware of this type of error (that's why people keep saying *irregardless*). If you are lucky, someone will point out your errors; if not, you have to make an effort to find them. You might want to buy a book about word usage or use the Internet to find lists of errors and their corrections. An excellent book source is *The American Heritage Book of English Usage: A Practical and Authoritative Guide to Contemporary English* (Boston: Houghton Mifflin 1996 and New York: bartleby.com, 2000). If you buy this book or log on to the website, you will find much more than just help with homonyms. The information addresses grammar, style, pronunciation, and spelling as well as other topics.

The following is a list of commonly misused or confused words and phrases.

aggravate (make worse), **annoy** (infuriate)

The third fall on the same knee really aggravated the injury.

The noise from the upstairs apartment finally began to annoy us.

among (compares three or more), **between** (compares two or more)

Among all six counties, ours is the most progressive.

Child care is divided between the parents.

amount (quantity), **number** (figure used in counting)

The amount of paper we use is staggering!

The number of sheets in a package is 200.

anxious (feeling nervous), **eager** (enthusiastic and excited)

anywhere (There is no such word as *anywheres*.)

We'll meet you anywhere you say.

As (adverb, equally), **like** (preposition, similar to)

We use *like* or *as* to say that things are similar. Use *like* before a noun or pronoun.

Incorrect: She looks as her sister.

Correct: She looks like her sister.

Correct: He ran like the wind.

On the other hand, *as* is used like a conjunction before a clause.

Correct: Nobody loves her as I do.

Correct: Do as I do.

In informal English, you will often hear *like* used as a conjunction instead of *as*. However, the following use of *like* is still neither standard nor accepted.

Incorrect: Nobody loves Gary like I do.

Correct: Nobody loves Gary as I do.

Correct: Monty does as Pat does.

Correct: Aidan looks like his mother.

bring versus **take**

Incorrect: When we go to the mountains on Saturday, let's bring our skis.

When you are viewing the movement of something from the point of departure, use *take*. When you think of moving something from the point of arrival, use *bring*.

Correct: When you come to the party, please bring a bottle of wine.

fewer versus **less**

Incorrect: *Ten items or less.* Sign at the checkout in a supermarket.

You can count the items, so you need to use the number word, which is *fewer*.

Correct: Ten items or fewer.

If you can't *count* the substance, then you should use *less*.

Correct: You should eat less meat.

This sentence is correct because meat is uncountable.

have versus of

Incorrect: I never would of thought that he'd behave like that.
Use *would have*.

Correct: I never would have/would've thought that he'd succeed.

Use *should* and *could* correctly.

Incorrect: He should of come with me.

Correct: He should have/should've come with me.

Incorrect: She could of had any job she wanted.

Correct: She could have had any job she wanted.

double negative

Incorrect: I'm not speaking to nobody at this party!

Since *not* is a negative, you cannot use *nobody* in this sentence.

Correct: I'm not speaking to anybody at this party!

went versus gone

Incorrect: I should have went to work yesterday.

The correct form is *should* + *have* + past participle (review Chapter 3 if you have any problem with this concept).

Correct: I should have gone to work yesterday.

awful (terrible) versus very (extremely)

Correct: His speech was awful.

Correct: His voice was very weak.

Incorrect: His voice was awful weak.

Correct: His voice was awfully weak.

Words That Sound *Almost* Alike but Have Different Meanings

Many words fall into this category. Errors sometimes occur as a result of incorrect spelling, but often they result from not saying or hearing the words correctly. The following is a list of common words that sound almost alike but mean different things.

accept (acknowledge), **except** (agree to)

I accept your apology.

Everyone except Martha was invited.

adapt (adjust to something), **adopt** (legally raise another's child)

I can adapt to almost any climate.

We're searching for families to adopt hard-to-place children.

advice (recommendation about an action or decision), **advise** (offer advice)

I appreciate constructive advice.

I don't advise others unless they ask me to.

affect (influence something or somebody), **effect** (result)

An antibiotic will not affect that disease.

However, it may have an adverse effect.

all ready (completely ready), **already** (happened before now)

Call me when you are all ready to leave.

My friend Tim has already left.

all right (*Alright* is not an acceptable word.)

Is it all right to add all the ingredients at once?

all together (all in the same place), **altogether** (totally, entirely)

We'll be all together for Thanksgiving.

This course is altogether too difficult.

allusion (indirect reference), **illusion** (mistaken idea)

Only a few people were aware of my allusion to Shakespeare's *Romeo and Juliet*.

You have the illusion that I like rap music; I don't.

climactic (the point of greatest intensity in a series of events), **climatic** (refers to meteorological conditions)

The *climactic* period in the dinosaurs' reign was reached just before severe *climatic* conditions brought on the ice age.

continually (regularly or frequently), **continuously** (uninterrupted)

I am continually late for work.

Any loud music that is played continuously is annoying.

emigrate (*Emigrate* begins with the letter *E*, as does *exit*. When you emigrate, you exit a country.), **immigrate** (*Immigrate* begins with the letter *I*, as does *in*. When you immigrate, you go into a country.)

Sylvia emigrated from the United States

Vivian immigrated to France from her native Canada.

Loose (not firmly attached, slack), **lose** (misplace)

The tree branches were left loose in the street.

If I lose my new watch, I'll be so sad.

moral (message of right and wrong), **morale** (confidence, spirits)

Children love stories that have a moral.

Shopping often lifts my morale.

personal (private, own), **personnel** (human resources department; staff)

Please don't open my personal correspondence.

We're trying to build our personnel department to a staff of six.

quiet (silence, calm), **quite** (entirely)

My work demands quiet.

I'm not quite ready.

Written Practice 11-6

Choose the correct word to complete each sentence.

1. I see you sweating: Does my decision make you feel (anxious/eager)?
2. You'll know you've lost weight when your jeans are (lose/loose).
3. My grandparents (emigrated/immigrated) from Russia.
4. I love the sound of (quite/quiet).
5. Your handwriting is (all together/altogether) too sloppy.
6. Everyone (accept/except) Martha finished the hike.
7. We never considered that Anil (would of/would have) left us with the bill!
8. They (should of /should have) eaten with us.
9. Take (fewer/less) clothes with you on this trip.
10. I'm not offering you any more (advise/advice).

Written Practice 11-7

Choose a word from the preceding list to complete each sentence correctly.

1. You're asking about a _____ matter; I don't discuss those.
2. I need a bookmark so that I don't _____ my place.
3. We all agree that keeping our troops' _____ high is important.
4. You know I get annoyed when you _____ interrupt me.
5. Your paper was excellent; I particularly enjoyed the _____ to rap music.
6. I said it was _____ for the children to stay outside for another ten minutes.
7. Seeing money in my account at the end of the month was simply an

   _____ .

8. Have the _____ certainty to go against popular opinion.
9. The bed slats are _____ again; the bed will fall!
10. _____ conditions seem to be producing more rain.

QUIZ

Choose the correct word to complete each of the following sentences.

1. Monet's color (pallet/palette) is distinctive.

2. The storyteller recited a (tail/tale) of terror.

3. We took our work problem to the (personal/personnel) department.

4. Mark and I hadn't done any business until we were (formally/formerly) introduced.

5. We certainly have a (bases/basis) upon which to continue.

6. My students received (they're/their) new books.

7. (Your/You're) books will arrive next week.

8. I was offered a gift of either a dress or shoes, and I chose the (latter/later).

9. My friend has the highest (morale/moral) standards; he proved it when he refused to keep the money he found.

10. You (to/too) can meet us each day for our morning run.

PART FOUR TEST

Choose the correct spelling for each misspelled word.

1. Be sure to ask for a reciept.
   - (a) resiet
   - (b) reciet
   - (c) rcccipt
   - (d) resceipt

2. Juan was refered to me for a job.
   - (a) refferred
   - (b) referd
   - (c) refurd
   - (d) referred

3. Ms. Santini, a piano teacher, has bought a number of pianoes.
   - (a) pianose
   - (b) pianos
   - (c) piannos
   - (d) pianoze

4. The lawmakers would go to any length to keep states from seceeding from the Union.
   - (a) seceading
   - (b) saceding
   - (c) seceding
   - (d) suceeding

5. Do you have a peferrence for one color over another?
   - (a) preference
   - (b) prefference
   - (c) preferennce
   - (d) preferense

6. Happyness is not always possible.

    (a) Hapiness

    (b) Happines

    (c) Happynes

    (d) Happiness

7. Max has an unatural love of alligators.

    (a) unaturall

    (b) unnattural

    (c) unnatural

    (d) unnaturale

8. Carefuly mix the dry and wet ingredients.

    (a) carfuly

    (b) carefully

    (c) carefuley

    (d) carfully

9. The loud and continueous music finally gave me a headache.

    (a) contenuous

    (b) continuous

    (c) continuious

    (d) conntinuous

10. Melanie was thiner than ever.

    (a) thinner

    (b) thinnur

    (c) thinur

    (d) thinnar

11. It was a releif to be finished with that task.

    (a) ralief

    (b) rulief

   (c) relief

   (d) rellief

12. Bright Airways flys to Chicago.

   (a) flyes

   (b) flyies

   (c) flis

   (d) flies

13. Two woman led the book club.

   (a) women

   (b) womin

   (c) womun

   (d) womane

14. Our children took huge handsful of Halloween candy.

   (a) handfulls

   (b) handsfull

   (c) handfuls

   (d) handfulls

15. We thought your actions were irresponsable.

   (a) iresponsable

   (b) iresponsible

   (c) irresponsablle

   (d) irresponsible

16. Your lack of enthusiasm is noticable.

   (a) notisable

   (b) noticeable

   (c) noticeabl

   (d) notisible

17. This memo superseeds all others.
    - (a) superseeds
    - (b) supersedes
    - (c) supraseeds
    - (d) suppersedes

18. Whatever you do, don't mispell this word.
    - (a) misspell
    - (b) mispel
    - (c) misspel
    - (d) mespell

19. She signed the letter, *Very truely yours*.
    - (a) trooley
    - (b) trulley
    - (c) trully
    - (d) truly

20. I was refering to the weather changes we've experienced.
    - (a) refuring
    - (b) reffering
    - (c) reffering
    - (d) referring

Choose the correct word or transliteration to complete each sentence correctly.

21. The teenagers managed to move a (stationary/stationery) stop sign to a different corner.

22. Many small children want fruit skins (paired/pared) away.

23. (There/Their) preference is not unusual.

24. Your joining the company was the (principal/principle) reason for my applying for the opening.

25. Without the (counsel/council) of an attorney, I wouldn't make the decision.

26. Have you told your children this? "Don't eat (to/too/two) many sweets!"

27. On his first solo skiing experience, he (braked/broke) his leg.

28. The (cent/scent) of flowers sends me into a sneezing fit.

29. A (hole/whole) watermelon is fun for a picnic.

30. The teacher said, "Learning by (wrote/rote) means memorizing, and what good is that?"

31. You have to decide (weather/whether) or not you want to participate in state government.

32. Selena and Camila wanted (SEPerATE/SEPret) rooms.

33. Our shopping is very convenient; it's (CLOZE/CLOS) to our home.

34. I'm so (anxious/eager) to leave; I've been waiting for so long to take this trip.

35. We're taking the trip (irregardless/regardless) of the economy.

36. Your choice of music (aggravates/annoys) me.

37. The (number/amount) of people in the restaurant was higher than the allowed limit.

38. I need your (advise/advice) about the color of paint for my house.

39. Sergio was under the (illusion/allusion) that keeping the children up later would make them sleep longer.

40. Mariso is (continually/continuously) late for work.

41. You can't recycle (lose/loose) papers; tie them up.

42. The container isn't (quiet/quite) high enough to hold all those papers.

43. The toddler loved hearing about the bunny with the soft (tail/tale).

44. Is it (alright/all right) for me to use the desk in front of the windows?

45. How many people have (immigrated/emigrated) from Europe?

46. Most people don't want to be accused of losing their (moral/morale) compass.

47. Camila took a day off to attend to all the (personal/personnel) business that is put off during the workweek.

48. There were (all together/altogether) too many references to unhappy happenings.

49. (You're/Your) opinion is very important to me.

50. We're trying to (adopt/adapt) to a greener lifestyle.

Circle the letter of the word, phrase, or sentence that *best* completes or corrects each sentence.

1. I'll call or e-mail you then you call Tony.
   (a) I'll call or e-mail you; then you call Tony.
   (b) I'll call or e-mail you? Then you call Tony.
   (c) I'll call or e-mail you call Tony then!
   (d) I'll call or e-mail you (then you call Tony).

2. When she tumbled.
   (a) When she tumbled, she screamed
   (b) When she tumbled, scraped her knees, and broke her wrist.
   (c) When she tumbled and screamed.
   (d) When she tumbled and scraped her knee.

3. Tables and chairs stands in the room.
   (a) standing
   (b) stand
   (c) standed
   (d) standded

4. My uncle thought he gave me a huge complement when he said, "You drive just like a man!"
   (a) My uncle thought he was giving me a huge complement when he said, "You drive just like a man!"
   (b) My uncle thought he gave me a huge complement when he said, "You drive just like a man!
   (c) My uncle thought he gave me a huge compliment when he said, "You drive just like a man!"
   (d) My uncle thought he gave me a huge complement when he said, "you drive just like a man!"

5. Course sand is so uncomforable under your feet.

   (a) Coarse sand is so uncomfortible under your feet.

   (b) Coarse sand is so uncomfurtable under your feet.

   (c) Coarse sand is so uncomfortable under your feet.

   (d) Course sand is so uncomfortible under your feet.

6. If you dessert the dinner table, we won't save any of this delicious desert for you.

   (a) If you dessert the dinner table, we won't save any of this delicious dessert for you.

   (b) If you dessert the dinner table, we won't save any of this delicious desurt for you.

   (c) If you desert the dinner table, we won't save any of this delicious desert for you.

   (d) If you desert the dinner table, we won't save any of this delicious dessert for you.

7. Music is an important part of my life (As I'm sure you know).

   (a) Music is an important part of my life (As I'm sure You know.)

   (b) Music is an important part of my life (as i'm sure you know).

   (c) Music is an important part of my life (as I'm sure you know).

   (d) Music is an important part of my life. (As I'm sure you know).

8. "I can't wait to visit you," Jenna said. "will you take me to the beach?"

   (a) "I can't wait to visit you," Jenna said? "will you take me to the beach?"

   (b) "I can't wait to visit you," Jenna said "will you take me to the beach?"

   (c) "I can't wait to visit you" Jenna said. "will you take me to the beach?"

   (d) "I can't wait to visit you," Jenna said. "Will you take me to the beach?"

9. Snowing hard and later lightly.

   (a) At first it was snowing hard, and then later it was snowing lightly.

   (b) Snowing hard and later lightly up to ten inches.

(c) Snowing hard and later lightly and then icy roads.

(d) Snowing hard but later lightly.

10. When there is piece in the Middle East.

   (a) When there is peace in the Middle East.

   (b) When will there be peace in the Middle East?

   (c) When there is peace in the Middle East and everyone is content.

   (d) When there is peace in the Middle East?

11. Each of the class members have one vote.

   (a) Each of the class members have one and only one vote.

   (b) Each of the class members have one votes.

   (c) Each of the class members has one vote.

   (d) Each of the class members have one vote to cast.

12. We have had more than the expected snow this winter and the snow removal has gone well.

   (a) We have had more than the expected snow this winter: and the snow removal has gone well.

   (b) We have had more than the expected snow this winter, and the snow removal has gone well.

   (c) We have had more than the expected snow this winter and also the snow removal has gone well.

   (d) We have had more than the expected snow this winter so you see and the snow removal has gone well.

13. Each received their semester grade.

   (a) Each student received their semester grade.

   (b) Each received all the semester grades.

   (c) Each received their semester grade.

   (d) Each received his or her semester grade.

14. Whom was the contest winner?

   (a) Who was the contest winner?

   (b) Whom were the contest winner?

   (c) Whom was the contest winners?

   (d) Whom was the winner of the contest?

15. Max takes the bus to school his teacher takes the subway.

   (a) Max takes the bus to school his teacher takes the subway?

   (b) Max takes the bus to school only his teacher takes the subway.

   (c) Max takes the bus to school; his teacher takes the subway.

   (d) Max takes the bus to school His teacher takes the subway

16. After I ate that huge meal.

   (a) After I ate that huge meal and a large bowl of ice cream.

   (b) After I ate that huge meal and took a walk.

   (c) When I finished eating that huge meal.

   (d) I felt sick after I ate that huge meal.

17. I digged my way through a large amount of old potting soil.

   (a) I digged my way through a large amount of really old potting soil.

   (b) I dug my way through a large amount of old potting soil.

   (c) I had digged my way through a large amount of old potting soil.

   (d) I have digged my way through a large amount of old potting soil.

18. On Sunday, I laid on the hammock for three hours.

   (a) On Sunday, I lain on the hammock for three hours.

   (b) On Sunday, I lay on the hammock for three hours.

   (c) On Sunday, I was lain on the hammock for three hours.

   (d) On Sunday, I layed on the hammock for three hours.

19. I have always mistook you for your sister.

    (a) I have always mistaken you for your sister.

    (b) I have always mistooked you for your sister.

    (c) I had always mistook you for your sister.

    (d) I will have always mistook you for your sister.

20. We thought your actions were iresponsible; please correct the problem you created.

    (a) We thought your actions were iresponsiblle; please correct the problem you created.

    (b) We thought your actions were iresponssible; please correct the problem you created.

    (c) We thought your actions were irresponsible; please correct the problem you created.

    (d) We thought your actions were iresponsable; please correct the problem you created

21. We did not expect to effect your behavior; we just hoped we would.

    (a) We did not expect to effect your behavior, we just hoped we would.

    (b) We did not expect to effect your behavior? We just hoped we would.

    (c) We did not expect to effect your behavior; we had just hoped we would.

    (d) We did not expect to affect your behavior. We just hoped we would.

22. There's a lot of reasons to argue!

    (a) There's a bunch of reasons to argue!

    (b) There's been a lot of reasons to argue!

    (c) There are a lot of reasons to argue!

    (d) There is a lot of reasons to argue!

23. It's to late to worry about that mistake.

    (a) It's more than to late to worry about that mistake.

    (b) It's too late to worry about that mistake.

(c) Its to late to worry about that mistake.

(d) It's much to late to worry about that mistake.

24. Yelling won't help you no more.

(a) Yelling won't help you anymore.

(b) Your yelling won't help you no more.

(c) Yelling won't help you no more?

(d) Yelling won't help you no more, no!

25. Our food-shopping list is longer than ever. Mostly because our children are on vacation this week.

(a) Our food-shopping list is longer than ever: mostly because our children on vacation this week.

(b) Our food-shopping list is longer than ever; mostly because our children on vacation this week.

(c) Our food-shopping list is longer than ever. And that's mostly because our children on vacation this week.

(d) Our food-shopping list is longer than ever, mostly because our children are on vacation this week.

26. She's much more intelligent than me.

(a) Is she much more intelligent than me?

(b) She's much more intelligent than I.

(c) She's much, much more intelligent than me.

(d) She's—not me—is much more intelligent than me.

27. I wish I could reclaim the amount of hours I've wasted on this project.

(a) I wish I could have the amount of hours I've wasted on this project.

(b) I wish I could reclaim the number of hours I've wasted on this project.

(c) I wish I could give away the amount of hours I've wasted on this project.

(d) Can I reclaim the amount of hours I've wasted on this project?

28. I will have had five different jobs before I will have retired.

   (a) I will have had five different jobs before I retire.

   (b) I will have had many different jobs before I will have retired.

   (c) I will have had five or more different jobs before I will have retired.

   (d) I will have had five different jobs before I will have begun to retire.

29. Millie picked up her new passport months before she had traveled.

   (a) Millie picked up her new passport and then it was months before she had traveled.

   (b) Millie will have picked up her new passport months before she had traveled.

   (c) Millie is going to pick up her new passport months before she had traveled.

   (d) Millie had picked up her new passport months before she traveled.

30. Neither of the girls know how to jump rope.

   (a) Neither of the two girls know how to jump rope.

   (b) Neither of the many girls know how to jump rope.

   (c) Neither of the three girls knows how to jump rope.

   (d) Neither of the girls knows how to jump rope.

31. Tony will fly anywheres to complete a business deal.

   (a) Tony will be flying anywheres to complete a business deal.

   (b) Tony will fly anywhere to complete a business deal.

   (c) Tony will fly anywheres to finish a business deal.

   (d) Tony will fly anywheres and everywheres to complete a business deal.

32. Gaby gave the concert tickets to Maggy and she carried them to the concert.

   (a) Maggy was to give Gaby the concert tickets after they arrived at the concert.

   (b) Gaby gave the concert tickets to Maggy, and then she arrived at the concert carrying them.

(c) Gaby gave the concert tickets to Maggy, who carried them to the concert.

(d) Gaby gave the concert ticket to Maggy, she carried them to the concert.

33. Ana performed the dance good.

(a) Ana performed the dance well.

(b) Ana performed the dance so good.

(c) Ana performed the dance so good and well.

(d) Ana performed the dance goodly.

34. Our motorboat was took in toe after the motor failed.

(a) Our motorboat was taken in toe after the motor failed.

(b) Our motorboat was being taken in toe after the motor failed.

(c) Our motorboat was taken in tow after the motor failed.

(d) Our motorboat will be taken in toe after the motor failed.

35. Emily doesn't go camping; she's too vane to travel without makeup and a mirror.

(a) Emily doesn't go camping; she's too vein to travel without makeup and a mirror.

(b) Emily doesn't go camping; she's much too vane to travel without makeup and a mirror.

(c) Emily doesn't go camping; she's to vane to travel without makeup and a mirror.

(d) Emily doesn't go camping; she's too vain to travel without makeup and a mirror.

36. As far as my parents were concerned, the concert was one continueous blast of noise.

(a) As far as my parents was concerned, the concert was one continueous blast of noise.

(b) As far as my parents were concerned, the concert was one continual blast of noise.

(c) As far as my parents were concerned, the concert, it was one continueous blast of noise.

(d) As far as my parents were concerned, the concert it was not one continueous blast of noise.

37. The girls played basketball the boys played tennis.

(a) The girls played basketball the boys played some tennis.

(b) The very capable girls played basketball well the boys played tennis.

(c) The girls played basketball the boys played tennis with great skill.

(d) The girls played basketball; the boys played tennis.

38. Einstein is famous for E = mc² Edison is famous for the invention of the lightbulb.

(a) Einstein is famous for E = mc², while Edison is famous for the invention of the lightbulb.

(b) Einstein is famous for E = mc² Edison is famous for the invention of the lightbulb?

(c) Einstein is famous for E = mc² Edison is not famous for the invention of the lightbulb.

(d) Einstein is famous for E = mc² you think Edison is famous for the invention of the lightbulb.

39. *Titanic* is my favorite movie, I love eating popcorn while I watch it.

(a) *Titanic* is my favorite movie, which I love eating popcorn while I watch it.

(b) *Titanic* is still my favorite movie, I love eating popcorn while I watch it.

(c) *Titanic* is my favorite movie. I love eating popcorn while I watch it.

(d) *Titanic* is my favorite movie, do I love eating popcorn while I watch it!

40. Americans shake hands when they meet the Japanese bow.

(a) Americans shake hands when they meet the: Japanese bow.

(b) Americans shake hands when they meet; however, the Japanese bow.

(c) Americans shake hands. when they meet the Japanese bow.

(d) Americans shake hands when they meet, however, the Japanese bow.

41. Cesar said, "If you asked to borrow money, I would have refused."

    (a) Cesar said, "If you have asked to borrow money, I would have refused."

    (b) Cesar said, "Even if you asked to borrow money, I would have refused."

    (c) Cesar said, "If you had asked to borrow money, I would have refused."

    (d) Cesar said, "If you will be asking to borrow money, I would have refused."

42. Mother's Day is always on a Sunday but Thanksgiving is always on a Thursday.

    (a) Mother's Day is always on a Sunday but you know Thanksgiving is always on a Thursday.

    (b) Mother's Day is always on a Sunday, but Thanksgiving is always on a Thursday.

    (c) Mother's Day is always on a Sunday but thanksgiving is always on a Thursday.

    (d) Mother's Day is always on a Sunday but Thanksgiving, it is always on a Thursday.

43. Josue, along with her four children, leave for the Grand Canyon on Sunday.

    (a) Josue, along with her four children, leave for the grand canyon on Sunday.

    (b) Josue along with her four children, leave for the Grand Canyon on Sunday.

    (c) Josue, along with her four children, leave for the Grand Canyon on sunday.

    (d) Josue, along with her four children, leaves for the Grand Canyon on Sunday.

44. William loved visiting Montreal Sally preferred just to stay in Quebec City.

    (a) William loved visiting Montreal "Sally preferred just to stay in Quebec City."

    (b) William loved visiting Montreal: Sally preferred just to stay in Quebec City.

    (c) William loved visiting Montreal, while Sally preferred just to stay in Quebec City.

    (d) William loved visiting Montreal Sally preferred just to stay in quebec city.

45. My car breaked down, so I need to buy a new one.

    (a) My car breaked down, will I need to buy a new one.

    (b) My car breaked down, will I need to buy a new one?

    (c) My car braked down, so I need to buy a new one.

    (d) My car broke down, so I need to buy a new one.

46. At one time few people had enough money to buy books however few people could read books.

    (a) At one time few people had enough money to buy books therefore few people could read books.

    (b) At one time few people had enough money to buy books so few people could read books.

    (c) At one time, few people had enough money to buy books; however, few people could read books.

    (d) At one time few; people had enough money to buy books few people could read books.

47. I made a decision to learn Korean Trudy wants to learn Turkish.

    (a) I decided to learn Korean; Trudy wanted to learn Turkish.

    (b) I made a decision to learn Korean with me Trudy wants to learn Turkish.

    (c) I decided to learn Korean, Trudy made a decision to learn Turkish.

    (d) I made a decision to learn Korean Trudy wants to learn Turkish.

48. We are all concerned about our children's education, our family's health care, and we worry about job stability, too.

    (a) We are all concerned about our children's education, our family's health care, and then there's job stability, too.

    (b) We are all concerned about our children's education, our family's health care, and our job stability, too.

    (c) We are all concerned about our children's education, our family's health care, and we worry about job stability, too?

    (d) We are all concerned about our children's education, our family and how their health care is, and we worry about job stability, too.

49. I know your concern is for my safty.

    (a) I know your concern is for my safty?

    (b) I know your concern is for my safety.

    (c) I know your concern is for my saftey.

    (d) I know your concern is four my safty.

50. Her referrence to my height was unkind.

    (a) Her reference to my height was unkind.

    (b) Her refference to my height was unkind.

    (c) Her refferrance to my height was unkind.

    (d) Her referrance to my height was unkind.

51. How come father-in-laws don't receive the same scrutiny as mother-in-laws?

    (a) How come fatheres-in-law don't receive the same scrutiny as motheres-in-law?

    (b) How come fatheres-in-laws don't receive the same scrutiny as mother-in-laws?

    (c) How come fathers-in-law don't receive the same scrutiny as mothers-in-law?

    (d) How come fathur-in-laws don't receive the same scrutiny as muther-in-laws?

52. "Procede to the exit immediately!" he shouted.

    (a) "Prosede to the exit immediately!" he shouted.

    (b) "Proceede to the exit immediately!" he shouted.

    (c) "Proseed to the exit immediately!" he shouted.

    (d) "Proceed to the exit immediately!" he shouted.

53. My friend he left me standing in the parking lot.

    (a) My friend he left me standing all alone in the parking lot.

    (b) My friend he left me standing in the parking lot in the rain.

    (c) My friend he left me for hours standing in the parking lot.

    (d) My friend left me standing in the parking lot.

54. Did you hear the toddler say, "Mommy, I hate this toy"!

    (a) Did you hear the toddler say, "Mommy, I hate this toy!"

    (b) Did you hear the toddler say, "Mommy, I hate this toy?"

    (c) Did you hear the toddler say, "Mommy, I hate this toy"?

    (d) Did you hear the toddler say? "Mommy, I hate this toy"!

55. Take your pencils pens and notepaper to the meeting.

    (a) Take your pencils, pens, and notepaper to the meeting.

    (b) Take your pencils pens, and notepaper to the meeting.

    (c) Take your pencils pens and notepaper, to the meeting.

    (d) Take your pencils pens (and notepaper) to the meeting.

56. "Theirs a fly in my soup!" she exclaimed.

    (a) "Theyrs a fly in my soup!" she exclaimed.

    (b) "There's a fly in my soup!" she exclaimed.

    (c) "Their's a fly in my soup!" she exclaimed.

    (d) "They'rs a fly in my soup!" she exclaimed.

57. According to the program notes, its going to be a long concert.

    (a) According to the program notes, it's going to be a long concert.

    (b) According to the program notes, its' going to be a long concert.

    (c) According to the program note's its going to be a long concert.

    (d) According to the program notes. its going to be a long concert.

58. If I had known how long it was going to be, I would of refused to attend.

    (a) If I had known how long it was going too be, I would of refused to attend.

    (b) If I had known, how long it was going to be, I would of refused to attend.

    (c) If I had known how long it was going to be, I would have refused to attend.

    (d) If I had known how long it was going to be, I could of refused to attend.

59. To do it correctly, place the tomato sauce on the bottom, follow that with lasagna, tomato sauce, and cheese.

    (a) To do it correctly, place the tomato sauce on the bottom: follow that with lasagna, tomato sauce, and cheese.

    (b) To do it correctly, place the tomato sauce on the bottom; follow that with lasagna, tomato sauce, and cheese.

    (c) To do it correct, place the tomato sauce on the bottom, follow that with lasagna, and don't forget tomato sauce, and cheese.

    (d) To do it correctly, place the tomato sauce on the bottom, follow that with lasagna tomato sauce, and cheese.

60. We lived in cleveland from july, 1990 to august, 2000.

    (a) We lived in Cleveland from july, 1990 to august, 2000.

    (b) We lived in cleveland from july, 1990 to August, 2000.

    (c) We lived in Cleveland from july, 1990 to auguast, 2000.

    (d) We lived in Cleveland from July 1990 to August 2000.

61. Have you read doris kearns goodwin's book, *team of rivals*?

    (a) Have you read doris kearns Goodwin's book, *team of rivals*?

    (b) Have you read Doris Kearns Goodwin's book, *Team of Rivals*?

    (c) Have you read Doris kearns Goodwin's book, *team of rivals*?

    (d) Have you read doris kearns goodwin's book, *team of rivals*!

62. One of the courses I'm taking is european history I which includes world war II.

    (a) One of the courses I'm taking is European History I, which includes World War II.

    (b) One of the courses I'm taking is European history I which includes world war II.

    (c) One of the courses I'm taking is European History I which includes world war II.

    (d) One of the courses I'm taking is european history I which includes World War II.

63. Known as a no-frills airline, southwest airlines serves most of the united states.

    (a) Known as a no-frills airline, southwest airlines serves most of the United States.

    (b) Known as a no-frills airline, SouthWest airlines serves most of the united states.

    (c) Known as a no-frills airline, Southwest Airlines serves most of the United States.

    (d) Known as a no-frills airline, Southwest Airlines Serves most of the United States.

64. A completely free food program is offered by the Food Bank.

    (a) A free food program of free food is offered by the Food Bank.

    (b) The Food Bank offers a free program.

    (c) A completely free food program is ofered by the Food Bank.

    (d) Do they offer a free program of free food at the Food Bank?

65. This year was the first time I finished my taxes before the last possible day.

    (a) This year was the first year I finished my taxes before the last possible day.

    (b) This year was the first time me and my friends finished my taxes before the last possible day

    (c) This year was the first time I finished my taxes and it was before the last possible day

    (d) This year was the first time I finished my taxes before the last day.

66. Tim is very bright: He always makes me make a justification for a decision regarding his curfew.

    (a) Tim is very bright: He always makes me justify my decision regarding his curfew.

    (b) Tim is very bright: (He always makes me make a justification for a decision regarding his curfew.)

    (c) Tim is very bright: He sometimes makes me make a justification for a decision regarding his curfew.

    (d) Tim is pretty bright: He always makes me make a justification for a decision regarding his curfew.

67. The chairman will attend and argue with the new proposition.

    (a) The chairman and his committee will attend and argue with the new proposition.

    (b) The chairman will attend and argue against the new proposition.

    (c) The chairman will be attending and argue against the new proposition.

    (d) The chairman will not attend and argue with the new proposition.

68. Geraldo is reliable and has honesty.

    (a) Geraldo is reliable and has some honesty.

    (b) Geraldo is reliable and usually has honesty.

    (c) Geraldo is reliable and has honestly.

    (d) Geraldo is reliable and honest.

69. At the end of the report it gave a conclusion.

    (a) At the end of the long report it gave a conclusion.

    (b) The report provided a conclusion at the end.

    (c) At the end of the report it provided a conclusion no one agreed with.

    (d) At the end of the report; it gave a conclusion.

70. We need the true facts to make an intelligent decision.

    (a) We need the facts to make an intelligent decision.

    (b) We need the true facts to make an intelligent decision?

    (c) We need the facts; to make an intelligent decision

    (d) We need the true facts in order for us to make an intelligent decision

71. My niece is a gifted softball player so she doesn't play on any team.

    (a) My niece is a gifted softball player, so she doesn't play on any team.

    (b) My niece is a gifted softball player consequently she doesn't play on any team.

    (c) My niece is a gifted softball player, yet she doesn't play on any team.

    (d) My niece is a gifted softball player instead she doesn't play on any team.

72. Will you repeat again what you told me on the phone last night?

    (a) Will you repeat once again what you told me on the phone last night?

    (b) I'm asking you to repeat again what you told me on the phone last night!

    (c) You repeat again what you told me on the phone last night

    (d) Will you repeat what you told me on the phone last night?

73. The traveler was late for his flight in the taxicab.

    (a) The traveler was very late for his flight in the taxicab.

    (b) The traveler was too late for his flight in the taxicab.

    (c) The traveler in the taxicab was late for his flight.

    (d) The traveler was late for his flight in the Redtop taxicab.

74. We helped Amaya and she fill out applications.

    (a) Did you help Amaya and she fill out applications?

    (b) We helped Amaya and her fill out applications.

    (c) We helped she and Amaya fill out applications.

    (d) Amadio helped Amaya and she fill out applications.

75. Me running for City Council was a big mistake.

    (a) Me running for our town's City Council was a big mistake.

    (b) Me running for City Council was an even biggger mistake.

    (c) My running for City Council was a big mistake.

    (d) Do you think me running for City Council was a big mistake?

76. All of the following day were ruined.

    (a) All of the following day were ruined, weren't they?

    (b) All of the following day were ruined.

    (c) All of the following day was ruined.

    (d) All of the following day were ruined for us.

77. Cecelia didn't know whom you were until today.

    (a) Cecelia didn't know who you were until today.

    (b) Cecelia didn't know which you were until today

    (c) Cecelia didn't know that you were until today.

    (d) Cecelia didn't really know whom you were until today

78. The delivery person which you saw is not the usual one.

    (a) The delivery person that you saw is not the usual one.

    (b) The delivery person whom you saw is not the usual one.

    (c) The delivery person who you saw is not the usual one.

    (d) The delivery person which you saw yesterday is not the usual one.

79. My car which is seven years old is overdue for new tires.

    (a) My car, that is seven years old, is overdue for new tires.

    (b) My used car which is seven years old is overdue for new tires.

    (c) My car which I think is seven years old is overdue for new tires.

    (d) My car, which is seven years old, is overdue for new tires.

80. Everything we've done are wrong!

    (a) All we've done are wrong!

    (b) Everything we've done are being wrong!

(c) Everything you've done are wrong!

(d) Everything we've done is wrong!

81. I decided it was time to give a break to myself.

(a) I decided it was time to give myself a break.

(b) I decided it was my time, to give a break to myself.

(c) I decided it was the right time to give a break to myself.

(d) Did I decide it was time to give a break to myself?

82. We can be on time for the train if we start out early enough.

(a) You and me can be on time for the train if we start out early enough.

(b) If we start out early enough, we can be on time for the train.

(c) We can finally be on time for the first train finally! if we start out early enough.

(d) We can finally get the train if we start out early enough.

83. The children have missed their bedtime everyday this week.

(a) The children have missed their bed time everyday this week.

(b) The children have missed they're bed time everyday this week.

(c) The children have missed their bedtime every day this week.

(d) The children have missed there bedtime everyday this week.

84. I seed the accident as it happened.

(a) I saw the accident as it happened.

(b) I seed the accident very good as it happened.

(c) I had seed the accident as it happened.

(d) I have seed the accident as it happened.

85. I had my name and address printed on my new stationary.

(a) I had put my name and address on my new stationary.

(b) I had my name and address printed on my very new stationary.

(c) I had my name and address printed on my new stationarys.

(d) I had my name and address printed on my new stationery.

86. The nuts and cranberries in my salad tastes so crunchy.

    (a) The nuts and cranberries in my salad tastes so crunchy and delicious.

    (b) The nuts and cranberries in my salad taste so crunchy.

    (c) The nuts and cranberry in my salad tastes so crunchy.

    (d) You know, the nuts and cranberries in my salad tastes so crunchy.

87. Yesterday my day is simple—until school was cancelled.

    (a) Yesterday my day is simple, until school was cancelled.

    (b) Yesterday my day was simple—until school was cancelled.

    (c) Yesterday my day is simple—until school is canceled.

    (d) Yesterday my whole day is simple—until school was cancelled.

88. I bended my finger back and it was so painful!

    (a) I had bended my finger back, and it was so painful!

    (b) I bended my finger back, and it was so painful!

    (c) I bent my finger back, and it was so painful!

    (d) I mistakenly bended my finger back, and it was so painful!

89. I decided to adapt a puppy from a shelter.

    (a) I decided to adept a puppy from a shelter.

    (b) I had decided to adapt a puppy from a shelter.

    (c) I decided to adopt a puppy from a shelter.

    (d) Did you decide to adapt a puppy from a shelter?

90. Heres' your chance to make some extra money.

    (a) Here's your chance to make some extra money.

    (b) Here are your chance to make some extra money.

    (c) Heres' your chance to make some extra money.

    (d) Finally, heres' your chance to make some extra money.

91. He ain't leaving until he finishes his work.

    (a) He ain't going nowhere until he finishes his work.

    (b) He ain't leaving untill he finishes his work.

    (c) He ain't leaving until he finished his work.

    (d) He isn't leaving until he finishes his work.

92. There's too many jobs for one person.

    (a) There's to many jobs for one person.

    (b) There's not too many jobs for one person.

    (c) There are too many jobs for one person.

    (d) Theres' to many jobs for one person.

93. Don't he have enough to do?

    (a) Don't he and she have enough to do?

    (b) Don't he have enough to do?

    (c) Doesn't he have enough to do?

    (d) Don't she have enough to do?

94. If I decide to go and I know I'm driving.

    (a) If I decide to go and I know I'm driving, I'll call you.

    (b) If I decide to go, and I know I'm driving.

    (c) If I decide, to go and I know I'm driving.

    (d) If I decide to go and I know, I'm driving.

95. The Christmas trees was grinded to a pulp.

    (a) The Christmas trees were grinded to a pulp.

    (b) The Christmas trees is grinding to a pulp.

    (c) The Christmas trees were ground to a pulp.

    (d) The Christmas trees was always grinded to a pulp.

96. The dress lost it's color after two washings.

    (a) The dress lost its color after two washings.

    (b) The dress lost its' color after two washings.

    (c) The dress lost i'ts color after two washings.

    (d) The dress lost it'ses color after two washings.

97. At first Paulina said, "I'll be there at noon," and then she continued, "So try to be on time."

    (a) At first Paulina said, "i'll be there at noon," and then she continued, "So try to be on time."

    (b) At first Paulina said, "I'll be there at noon," and then she continued, "so try to be on time."

    (c) At first Paulina said, "I'll be there at noon," and then she continued; So try to be on time."

    (d) At first Paulina said "I'll be there at noon" and then she continued "So try to be on time."

98. The captain thought he had delivered a stern warning, nevertheless the driver sped off with a screech.

    (a) The captain thought he had delivered a stern warning, nevertheless, the driver sped off with a screech.

    (b) The captain thought he had delivered a stern warning; nevertheless, the driver sped off with a screech.

    (c) The captain thought he had delivered a stern warning, nevertheless; the driver sped off with a screech.

    (d) The captain, he thought he had delivered a stern warning, nevertheless the driver sped off with a screech.

99. My reason for going to the mall on Monday was that I knew it would be less crowded.

    (a) My reason for going to the mall on Monday was really that I knew it would be less crowded.

    (b) My reason for going to the mall on Monday was that I knew from the last time it would be less crowded.

(c) My reason for going to the mall on Monday at 10 A.M. was that I knew it would be less crowded.

(d) I went to the mall on Monday because I knew it would be less crowded.

100. We were searching for a builder who had experience.

(a) We were searching for an experienced builder who had lots of experience.

(b) We were searching for a builder who had some experience.

(c) We were searching for an experienced builder.

(d) We were searching for a builder who was experienced.

APPENDIX A

Most Commonly Misspelled Words

The text below of the most commonly misspelled words in English is copyrighted © 2008 by Lexiteria LLC. It was created by Prof. Robert Beard of Bucknell University and alphadictionary.com and is used here by permission.

a while: It should only take a little while to learn that this expression is two words, not one.

awhile: With the two words joined, this is an adverb. Be sure the adverb has a verb, adjective, or another adverb to modify. "Earth takes us in *awhile* as transient guests . . ."

acceptable: Unfortunately, there is no rule that predicts when to use *-able* and when to use *-ible*. But if you can accept a table in a cafe, you should be able to remember this one.

accidentally: It is no accident that if an adjective may end with the suffix *-al*, this suffix must be in the adverb—that is the *al*-rule. *Theatric* may be *theatrical*, so the adverb must be *theatrically*. There is no *publical*, so *publicly* is OK.

accommodate: This word is large enough to accommodate two *c*'s and two *m*'s. Don't forget.

accordion: Since accordions do not come from Accordia, you spell the ending on this word *-i-o-n*, not *-i-a-n*.

acquire: You should acquire the habit of adding a silent *c* before the *q* in this word.

acquit: Don't quit before adding a *c* before the *q* in this word, either.

a lot: If you allot some time for learning that this expression is two words, you should master it after a while.

altar: Be sure you do not alter (change) the spelling of *altar* when writing about churches.

amateur: Amateurs may or may not be mature, but you always spell these two words differently.

apparent: It should be apparent to all that *apparent* has two *p*'s and a *parent* in it.

argument: The silent *e* at the end of *argue* can't argue with a suffix bigger than it is, so it gets out of *argument*.

atheist: Remember religiously that this word is built on the same -the- "god" that we find in theology.

believe: You must believe the "*i*-before-*e* rule": that *i* comes before *e* except after *c* or when it is pronounced like "ay" as in *neighbor* and *weigh*. However, beware of exceptions like *foreign*.

bellwether: A bellwether is not a bell that predicts the weather but a gelded ram (= a wether) with a bell around his neck, chosen to lead the herd by virtue of the greater likelihood that he will remain ahead of the ewes.

broccoli: You don't have to like broccoli to spell it correctly with two *c*'s and one *l*.

calendar: You might put a review of this word on your calendar: remind yourself that it ends with -*ar*, not -*er*.

camouflage: Even though we shorten this word to *camo*, we should always remember *u* in the middle of the full form.

cantaloupe: Here is another place we often forget *u*: don't be misled by signs that say "Lopes for sale."

Caribbean: As any Carib bean tells you, this word has one *r* and two *b*'s.

category: Spelling *category* like *catastrophe* isn't catastrophic, but it could be embarrassing.

cemetery: Don't let this word bury you: except for the final *y*, the only vowel in it is *e*.

changeable: The silent *e* on *change* is able to live with the suffix -*able*, so it remains to remind us that the *g* is soft, pronounced like *j*. (See also *noticeable*.)

chili: You'll never find a chilly chili, but do keep their spellings straight.

collectible: Even if you collect tables, what you collect is collectible, with an *i*. Unfortunately, there is no rule for this one.

colonel: There is more than a kernel of truth in the claim that *colonel* is pronounced exactly like *kernel*—but spelled *colonel*.

column: *E* is not the only letter in English that can be silent: column has a silent *N*.

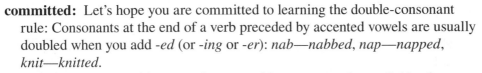

committed: Let's hope you are committed to learning the double-consonant rule: Consonants at the end of a verb preceded by accented vowels are usually doubled when you add *-ed* (or *-ing* or *-er*): *nab—nabbed, nap—napped, knit—knitted.*

conscience: No one with a conscience would try to con science. *Sci* is often pronounced "ch" after an *n*.

conscientious: Here is a word where both *sci* and *ti* are pronounced "ch" after an *n*. Be a conscientious speller and remember that.

conscious: I hope that by now you are conscious of the fact that *sci* after *n* is pronounced "ch" in English.

consensus: The consensus (majority opinion) is that the census is a good idea, even though they are not spelled alike.

coolly: You will coolly spell this word correctly if you remember that it is the adjective *cool* with the adverb suffix *-ly.*

cupboard: Just because we don't hear the *p* in this word when we pronounce it, "kuhburd," doesn't mean it's not there.

definite(ly): This word definitely sounds like it ends with *t* but that is because the *e* behind it remains silent no matter what.

descendant: This word may also be spelled *descendent*, but this spelling usually indicates an adjective (e.g., a descendent vine), while a person in a family tree is a descendant of his or her ancestors.

deterrence: Four common English words ending on an accented vowel + *r*, double the *r* before the suffixes *-ence* and *-ent*: *deterrence, abhorrence, occurrence*, and *concurrence.*

discipline: A little discipline in spelling habits will help you remember the silent *c* in the middle and silent *e* at the end of this word.

drunkenness: Even sober writers sometimes forget one of the *n*'s in this word.

embarrass(ment): This word has an embarrassment of *r*'s and *s*'s—two of each.

equipment: This word is easier to spell than you think if you avoid sticking a *t* between the *p* and the *m*: not *equiptment*!

exceed: Exceed all expectations and master spelling this word like *proceed* but not like *precede* or *supersede.*

exhilarate: Just think of the exhilaration knowing that you are one of those good writers who know this word contains an *h*.

existence: Putting an *a* rather than an *e* before the *nce* in this word can make your existence miserable.

experience: Avoid the embarrassing experience of spelling this word with an *a* before the final *nce*, too.

fiery: The final *e* in *fire* jumped over the *r* to get away from the *y*. Wouldn't you?

foreign: The *i*-before-*e* rule is foreign to the spelling of *foreign.*

fulfill: *Full* is not fully spelled in this word, but *fill* is.

gauge: Learn to gauge the positions of the *a* and *u* in this word; they are in alphabetical order.

grateful: Spelling *grateful* as *greatful* grates on the eyes. Spelling it *grateful* is great.

guarantee: I guarantee you that this word does not end like *warranty* and *warranty* does not end like *guarantee*.

handkerchief: Remember that handkerchiefs go in your hand and not on your head, and you won't forget the silent *d*. The *i*-before-*e* rule works in this word.

harass: Don't let the single *r* in this word harass you—only double the *s*.

height: English reaches the height (not heighth!) of absurdity when it spells *height* and *width* so differently—and ignores the *i*-before-*e* rule.

hierarchy: The *i*-before-*e* rule works in this word, just as it does in *hieroglyph*.

humorous: Humor us by spelling this word *humorous*: don't forget the *o* and the *u*, and no one will say, "Forget you!"

hypocrisy: It isn't just hype to say this word has nothing to do with hippos: it's hip to spell it *hypocrisy*.

ignorance: Don't let ignorance becloud the fact that this word ends with -*ance*, not -*ence*.

imitate: Be sure not to imitate those who write this word with two *a*'s rather than two *i*'s.

immediate: This word contains two *m*'s in immediate proximity of each other—side by side.

incredible: It is simply incredible that no rule tells us when to use -*ible* and when to use -*able*. Just remember: incredible.

independent: There is no independent way to spell this word: it ends with -*ent* not -*ant*.

indispensable: The *a* in the suffix -*able* is indispensable if you want to spell this word correctly.

inoculate: You should inoculate yourself against the temptation to double any letter in this word.

intelligence: Let's use our intelligence to remember the double *l* in this word and the ending -*ence*.

its/it's: Sometimes it's hard to remember that *it's* is a contraction of *it is* and *its* means "belonging to it," as in, "It's too bad that its leg is broken."

jewelry: Jewelry is made by a jeweler but the ending *y* is a thief that pilfers the *e* from *er*.

just deserts: We would not get our just deserts if we ate just desserts for our meals. *Deserts* with one *s* means "that which is deserved," as is dessert when we finish our vegetables.

kernel: There is more than a kernel of truth in the claim *colonel* is spelled peculiarly to be pronounced the same as *kernel*. English spelling can be chaotic.

leisure: We can't leisurely apply the *i*-before-*e* rule to this word: it does not follow it.

liaison: The *a* is a liaison between the *i*'s in this word. It has three—count them—three vowels in a row.

library: Pronouncing this word correctly helps with the spelling: you will find no berry in *library*.

license: We'll give you a license to spell this word with both letters for the sound "s": *c* and *s*.

lightning: Even though lightning is capable of lightening the sky, it contains no *e*.

maintenance: Help us maintain the correct spelling of maintenance by never forgetting the *e* in the middle: maintain but maintenance.

maneuver: Always maneuver an *eu* into the middle of this word, and if you live outside the United States, *oeu*: the British spelling of this word is *manoeuver*.

marshmallow: No matter how mellow your marshmallow gets, it is still spelled with two *a*'s and an *o*, no *e*'s.

medieval: Take this memory med to remember that the adjective referring to the Middle Ages begins with *med* and follows the *i*-before-*e* rule.

memento: Don't hesitate a moment to spell this word with two *e*'s and one *o*.

millennium: Never in a thousand years could we spell millennium with fewer that two *l*'s and two *n*'s.

miniature: It is only a miniature task to write (and pronounce) the *a* in the middle of this word.

minuscule: And it is but a minuscule task to remember that *minuscule* begins with a minus.

mischievous: It would be very mischievous to ignore the *i*-before-*e* rule when spelling this word.

misogyny: Of course, we all love women but the word for hating them ends with the same *gyn* seen in *gynecology*.

missile: You can send a missal to your friend about launching a missile; just keep the missile in its silo.

misspell: Misspelling *misspell* can be embarrassing, so remember both *s*'s and both *l*'s.

nauseous: This word has enough vowels to make you nauseous, another one with three vowels in a row, this time in alphabetical order.

neighbor: Just remember, the neigh of a horse plus *-bor*, and you will always spell this word correctly in the United States.

necessary: It is necessary to use two *s*'s but only one *c* to write this word right every time.

no one: Let no one tell you this is one word; it is always two.

noticeable: Don't forget to leave the final *e* of *notice* before the suffix *-able* so everyone will know the *c* is soft (pronounced like *s*.) See also *changeable*.

occasion: Now is a good occasion to remember that this word has two *c*'s and one *s*.

occasionally: Ditto for this word, but also remember the *al*-rule: if an adjective may end with *-al*, its adverb must contain *-al* before *-ly*.

occurrence: Never forget the two occurrences of *c* and the two occurrences of *r* in this word. (See other words that double *r* before *-ence*.)

pastime: Even though a pastime is a good way to pass time, you need only one *s* to spell it correctly.

perseverance: Too much perseverance of the *e* is bad for the spelling of this word: all *e*'s except the next to the last. Also notice that there is no *r* before the *v*.

personnel: Funny story: The assistant vice-president of personnel notices that his boss, the vice-president himself, upon arriving at his desk each morning, opens a small locked box, looks inside, smiles, and locks it up again. Some years later when the assistant is promoted to his boss's position, he comes to work early one morning and opens the secret box to see what was inside. He finds a single piece of paper on which is written: "Two *n*'s, one *l*." That's the way you spell *personnel*.

pigeon: If you aren't speaking pidgin English, you must spell *pigeon* without a *d* and with an *-eon*.

playwright: If you play right, you are a right player, but folks who write plays were first called "play-makers" or to use the word of the time, playwrights, like cartwrights, wagonwrights, wheelwrights.

plenitude: It takes a plenitude of self-restraint to resist the temptation of including a *t* in this word: *plenty* but *plenitude*.

possession: The word *possession* possesses more *s*'s than a snake—four altogether.

precede: Coming before is to precede; coming after is to succeed. Don't you love the consistency of English spelling? *Precede* is spelled like *accede*, *antecede*, *concede*, *intercede*, *recede*, and *secede*, but not like *proceed* or *supersede*.

principal: Just remember your principal is a prince and a pal in principle, especially if your principal is a man or woman of principles.

privilege: Consider it a privilege to know that this word contains two *i*'s in a row followed by two *e*'s.

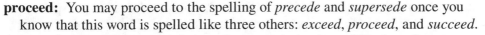

proceed: You may proceed to the spelling of *precede* and *supersede* once you know that this word is spelled like three others: *exceed*, *proceed*, and *succeed*.

pronunciation: The pronunciation of *pronunciation* is not like that of *pronounce*—nor is the spelling.

publicly: The *al*-rule works here, too: if *publical* is impossible, the adverb will be *publicly*.

queue: This word sets a record: four vowels in a row forming a double *ue*! Speaking of rows, it refers to a line you stand in. It is pronounced the same as *cue*.

questionnaire: Double up on the *n*'s in this word, and don't forget the silent *e* on the end. This is another French word causing problems for English spelling.

raspberry: If you can remember that the skin of a raspberry looks a little like a rasp, it will help you to remember the *sp* in this word that sounds like "z."

receive/receipt: The *i*-before-*e*-except-after-*c* rule works on all words ending in -*ceive*, including this one, *deceive*, *perceive*, and *conceive*.

recommend: We strongly recommend that you write this word with two *m*'s but only one *c*.

referred: According to the double-consonant rule, single consonants at the end of verbs usually double before -*ed* if preceded by an accented vowel.

reference: *Reference* contains only one vowel, *e*. The *r* is not doubled before -*ence*, because the *er* is not accented as it is in *deterrence*.

relevant: The *a* in this word is very relevant to its spelling; do not replace it with *e*. Of course, the *l* always precedes the *v* even though *revelant* looks like a real word.

restaurant: Restaurants aren't for resters, so you don't spell it that way. The middle of this word is *au* as in *Australia*.

rhyme: This word was originally spelled *rime* but not anymore; it looked so much like *rhythm* that ancients decided it should be spelled that way.

rhythm: This word was borrowed from Greek (and never returned) so the "r" sound is spelled the Greek way, *rh*.

sandal: Sandals won't keep out the sand, Al, but if you spell the word with two *a*'s, you will at least spell it correctly.

schedule: School should schedule a time to learn how to spell this word since *school* and *schedule* start with the same letters. Outside the United States, this word is pronounced "shedjule," not "skedjule."

scissors: See the *c* in *scissors*? You can't snip it out when you spell this word.

seize: Pronounced like two *c*'s, this word roundly breaks the *i*-before-*e* rule.

separate: Never forget that two *a*'s separate the *e*'s when spelling *separate*.

sergeant: The sergeant's nickname is Sarge but his full name is sergeant. (Don't ask why.)

succeed: If you want to succeed in this world, you must learn how to spell *succeed*. Remember, it is spelled double *c* and double *e*, like *proceed* but not like *precede* and *supersede*.

supersede: This word supersedes all others in spelling perversity. Spelling words like *proceed* and *precede* raise problems enough. The good news is, this is the only English word spelled *-sede*.

their/they're/there: Their pronunciations are the same but not their spellings. Possessive *their* means "belonging to them" and *they're* is a contraction of *they are*. That leaves *there* for everywhere else.

threshold: This one looks like a compound *thresh* + *hold* but it isn't. Two *h*'s in the middle of this word pushes you over the threshold of bad spelling.

tomorrow: One *m* and two *r*'s yesterday, today, and tomorrow.

turmeric: The *r* before *m* in *turmeric* is all but forgotten—but it is still there.

twelfth: Remember the little elf in the middle of *twelfth*, and you should write this word right every time.

tyranny: Remember how *tyrant* is spelled, and the correct spelling of *tyranny* follows. Of course, we mustn't forget to double the *n*.

until: I won't stop saying that this word ends with only one *l* until everyone is spelling it correctly!

vacuum: A vacuum holds a large volume of dust, but the two words do not end the same.

weather: In good weather or bad, we must write an *a* after the *we*.

weird: It's so weird to see how this word breaks the *i*-before-*e* rule.

APPENDIX B

The 50 Most Deadly Common Errors

Some errors are so common that many people accept them as correct—but they're not.

For example, *between you and I* will never be correct. People say it or write it because it's so often used. It is important to try extra hard not to make these errors because they make the writer appear undereducated. These errors are so pervasive that they merit a special section.

Interestingly, the following most common errors are all taken from actual conversations (overheard), written communications, and (oh, what a treasure trove!) from television news anchors, commentators, and TV audiences. The error appears on the first line followed by the correct usage on the second. To review any concepts in more detail, each entry includes the type of error and a reference to the chapter(s) that addresses the error.

Incorrect: Me and my friends spent the day at the mall.

Correct: My friends and I spent the day at the mall. (pronoun, 2, 3)

Incorrect: There's a lot of people who like that candidate.

Correct: There are a lot of people who like that candidate. (verb, 2)

Incorrect: It's never to late to go back to school.

Correct: It's never too late to go back to school. (word usage, 11)

Incorrect: They had broke down the door.

Correct: They had broken down the door. (irregular verb, 1)

Incorrect: His parents expected to go with he and myself.

Correct: His parents expected to go with him and me. (pronoun, 2, 3)

Incorrect: Every winter morning, I tell the children to dress warm.

Correct: Every winter morning, I tell the children to dress warmly. (adverb, 2)

Incorrect: In that category, the differences is very small.

Correct: In that category, the differences are very small. (subject-verb agreement, 1)

Incorrect: The flowers in my garden is so colorful.

Correct: The flowers in my garden are so colorful. (subject-verb agreement, 1)

Incorrect: Time was moving too slow.

Correct: Time was moving too slowly. (adverb, 2)

Incorrect: My schedule rarely goes smooth.

Correct: My schedule rarely goes smoothly. (adverb, 2)

Incorrect: I've spoke to that child many times.

Correct: I've spoken to that child many times. (verb, 2)

Incorrect: Everybody in the country think things are going badly.

Correct: Everybody in the country thinks things are going badly. (subject-verb agreement, 1, 3)

Incorrect: Our company can handle everything quick and easy.

Correct: Our company can handle everything quickly and easily. (adverb, 2)

Incorrect: He should have came right back.

Correct: He should have come right back. (verb, 2)

Incorrect: Her mother and her agreed on a curfew.

Correct: Her mother and she agreed on a curfew. (pronoun, 2, 3)

Incorrect: We were so glad that the principal had chose us for early dismissal.

Correct: We were so glad that the principal had chosen us for early dismissal. (irregular verb, 1)

Incorrect: We was all ready to leave.

Correct: We were all ready to leave. (subject-verb agreement, 1)

Incorrect: Take the food with you leave your bathing suit in the car.

Correct: Take the food with you; leave your bathing suit in the car. (run-on sentence, 1)

Incorrect: If they packed to little food, it was there own fault.

Correct: If they packed too little food, it was their own fault. (spelling, 10)

Incorrect: Our political campaigns are longer than any others. Partly because we're willing to spend so much more money.

Correct: Our political campaigns are longer than any others, partly because we're willing to spend so much more money. (fragment, 1)

Incorrect: We'll close for the whole entire time.

Correct: We'll close for the entire time. (unnecessary words, 7)

Incorrect: Mara arranged her desk first then in a real fit of neatness she started organizing her file cabinet.

Correct: Mara arranged her desk first; then, in a real fit of neatness, she started organizing her file cabinet. (coordinating conjunction, 7)

Incorrect: I want to make the meal real quick.

Correct: I want to make the meal really quickly. (adverb, 2)

Incorrect: She's funnier than me.

Correct: She's funnier than I am. (pronoun, 3)

Incorrect: Bad feelings creeped into our relationship.

Correct: Bad feelings crept into our relationship. (irregular verb, 2)

Incorrect: I was looking for a present for you and I.

Correct: I was looking for a present for you and me. (pronoun, 2, 3)

Incorrect: When you go to the party, will you bring me with you?

Correct: When you go to the party, will you take me with you? (word usage, 11)

Incorrect: Some of the greatest musicians was there.

Correct: Some of the greatest musicians were there. (subject-verb agreement 1, 3)

Incorrect: Newspaper headline: Less frowns. More smiles.

Correct: Newspaper headline: Fewer frowns. More smiles. (word usage, 11)

Incorrect: There's enough people for our game tonight.

Correct: There are enough people for our game tonight. (subject-verb agreement, 1)

Incorrect: They do things very different.

Correct: They do things very differently. (adverb, 2)

Incorrect: Each of us have the opportunity to serve.

Correct: Each of us has the opportunity to serve. (subject-verb agreement, 1, 3)

Incorrect: There is a fundamental difference between these three candidates.

Correct: There is a fundamental difference among these three candidates. (word usage, 11)

Incorrect: I'm not afraid of nothing.

Correct: I'm not afraid of anything. (pronoun, double negative, 3)

Incorrect: Who likes who?

Correct: Who likes whom? (pronoun, 3)

Incorrect: It works so good.

Correct: It works so well. (adjective, 2)

Incorrect: These are repetitions that you hear repeatedly.

Correct: You hear these repeatedly. (unnecessary words, 7)

Incorrect: We could have went anywhere.

Correct: We could have gone anywhere. (irregular verbs, 2)

Incorrect: The President would describe the problem different.

Correct: The President would describe the problem differently. (adverb, 2)

Incorrect: Drew took his medication washed dressed and started reading a new book.

Correct: Drew took his medication, washed, dressed, and started reading a new book. (punctuation, 4)

Incorrect: There'll be a big contest between John and he.

Correct: There'll be a big contest between John and him. (pronoun, 3)

Incorrect: Sheila said, "Between you and I, I know his plan won't work."

Correct: Sheila said, "Between you and me, I know his plan won't work." (pronoun, 3)

Incorrect: None of us want to be in this position.

Correct: None of us wants to be in this position. (pronoun, 3)

Incorrect: Did she ask you if you were ready to leave.

Correct: Did she ask you if you were ready to leave? (punctuation, 4)

Incorrect: Don't touch those lights, the director yelled!

Correct: "Don't touch those lights!" the director yelled. (punctuation, 4)

Incorrect: The magna carta must be one subject in american history.

Correct: The Magna Carta must be one subject in American history. (capitalization, 6)

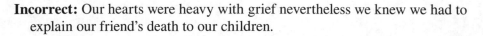

Incorrect: Our hearts were heavy with grief nevertheless we knew we had to explain our friend's death to our children.

Correct: Our hearts were heavy with grief; nevertheless, we knew we had to explain our friend's death to our children. (punctuation, 5)

Incorrect: The neighbors, we took a survey of the neighborhood about having a block party.

Correct: The neighbors took a survey about having a block party. (unnecessary words, 7)

Incorrect: Marcel dropped the tomato juice jar on the glass scanner and broke it.

Correct: Marcel dropped the tomato juice jar and broke the glass scanner. (descriptive phrase placement, 3)

Incorrect: Your tactless response was unecessary!

Correct: Your tactless response was unnecessary! (spelling, 10)

ANSWER KEY

CHAPTER 1

Written Practice 1-1
Sample answers are provided.
1. . . . California, I need to make a hotel reservation. 2. . . . rain stops, I'll plant annuals and herbs. 3. . . . a promotion, I'm building a personal work file.
4. . . . a week, I feel better. 5. . . . course, I cleaned out many of my food supplies.
6. . . . the weather, we'll know what to wear. 7. . . . looking for one, I had many interviews. 8. . . . early shift, we can start our day earlier. 9. . . . stayed awhile, we'll leave. 10. . . . he was precinct captain, is retiring this year.

Written Practice 1-2
Sample answers are provided.
1. . . . 9 A.M. to 5 P.M.; yours will be . . . 2. . . . exhausting. We really prefer . . . 3. . . . of the trip because it's busy. . . 4. . . . 10 percent of our brain although studies . . . inactive. Don't believe . . . 5. . . . on time tomorrow. I'll believe . . . 6. . . . unpacking, call me and we'll go out to dinner. 7. . . . a very tight budget, I hope other costs don't rise too quickly. 8. . . . swiftly through the park scared everyone in his path. 9. . . . food donations and many people joined the march as it progressed. We were too . . . 10. . . . my new knitting project, so I turned . . .

Written Practice 1-3
1. No, it doesn't. 2. They suggested . . .

Written Practice 1-4
1. learns/present 2. will avoid/future 3. turned off/past 4. decided/past 5. uses/present 6. eats/present 7. will play/future 8. ate/past 9. collected/past 10. keep/present 11. will ask/future 12. completed/past 13. played/past 14. will start/future 15. stops/present

Written Practice 1-5

1. checks 2. appear 3. knows

Written Practice 1-6

1. prices change 2. family goes 3. men take 4. interferences keep 5. friend takes
6. development gives 7. fiber rates 8. some include 9. fabric pays 10. plants give

Written Practice 1-7

1. expect/present tense 2. received/past tense 3. have expected/present perfect
tense 4. will come/future tense 5. have read/present perfect 6. slid/past tense
7. will know/future 8. wrote/past 9. will implement/future 10. avoided/past

Written Practice 1-8

1. will lie 2. woke 3. swam 4. laid 5. had run

Written Practice 1-9

1. lain 2. swum 3. raised 4. paid 5. forbidden 6. swung 7. chosen 8. drunk 9. threw
10. seen

Written Practice 1-10

1. change *went* to *go* 2. change *existed* to *exist*

Quiz

Sample answers are provided.
1. Fragment. If you decide on which route to take, call me. 2. Fragment. He was
looking back at his childhood. 3. Run-on. You're ready. Don't hesitate.
4. Agreement of subject and verb in number. Mark and Amy run a very organized
household. 5. Fragment. I love buying a new piece of clothing. 6. Irregular verb
form. If you had ridden to work with us, you would have been on time.
7. Fragment. When my time on the meter ran out, I raced back to my car. 8. Run-
on/comma fault. I'll be there. The children will arrive later, and we'll all have
lunch. 9. Agreement of subject and verb. He complained, "These cars park in the
wrong spaces every day." 10. Fragment. Because I had written, word-processed,
corrected, and approved the report, my job was done.

CHAPTER 2

Written Practice 2-1

1. He and I . . . 2. Tim and he . . . 3. . . . for Betsy and me. 4. . . . between Marcus
and me. 5. Tim and I . . .

Written Practice 2-2
1. verb 2. subject 3. modifier 4. object 5. subject 6. subject 7. object 8. verb
9. verb 10. subject

Written Practice 2-3
1. Psychologists, people 2. Dr. Daniel Gilbert, psychologist, future, choices
3. choices, today, future 4. cards, convenience 5. credit, year 6. lawyer, case
7. designer, glass, Chihuly 8. carpet, space 9. environmentalists, area, clams,
ponds, success 10. lawmakers, hearings, deficit

Written Practice 2-4
1. flies 2. glitter and gleam 3. is 4. felt 5. am 6. closed 7. will merge 8. are
9. seared 10. produced

Written Practice 2-5
1. was 2. appears 3. seems 4. grew 5. smell 6. were 7. are 8. remain 9. seem
10. was

Written Practice 2-6
Sample answers are provided.
1. is 2. could be 3. were 4. will be/was 5. was 6. to be 7. smell 8. taste 9. are
10. will be

Written Practice 2-7
1. We're 2. Here's 3. It's 4. You're 5. You'll, it's 6. I'm 7. He's 8. They're
9. You're 10. It's

Written Practice 2-8
1. smooth-haired 2. organized 3. well-informed 4. tall, tan, long 5. sleek, front
6. strapping 7. right, injured 8. loud, pulsing, small 9. angry 10. gesturing, smiling

Written Practice 2-9
1. . . . is more valuable . . . 2. . . . the most efficient . . . 3. . . . worst. 4. . . . are the
best. 5. . . . a more difficult piece . . . 6. . . . the most enormous . . . 7. . . . most
legible . . . 8. . . . more tenacious. 9. . . . is more sympathetic . . . 10. . . . most
beautiful . . .

Written Practice 2-10
1. well 2. good 3. well 4. good 5. well 6. good 7. well 8. well 9. good 10. good

Written Practice 2-11
1. My friends and I . . . 2. He and I . . . 3. . . . gave him and me . . . 4. . . . to
him . . . 5. . . . from Alex and me.

Written Practice 2-12

1. in town/opened 2. against the walls/position 3. inside the carton/bottle
4. between the doors/place 5. on top/left 6. about Larry/tell 7. in the adult school/
class 8. at the park/laugh 9. on TV/program 10. in the fireplace/logs

Written Practice 2-13

1. bottles are 2. newspaper is 3. cans were 4. friend is 5. movies are

Written Practice 2-14

1. and/coordinating 2. or/coordinating 3. but/coordinating 4. neither, nor/
correlative 5. until/subordinating 6. Because/subordinating 7. neither, nor/
correlative 8. not only, but also/correlative 9. and/coordinating 10. Since/
subordinating

Chapter 2 Quiz

1. She and I 2. really well 3. feel well 4. Ted and I share 5. Ted and me 6. is the
best 7. I won't leave until you call 8. we're 9. You've 10. Isn't spring . . .

CHAPTER 3

Written Practice 3-1

1. Lacey has banked . . . 2. I have banked at Yardley Trust . . . 3. I have been
writing business . . . 4. The Tomkins have owned . . . 5. I have watched
baseball . . .

Written Practice 3-2

1. had finished 2. had taken yoga 3. I had never seen . . . 4. If you had
remembered . . . 5. I had chosen the menu . . . 6. Bill said "If you had
screamed . . . " 7. I had owned a small car . . . 8. My niece had participated . . .
9. I had worked . . . 10. Eli and Eleanor had eaten

Written Practice 3-3

1. . . . before I consider stopping 2. before I retire. 3. I will have flown one
million miles before I retire. 4. By the time you arrive, I will have baked the cake.
5. . . . before you move in.

Written Practice 3-4

1. rose 2. will have commuted 3. swelled 4. saw 5. will have left 6. decided
7. filed 8. had picked up 9. went out 10. will have prepared

Written Practice 3-5

1. love 2. had read 3. he had started, we started 4. had known 5. we met 6. climbs
7. we walked 8. will have visited 9. we learned 10. he realizes

Written Practice 3-6

1. (inside the carton) bottles are 2. (between the doors) newspaper is 3. (against the walls) cans were 4. (among all my classmates) friend is 5. (in the list) movies are

Written Practice 3-7

1. I did not see a huge crash . . . 2. The hamster with the shortest legs . . . 3. That antique roadster with 50,000 miles on it . . . 4. The prospective voters completed their registration for the election on the table. 5. You should hang some of your new artwork on the wall. 6. The banana-nut bread in the oven smells wonderful. 7. Ned lined up furniture and boxes under the deck. 8. You probably received a letter in the mail about the dangers of contaminated water. 9. We drove in a red convertible along the endless highway toward the setting sun. 10. With the pliers, remove the filter from the furnace.

Written Practice 3-8

1. Mac and I . . . 2. . . . salesperson and her. 3. . . . dinner than she (did) . . .
4. . . . to Bonnie and her. 5. You and they play . . . 6. . . . elections than he (did).
7. . . . give him. . . 8. . . . Cat and he are . . . 9. . . . him and me. 10. . . . more than he (does).

Written Practice 3-9

1. My buying a car . . . 2. Their charging me . . . 3. . . . about her choosing . . .
4. Her staying one extra . . . 5. Their fighting . . .

Written Practice 3-10

1. . . . their cat and themselves . . . 2. Larry and I . . . 3. Marty asked himself . . .
4. All of you have to make that decision yourselves . . . 5. . . . to the team leader and us.

Written Practice 3-11

1. demonstrative pronoun (These) 2. adjective (Those) 3. adjective (this)
4. demonstrative pronoun (That) 5. demonstrative pronoun (This)

Written Practice 3-12

Sample answers are provided.
1. Who is . . . 2. The food that . . . 3. Timothy whom I have known . . .
4. The medicines that arrived . . . 5. Who is the new . . . 6. One . . . lifts. 7. . . . that arrive every afternoon . . . 8. The puppy that . . . 9. Everybody . . . receives . . .
10. . . . received his or her certificate. 11. . . . participants received their certificates.

Written Practice 3-13
1. (me)/I 2. (I)/me 3. (nothing) anything 4. (me) Cari and I 5. (she) her
6. (her) she 7. (me) my 8. (myself) me 9. (their) her 10. (Whom) Who

Quiz
1. had driven 2. will have word processed 3. smelled 4. is 5. We 6. He and I
7. my 8. himself 9. that 10. Who

PART ONE TEST

1. b 2. c 3. d 4. b 5. b 6. b 7. c 8. a 9. d 10. d 11. d 12. b 13. c 14. d 15. a 16. b
17. b 18. d. 19. c 20. b 21. b 22. c 23. d 24. c 25. a 26. b 27. d 28. b 29. c 30. c
31. a 32. b. 33. c 34. c 35. a 36. d 37. c 38. c 39. d 40. b 41. a 42. d 43. c 44. b
45. d 46. c 47. b 48. d 49. a 50. c

CHAPTER 4

Written Practice 4-1
1. . . . results. 2. . . . state. 3. . . . know). 4. . . . 1 tbsp. of butter and 1 tsp. of salt.
5. . . . game. 6. . . . the bike." (. . . shrinking budget.) 7. . . . by 6 P.M. 8. Mr. and
Mrs. . . . lunch. 9. . . . Capt. and Mrs. Murphy. 10. . . . Rd. . . . me.

Written Practice 4-2
Paragraph 1
Scientists have reached important conclusions regarding the connection between
children's social disadvantages and their health risks. Doctors considered three
main social disadvantages: poverty, low parental education, and single parent
household. According to Dr. Ruth S. Stein, children with all three risk factors
were twice as likely as children with none to have a chronic health condition such
as diabetes, asthma, or mental retardation.

Paragraph 2
Where does chocolate come from? Actually, it does grow on trees. It all starts
with a small tropical tree, the Theobroma cacao, usually simply called "cacao."
(It is pronounced ka-KOW. *Theobroma* is Greek for "food of the gods.") Cacao is
native to Central America and South America, but it is grown commercially
throughout the tropics. About 70 percent of the world's cacao is grown in Africa.

A cacao tree can produce close to two thousand pods per year. The ridged, football-
shaped pod, or fruit, of the cacao grows from the branches and, oddly, straight out of

the trunk. The pods, which mature throughout the year, encase a sticky, white pulp and about thirty or forty seeds. The pulp is both sweet and tart; it is eaten and used in making drinks. The seeds, were you to bite into one straight out of the pod, are incredibly bitter. Not at all like the chocolate that comes from them.

It's actually a perfect design. The fruit attracts forest animals, like monkeys, who eat the fruit but cast the seeds aside, dispersing them and allowing new trees to sprout up. (One of my favorite memories of a recent trip to Costa Rica was watching monkeys eating in a "chocolate" tree.) It's hard to imagine why humans ever thought to do anything with the seeds.*

Written Practice 4-3

1. . . . at 10:00 P.M."? 2. . . . to plant flowers?" Elsa asked. 3. . . . your insurance card?" 4. . . . of ID as well. 5. . . . for our appointments?"

Written Practice 4-4

Paragraph 1

My friend asked, "Have you heard about the link of lead exposure to Alzheimer's disease?" She had just read the study from the University of Rhode Island that found a link between early exposure to lead in the environment and the onset of Alzheimer's disease much later in life. The scientists cautioned lead poisoning patients not to fear that their lead exposure would definitely lead to Alzheimer's disease. They said, "There are, after all, many other things that can affect a person between youth and old age, aren't there?"

Paragraph 2

Do you see the world around you going green? Has your supermarket started charging for bags—either plastic or paper? Will you finally decide to ride your bicycle to the office to help reduce carbon emissions (not even considering the cost of gas)? Did you remember to turn off the lights before you left home? (And if you didn't, will it bother you all day?) Surely, you have switched to energy-efficient lightbulbs, or have you? I guess we can agree that going green is not an easy thing to do, or can we? There's a popular children's song that says it all: It's not easy being green!

Written Practice 4-5

1. . . . nuts in it?" Rosa asked. 2. . . . harm you!" 3. . . . restaurant? I'm starving. 4. . . . before we leave? 5. . . . requests!" 6. . . . in the car? 7. . . . mine, are you? 8. . . . taking Vitamin D. 9. . . . the game! Isn't that sad? 10. . . . correctly. Yea!

---

*Adapted with permission from facts-about-chocolate.com.

Written Practice 4-6

1. All national elections bring change; the 2008 presidential election was historic in bringing an African-American into the White House Oval Office. 2. We kept hearing people ask, "Did you vote?" 3. Don't you think that this was one of the most important statements uttered by President-Elect Obama: "I will always be honest with you about the challenges we face"? 4. When we went camping last summer, we saw a bear. We wanted to scream, "Run!" 5. When we finally agreed to go (remember my reservations), it was too late in the day. 6. "Wait!" he cried, "There's contamination in there." 7. Chef Antonia said, "I'll be back at 6 P.M. to serve the main course. Don't disappoint me!" 8. If you're really late, you'll find us at 100 Linden St. 9. Address that letter to Newark, NJ. 10. We left a note on the door regarding suspending deliveries. (Anyone would understand not to leave packages while we were away.)

Written Practice 4-7

1. Having a new, sleek sports car is still just a dream. 2. This summer, I'm going to paint the house, get estimates for a fence, and lose ten pounds. 3. While I waited for the estimator to arrive, I looked at many paint colors. 4. A friend of mine, a recent graduate, is working hard to write an excellent résumé. 5. Your job, however, will be to finish cleaning the basement.

Written Practice 4-8

1. . . . August 15, 2010. 2. . . . Bend, Oregon. 3. . . . room,". . . 4. Dear Eileen, . . . job search, so I'll . . . My best, 5. . . . Andy, . . . batteries, barbecue, and tent. 6. A detailed, lengthy . . . 7. March, a month just before real spring, . . . 8. . . . was, nevertheless, our . . . 9. . . . Auden, however, 10. . . . meeting,

Written Practice 4-9

Paragraph 1

Founded in 1981 as Students Against Driving Drunk, SADD's focus initially was to combat teen deaths due to drinking and driving. SADD has expanded its mission and name and now sponsors chapters called Students Against Destructive Decisions. SADD now focuses on prevention of all destructive behaviors and attitudes that are harmful to young people, including underage drinking, substance abuse, violence, reckless driving, depression, and suicide. SADD's unique approach involves young people delivering education and prevention programming to their peers through school- and community-wide activities and campaigns responsive to the needs of their particular locations. Since its formation, SADD has spread to all fifty states, Canada, New Zealand, and many other international locations.

Paragraph 2

Are you ready for a substitute for the mind-bending, compelling puzzle Sudoku? Psychologists now assure us that 10 minutes of talking, visiting, and establishing social contacts boost intellectual performance as much as doing crossword puzzles. A team of researchers asked more than 3,500 people between 24 and 96 years old about their social interactions and tested their memories. One researcher offered, "We found the more the social contacts, the higher the level of mental functioning."

Paragraph 3

You've heard the 30-minutes-of-exercise-per-day recommendation for some time, but you can't seem to fit that into your schedule. Is all hope lost? No, say the experts. Will short spurts of moderate exercise help your fitness level? If you're doing nothing and you decide to walk briskly five days a week or even three days a week for 30 minutes, you will experience positive results. In addition, you can do the 30 minutes all at once or in shorter segments of at least 10 minutes each. After three months, you'll probably experience lower blood pressure and a smaller waistline.

Written Practice 4-10

1. Jim Hanfry, a weekly player, finally won the office lottery. 2. My summer garden always includes squash, tomatoes, and cucumbers. 3. Can we, therefore, consider the matter closed? 4. The oldest theater in town was torn down, and a parking lot was built in its place. 5. Before the cold weather arrives, I turn off the outdoor water spout. 6. You will have driven 1,500 miles by the time you reach Detroit, Michigan. 7. "I understand how you feel about homework," Miss Emry said, "but I still have to assign it." 8. When Lenny arrived, the party became lively. 9. We had accepted the invitation a week earlier, but we cancelled when two of our children became ill. 10. Send us a current, skill-related résumé, and we will schedule an interview for you.

Quiz

1. John, my friend, will march at the wedding. 2. . . . expenses, but I can't," Mona said. 3. . . . in Seoul, South Korea. 4. . . . met, however, in Nashville, Tennessee. 5. That was on November 25, 2008. 6. Are you my friend, or not? 7. . . . your lives!" He screamed . . . building. 8. . . . Muir Woods, a kayak ride, and a mountain-climbing expedition. Whew! That was a long day. 9. . . . vacation, we needed a rest. 10. . . . global warming, can we, therefore, call . . . problem?

CHAPTER 5

Written Practice 5-1

1. . . . those Olympics; so many. . . 2. . . . American winning; my dream . . .
3. . . . we had lost, I watched . . . 4. . . . the weekend; a week later . . .
5. . . . Pacific region; meanwhile, Russian . . .

Written Practice 5-2

1. . . . gas tank; so we . . . 2. . . . gifts; but when . . . 3. . . . right lane; but cars . . .
4. . . . needed them; but . . . 5. . . . blood; yet we . . .

Written Practice 5-3

1. . . . time; nevertheless, we . . . 2. . . . door; otherwise, you'll . . . 3. . . . decision;
therefore, we . . . 4. . . . expected; however, you still . . . 5. . . . an expensive
houseplant, ask . . . needs; moreover, . . .

Written Practice 5-4

1. . . . work, while Chico. . . 2. . . . only in England; it did not . . . 3. . . . house;
however, we . . . 4. . . . cloudy; we cannot . . . 5. . . . call me, and I, although still
at work, will meet you. 6. . . . sales now, I can't . . . 7. . . . budget, you know how
I feel; therefore, no one . . . 8. . . . left home. 9. . . . to begin; consequently, we're
busier . . . 10. For the longest time, . . . her bedroom; finally, she had an . . .

Written Practice 5-5

Paragraph 1

1. . . . big eater; however, chocolate . . . downfall. 2. . . . good for me, but how
much . . . "for my health"? 3. . . . that I love (add almonds and it's even better).
4. . . . that pleasure; my waistline . . . results. 5. . . . good it is for me; moreover, I
want . . .

Paragraph 2

1. . . . bulbs; they want 2. . . . believe that the growing and killing 3. . . . a pound
of wheat, it takes

Written Practice 5-6

1. . . . open for the delivery"? 2. . . . are already bored with their Christmas
presents," and added, "We'll reintroduce them in a month or so." 3. . . . your credit
card number." 4. . . . your correct card number?" the associate asked.
5. . . . tonight?" my wife asked.

Written Practice 5-7

1. . . . asked, "Are you having . . . budget?" 2. "Do you have a computer?"
he asked. "There are websites . . . money is going," he continued. 3. . . . said,
"Websites have been used . . . online." 4. "If you're going to use . . . shopping,
please check . . . measures," my wife continued. 5. "May I . . . account?" the teller

asked. 6. "First I . . . banking," I told him. 7. He said that was a really good idea. 8. "Let me . . . own," I . . . instructor, "then . . . wrong." 9. "That's . . . idea," she said, "because . . . acquired." 10. "Did you know . . . hysterically?" Fred asked.

Written Practice 5-8

1. . . . your job: Open the office . . . mail. 2. . . . you leave: Premium Plumbers . . . Management. 3. . . . information: an agenda . . . bylaws. 4. . . . much-too-much information: He was asking . . . new car. 5. . . . buy these: hammer, nails . . . tiles.

Written Practice 5-9

1. . . . the following: warm clothes, boots, and raincoat. 2. . . . dismisses at 11:45 A.M. 3. . . . trip: a tent, bug spray, a flashlight, and easily prepared foods. 4. Dear Professor Keene: 5. Dear Ms. Boxer: 6. . . . Dad, 7. . . . after 9:00 A.M. . . 8. We'll meet at 12 noon. 9. . . . following: Prepare your home . . . 10. . . . a choice: We could eat out . . .

Written Practice 5-10

Paragraph 1

1. . . . Hubble Space Telescope; in fact, they . . . there. 2. . . . in 1990, and it has already . . . span. 3. In addition, it has seen . . . mission.

Paragraph 2

1. Hubble entered . . . 1990s; its advent . . . Internet. 2. As a result, everyone's . . . close. 3. However, . . . pictures; interestingly, it has generated . . . instrument. 4. Before Hubble, . . . universe; some had said . . . 20 billion. 5. Hubble did the correct calculations: Our universe . . . ago. 6. Hubble accomplishments include the following: measuring the age of the universe . . . expanding universe.

Written Practice 5-11

1. . . . home's 2. . . . wasn't 3. . . . its 4. . . . *i*'s . . . your *t*'s? 5. It's . . . isn't it?

Written Practice 5-12

Sample answers are provided.
1. . . . (Can you feel it in your mood?), and we really 2. . . . clothes—slacks, shirts, underwear, shoes—when the airline . . . 3. . . . store [California, Washington, and Arizona] and . . . until Monday" 4. . . . store (California [wines], Washington [apples], and Arizona [jicama]) and . . . 5. . . . a restaurant—you know what she likes—and we'll . . .

Written Practice 5-13

1. . . . shout, "Sound the alarm"? 2. Her mother said, "I agree to finish your work; however, you'll have to pay me for my time." 3. It's not . . . 4. . . . him—your dad—and he agreed . . . 5. It's warmer . . . degrees; we can 6. Although I've read through today's newspaper, I'm not ready to throw it away. 7. . . . paper—the one

you just handed in—shows great effort. 8. . . . most people's . . .1941; . . . 1975; . . . 2001. 9. The train stopped in Atlanta, Georgia; Newark, New Jersey; and New Paltz, New York. 10. . . . made in Europe (Italy [Milan], France [Paris], and Denmark [Copenhagen]).

Quiz
1. . . . unexpected results: Teens feel . . . 2. . . . garage said, "You need . . . days." 3. . . . thoughts; use a semicolon . . . 4. . . . newest $1 coins; and they will join . . . 5. . . . mint said, "We want these . . . in all transactions," and he added, "They will be given out as change as well." 6. . . . printed on it: "Do not drive with . . . in place." 7. . . . says that really successful . . . they want. 8. . . . mental functioning: socializing helps; exercising is also beneficial. 9. . . . entitled, "Exercise and the Mind," I was bored. 10. . . . of American adults: Just three of every ten get enough physical activity.

CHAPTER 6

Written Practice 6-1
1. . . . Chicago, . . . the Windy City. 2. . . . "Oh . . . 3. . . . Mother . . . Chicago 4. . . . French . . . World History 101 5. I'm . . .

Written Practice 6-2
1. . . . Seattle . . . Northwest . . . 2. . . . Eiffel Tower . . . Paris. 3. . . . War of the Roses . . . England . . . 4. Baptist . . . Buddhism . . . I . . . 5. Supreme Deity . . . Christ, Allah, or Buddha.

Written Practice 6-3
1. . . . Representative Stephanie Brown . . . 2. I . . . "May . . . 3. . . . "Where, . . . "You'll . . . 4. . . . Officer Kent . . . 5. I . . . "You . . . now,". . .

Written Practice 6-4
1. Corporal Marylou Ryan . . . "I . . . Ford . . . I'm . . . 2. Captain and Mrs. Talbott . . . Memorial Day . . . 3. Be. . . *Gone With the Wind* . . . 4. We took Jack's . . . an Italian . . . Saturday . . . 5. He . . . Southwest . . . Maine . . .

Written Practice 6-5
1. Each . . . Fourth of July . . . We hire a professional fireworks company. The displays . . . My son, Matt, . . . 2. This year, Matt . . . Alex. We're . . . Alex . . . 3. We've . . . New York . . . September . . . . I've . . . Empire State Building. That is first on my agenda. We'll . . . a hotel . . . 4. I. . . *Reader's Digest.* If I had . . . publisher. 5. In Modern American History II . . . World War II . . . Atomic Age. 6. Jeff . . . Ford Motor Company . . . 7. Center City. 8. Americans . . . Declaration of

Independence. 9. My children . . . Chinese and Spanish. 10. "I . . . " You're . . .
11. We . . . Claire McCaskill . . . Missouri, . . . Senate Building. 12. Mr. Reed,
senator from RI . . . 13. "Oh. . . 14. The American Red Cross. . . 15. The
Jamestown Bridge . . .

Written Practice 6-6

1. . . . spring . . . 2. . . . Department . . . 3. . . . Orient . . . 4. . . . *Experience.*
5. . . . Friday.

Written Practice 6-7

Paragraph 1

1. The terms . . . 2. Discussions . . . a Swedish scientist, Svante Arrhenius . . .
fossil. 3. He further . . . and temperature gains. 4. Arrhenius . . . the average
surface temperature. 5. This is what . . . 6. However, Arrhenius . . .

Paragraph 2

1. Arrhenius . . . Thomas Chamberlin . . . Human . . . 2. Years passed . . .
3. Then . . . natural forces. 4. In fact . . .

Paragraph 3

1. This is a new one. Eco-anxiety is taking hold of many many well-meaning
consumers. "What is it?" you ask.

Quiz

1. . . . Elmgrove Avenue, east of Wayland Avenue. 2. . . . "All . . . 3. To . . . Time
Magazine . . . and a Sunday . . . 4. . . . John Singer Sargeant. 5. . . . Aunt Polly . . .
6. . . . Forest Camping Supplies, Inc., in Boston. 7. . . . I'll . . . 8. . . . Robert T.
Masters, president of the division . . . 9. . . . "Oh no! . . . 10. . . . *The Last Lecture.*

PART TWO TEST

1. d 2. c 3. d 4. a 5. b 6. a 7. c 8. a 9. d. 10. d 11. d 12. b 13. a 14. c 15. b 16. b
17. a 18. c 19. d 20. b 21. c 22. a 23. b 24. d 25. d 26. d 27. c 28. b 29. a 30. d
31. c 32. b 33. a 34. a 35. d 36. b 37. b 38. c 39. a 40. a 41. a 42. c 43.c 44. d
45. b 46. a 47. c 48. c 49. d 50. d

CHAPTER 7

Written Practice 7-1

1. . . . hot, and inexpensive. 2. . . . truth and provide evidence. 3. . . . and soaks
the porch. 4. . . . calories, and fattening. 5. . . . dishes, and sometimes boring.

6. . . . suffering, and teaching other . . . 7. . . . equipment, and install . . . 8. . . . ingredients, whip the eggs, and preheat . . . 9. . . . the heat, turn off . . . 10. . . . jazz guitar, and rhythm and blues.

Written Practice 7-2
Sample answers are provided.
1. . . . my dog, clean the car . . . 2. . . . shrubs, and planning to add another room.
3. . . . it, and threw it . . . 4. . . . second, and breakfast last. 5. . . . and rainy.
6. . . . safe, and took care of her own household as well. 7. . . . faster, and higher in resolution. 8. . . . homework, and stays . . . 9. . . . loyalty, and perfect attendance.
10. . . . tank, and the children get up on time.

Written Practice 7-3
Sample answers are provided.
1. . . . energetic but also punctual. 2. . . . truthfully and humbly. 3. . . . puddles but also jumps . . . 4. . . . neither colorful nor well-fitting either. 5. . . . flowers or build a deck. 6. . . . nor willing to sacrifice her career. 7. . . . not only delicious but also energizing. 8. . . . shift, or I'll leave the house . . . 9. . . . not only busy but also rainy. 10. . . . family's rules and doing well in school.

Written Practice 7-4
Sample answers are provided.
1. . . . on sale, but the sale . . . 2. . . . the area, so he advertised . . . 3. . . . on the grounds, but we couldn't . . . 4. . . . stated, then gather . . . 5. . . . depot, but he quickly . . . 6. . . . at 1 P.M., but heavy . . . 7. . . . with you, or stop . . . 8. . . . pay, so I'll be . . . 9. . . . me $50, and I'll pay . . . 10. . . . for the test, yet I feel . . .

Written Practice 7-5
1. When 2. Unless 3. since 4. After 5. though 6. If 7. as 8. Although 9. whenever
10. If

Written Practice 7-6
Sample answers are provided.
1. instead 2. in fact 3. incidentally 4. however 5. next 6. otherwise 7. on the contrary 8. meanwhile 9. as a result 10. incidentally

Written Practice 7-7
Sample answers are provided.
1. then 2. instead 3. consequently 4. furthermore 5. otherwise 6. meanwhile
7. however 8. therefore 9. in addition 10. sometimes

Written Practice 7-8
Sample answers are provided.

1. The buggy tour of Charleston was enlightening. 2. We left the party early because we knew . . . 3. This is the new hybrid vehicle introduced . . . 4. This report analyzes our town water. 5. I suspect that . . . 6. We were looking for a skilled house painter. 7. While we waited for the train . . . 8. We sent the paperwork demanded . . . 9. Hire only certified welders. 10. Store these foods in an accessible place.

Quiz

Sample answers are provided.
1. . . . start college or go to work. 2. . . . was joyous yet tearful. 3. . . . reading, and history . . . 4. . . . for the environment, he never did anything to improve it. 5. . . . the subject but also footnoting sources. 6. . . . before, please suggest something from this menu. 7. Hillary Clinton was the first woman . . . 8. Our town interviewed for a new town manager. 9. Both options are expensive, 10. . . . space, but it . . .

CHAPTER 8

Written Practice 8-1

  (S)   (S) (V)   (O)   (O) (of prep.)
1. Matthew and I found our seats in the theater.

      (S)   (V)   (O)
2. Late arrivals caused a stir.

        (O) (of prep.)   (S)   (V)   (O) (of prep.)
3. On the stage, the main character, Bess, looked fleetingly at the audience.

  (S)   (V)   (O)
4. She continued her dialogue.

        (S)   (V)   (O)
5. The audience members regained their composure.

Written Practice 8-2

Sample answers are provided.
1. . . . products, but all . . . 2. . . . at 6 P.M., and we'll have . . . 3. . . . and newspapers, yet our town . . . 4. . . . tomorrow, but my office . . . 5. . . . at home, so we've lowered . . .

Written Practice 8-3

Sample answers are provided.
1. A hurricane threatened the coast; still, we made plans to drive home. 2. If you need me, please call; furthermore, you'll find the doctor's telephone number

next to the phone. 3. I've already cleaned my closets for winter; incidentally, I'm saving some perfectly good clothes for you. 4. I'm really low on energy these days; nevertheless, I keep up with my exercise routine. 5. My children aren't accepting any more gifts; in fact, they're giving extra toys and clothes to charity.

Written Practice 8-4

1. . . . the *Times*; his friend . . . 2. . . . to Massachusetts, or we'll stop . . .
3. . . . overheated; therefore, we . . . 4. . . . bumper; nevertheless, we . . .
5. . . . a week; my friend . . .

Written Practice 8-5

Sample answers are provided.

1. Because of my excellent advice, Marla and Darren had a great trip. 2. Although many people advised against it, we read the book and saw the movie. 3. When you arrive, we'll have dinner. *or* We'll have dinner when you arrive. 4. If Daria arrives on time, we'll have time to get to the late movie. 5. After we passed the construction site, the traffic began to flow.

Written Practice 8-6

Sample answers are provided.

1. We have always bought our baby educational toys because manufacturers make extravagant claims about verbal skill building. Researchers have studied the toys; however, they concluded that toys did not increase vocabulary. We buy expensive toys; consequently, we expect them to live up to their advertising. 2. As a result of our walking upright, back problems are common. Degenerative changes in the spine occur because walking upright places a great deal of weight on the lower spine. In addition, in middle age, some other problems can occur since arthritis and other changes affect the disks.

Written Practice 8-7

Sample answers are provided.

1. Ani, who plays the piano, rarely listens to any other kind of music; however, Mal plays no instruments and listens to all kinds of music. 2. We knew the prize was hidden in the house somewhere; nonetheless, even with that knowledge, we couldn't find it. 3. Jake and Leela never told us they were not coming, so even though we had planned carefully, we had much too much food.
4. Halloween never ceases to amaze me; although it appears year after year, both children and their parents exhibit unrelenting enthusiasm. 5. By the time he was fourteen, he had begun a professional career; from the Atlantic City boardwalk to touring in vaudeville, he rose by force of his extraordinary ability to star billing as W. C. Fields Tramp Juggler. 6. While Stephen Douglas maintained a popular sovereignty stance, Lincoln stated that the United States could not survive as

half-slave and half-free states; consequently, the Lincoln–Douglas debates drew the attention of the entire nation. 7. Because of the delays we've experienced, we are no longer using the U.S. mails; hence, you will receive our next catalog via e-mail. 8. When the contaminated water had finally drained out of the pool, the special cleaning crew climbed in and began to scrub all surfaces. 9. As I've told you before, I'm not perfect; nevertheless, I never turn down an opportunity to try something new even if I think I might not succeed. 10. Eighteenth-century cities were not models of cleanliness; furthermore, crime and poverty were rampant while public sanitation was clearly nonexistent.

Chapter 8 Quiz
Sample answers are provided.
1. The 100-acre Busch Gardens in Williamsburg, VA, is open to the public from March to the end of October. 2. Whenever he professed his love for her, she blushed. 3. I planted the flowering perennial plant that you gave me. 4. Even though I said I wanted to be alone, Jimmy insisted on joining me; consequently, I hated the movie. 5. Her husband, because he is the opposite of a chauvinist, cares deeply about her career; therefore, he even writes her résumé for her. 6. I wore my new black suit and coat to the interview. 7. Itemize all the food in your refrigerator; you'll be amazed at the quantity and variety of things.
8. Except for the pots and pans, I've itemized my entire kitchen. 9. Although he had been walked and fed, the dog barked loudly for a long time; finally, we realized that he was afraid of the dark. 10. My teenage son should have been studying for exams; instead, he was outside playing basketball with his friends.

CHAPTER 9

Written Practice 9-1
Sample answers are provided.
1. This year we realized a profit for the first time. 2. They played their strongest people at the beginning of the game. 3. You need to take a shopping list with you. 4. As the next step, build your speed on the treadmill. 5. Use the electric pen to sign the documents.

Written Practice 9-2
Sample answers are provided.
1. That gas station raised the price of gas for the second time this week. 2. Amelia can choose a pet from a recently born litter of puppies. 3. The spring flowers that I planted last month have bloomed. 4. Many people believe that global warming will eventually affect everyone. 5. The new automotive equipment detected the

weaknesses. 6. Our family sees a favorite Christmas movie every year. 7. That agency offers many dogs and cats for adoption. 8. A tall fence will stand between the Corbett and Balise properties. 9. Meteorologists use radar to forecast weather. 10. The house needs new sheets and blankets for all the beds.

Written Practice 9-3

1. In a depressed economic climate, how can I prepare for the future? 2. Let's make a deposit before the banks close. 3. If you are in a collision, you should file a police report. 4. You need to look at improving style and clarity in your sentences. 5. After you take time to think about other things for a while, sit down and reread your essay. 6. The first draft is an opportunity to put your words on paper while your creativity is flowing. 7. After the first of the year, each department should review our joint goals. 8. The important topic of the day remains the likelihood of growing food locally. 9. In the middle school, the need for better art supplies exists. 10. Because of the delays we have experienced, we have stopped using that truck company.

Written Practice 9-4

Sample answers are provided.

1. I will invite all your friends. 2. When you decide, let me be the first to know. 3. Do I always have to justify my actions? 4. A long time ago, I concluded that I . . . 5. We can inspect the house before we move in. 6. We shouldn't move on until we plan for the future. 7. Don't answer unless you are absolutely sure how you feel. 8. I apologize any time I offend someone. 9. Your father believes that you shouldn't drive . . . 10. I'll help you clean up when you finish the project.

Written Practice 9-5

Sample answers are provided.

Unless you see it in action, this advancement in science is hard to believe. People who are completely paralyzed due to illness or trauma will get help in the future thanks to the new Brain Computer Interface. Scientists can help these patients communicate with others and even use their paralyzed limbs by connecting patients' brains to a computer. Scientists have experimented with several people. Teaching a patient to move with his or her mind is neither fast nor fluid, but it can be done.

Written Practice 9-6

1. Don't give new uniforms to employees until the uniforms have name tags.
2. Myrna told Jodi not to go to the PTA meeting because of her terrible cold.
3. Although our new water tank holds 20 percent less than our old one, it cost 30 percent more. 4. My daughter wrote a long report and studied for a spelling test.
5. The chart at the end of the magazine article was the original.

Written Practice 9-7

1. Because he is so kind, my neighbor frequently buys my family food. 2. . . . and now the nail is crooked. 3. . . . played with Priscilla's children. 4. The turkey platter was empty, but we were tired of eating turkey anyway. 5. . . . to Jason, and Jason looked unhappy. 6. . . . cake shop, she never eats cake herself. 7. . . . the tree, the car was not damaged. 8. . . . teachers, I realized that the school was not for me. 9. my grandfather, and my grandfather told me his latest health problem. 10. White and Smith made their presentation.

Written Practice 9-8

1. The man found his glasses in his desk. 2. The student hung a picture of a favorite music group on the wall of her room. 3. The horse with the brown spots belongs to that rider. 4. The teacher posted the notes covered in class for the students. 5. My old car in the driveway has driven 100,000 miles.

Written Practice 9-9

When you take your child to the doctor because the child is coughing and sneezing with asthma-type symptoms, do you really know what's wrong? Up to now, in an office visit, doctors have depended on physical exams, symptoms, and the child's history to explain the illness. Doctors use their best judgment to prescribe antibiotics, but often the antibiotics don't cure the child because the cause of the ailment cannot be pinpointed. Now, however, a new test uses the Virochip, which gives hope of understanding viruses associated with asthma attacks. A new study led by University of California–San Francisco scientists has found an unexpected number of viruses and viral subtypes in patients with respiratory tract infections (RTIs). The technique used in the study may help identify new viruses associated with human diseases and lead to specific strategies for treatment and prevention.

Written Practice 9-10

1. repeat 2. refer 3. facts 4. consideration 5. status 6. complete 7. history 8. between 9. in ten years 10. then

Written Practice 9-11

1. Juana's mother agreed to bake . . . 2. Mickey . . . play was imaginative. 3. Now we need to consider a significant budget cut. 4. I'm looking for a job because I heard that the company I work for is downsizing. 5. The department head said, "We're not . . ."

Written Practice 9-12

1. Your schedule is full, so you won't be going out for lunch. 2. I didn't return the book to the library because I hadn't finished it. 3. We were happy not to leave the house on a rainy day. 4. Now I've decided to adopt a kitten from the local animal shelter. 5. A vacation is out of the question now. 6. Then we still had our out-of-date computers. 7. Between my house and yours is a beautiful park. 8. My car has

80,000 miles on its odometer. 9. Before you offer your opinion, at least get the facts. 10. We're looking for a new store.

Written Practice 9-13

1. The carriage tour around Charleston was fascinating. 2. I enjoyed the ride because I love historical architecture. 3. The carriage driver was full of intriguing stories. 4. The highlight of the tour was seeing the outdoor crafts market. 5. Because it was a wonderful tour, I signed up for another one for next year.

Written Practice 9-14

Sample answers are provided.
1. At the end of the season, the team gave a party for its supporters. 2. I bought this TV because it was on sale. 3. I couldn't afford one then. 4. All of the new graduates from the citizenship class met at the school for an awards ceremony. 5. Even though I despise that band's kind of music, I attend their concerts frequently. 6. My favorite part of the afternoon was going through the bead museum. 7. The pen was given to one of the senators after the bill was signed. 8. Complicated computer problems are solved by precise corrections.
9. The voters completed registration forms on the desk. 10. The applicant's status is perfect for our needs.

Written Practice 9-15

Sample answers are provided.
The President gives the Presidential Medal of Freedom each year. Because it is considered so important, it is the highest civilian award in the United States. In 1945, Harry Truman honored people who served in WWII, and John F. Kennedy revived the medal in 1963 on or near July Fourth when it became a yearly tradition to give it. President George W. Bush honored two doctors, one congressman, a retired general, a university chancellor, and a judge in 2008.

Written Practice 9-16

Sample answers are provided.
1. The astronauts will launch from the space center, capture the telescope, service it, and repair it. 2. They will service the Hubble Telescope, upgrade its parts, and replace broken parts. 3. The Hubble was launched in 1990 and has outlived its 15-year life expectancy. 4. Hubble gives us colorful, crisp, and detailed images of the cosmos. 5. Our drama teacher taught us how to stand, project our voices, and move on stage. 6. My son learned how to play the guitar, the trumpet, and the drums. 7. This new car is faster, sleeker, and more fuel efficient. 8. We'll know our new program is working when staff arrive on time, keep their equipment in good repair, and use fewer sick days. 9. The leaves are greener, the grass is more lush, and the flowers are taller than ever. 10. Angie is pleasant and intelligent.

Quiz
Sample answers are provided.
1. The preschoolers took a rest period. 2. My friend left before I did. 3. Mr. Bacari recommended that the company hire me. 4. The visitors gave the animals peanuts, and the animals continued to play. 5. Your travel directions were precise. 6. Although the building was old and dilapidated, the city planner decided to use it for students. 7. I took the bus because I had no money for gas. 8. I'm acquainted with and devoted to that charity. 9. The creditors closed the store. 10. The police believe that Wally drove the car.

PART THREE TEST
1. c 2. a 3.d 4. b 5. a 6. b 7. d 8. d 9. b 10. c 11. b 12. c 13. a 14. d 15. a 16. c 17. c 18. d 19. b 20. a 21. b 22. d 23. a 24. c 25. b 26. d 27. d 28. c 29. d 30. b 31. c 32. a 33. b 34. a 35. b 36. a 37. c 38. d 39. a 40. d 41. d 42. b 43. b 44. b 45. a 46. a 47.c 48. d 49. c 50. b

CHAPTER 10

Written Practice 10-1
1. **Span**-ish 2. **Tel**-e-phone 3. to-**day** 4. **yes**-ter-day 5. **pre**-sent 6. con-**ta**-gious

Written Practice 10-2
1. impossible 2. illogical 3. irreplaceable 4. uncomplicated 5. unnecessary

Written Practice 10-3
1. carelessness 2. noticeably 3. happiness 4. truly 5. famous

Written Practice 10-4
1. spotting 2. carelessness 3. developed 4. preference 5. badly

Written Practice 10-5
1. occurred 2. referred 3. *none* 4. runner 5. sunning

Written Practice 10-6
1. relief 2. niece 3. seize 4. deceived 5. leisure

Written Practice 10-7
1. shoes 2. crashes 3. trains 4. heroes 5. stories

Written Practice 10-8
1. knives 2. fathers-in-law 3. children 4. radios 5. handfuls

Written Practice 10-9
1. supersedes 2. Proceed 3. preceded 4. secede 5. exceeds

Quiz
1. irresponsible 2. misspelling 3. pianos 4. planting 5. biographies 6. referring
7. Mothers-in-law 8. thieves 9. thinner 10. truly

CHAPTER 11

Written Practice 11-1
1. fawn 2. grave 3. Down 4. just 5. lead 6. bark 7. exact 8. dear 9. peak 10. bear
11. trip 12. order 13. bats 14. left, left 15. wave

Written Practice 11-2
1. aisle 2. basses 3. does 4. palette 5. carat 6. sow 7. they're 8. you're 9. pallet
10. caret

Written Practice 11-3
1. principal 2. pare, pear 3. stationary 4. It's 5. currants 6. plane, ascent 7. capitol
8. Too 9. Peace, past 10. counsel

Written Practice 11-4
1. chute 2. fined 3. kneading 4. mince 5. sale 6. peace 7. scene 8. soul 9. waive
10. whine

Written Practice 11-5
1. ehFEKT 2. SEPret 3. ALternit 4. myNOOT 5. INvallid 6. RECKORD 7.
WOWND, WOOND 8. reKORD 9. proDOOS 10. EKSKYOOS

Written Practice 11-6
1. anxious 2. loose 3. emigrated 4. quiet 5. altogether 6. except 7. would have
8. should have 9. fewer 10. advice

Written Practice 11-7
1. personal 2. lose 3. morale 4. continually 5. allusions 6. all right 7. illusion
8. moral 9. loose 10. Climatic

Quiz
1. palette 2. tale 3. personnel 4. formally 5. basis 6. their 7. Your 8. latter 9. moral
10. too

PART FOUR TEST

1. c 2. d 3. b 4. c 5. a 6. d 7. c 8. b 9. b 10. a 11. c 12. d 13. a 14. c 15. d 16. b
17. b 18. a 19. d 20. d 21. stationary 22. pared 23. Their 24. principal 25. counsel
26. too 27. broke 28. scent 29. whole 30. rote 31. whether 32. SEPret 33. CLOS
34. eager 35. regardless 36. annoys 37. number 38. advice 39. illusion
40. continually 41. loose 42. quite 43. tail 44. all right 45. emigrated 46. moral
47. personal 48. altogether 49. Your 50. adapt

FINAL EXAM

1. a 2. a 3. b 4. c 5. c 6. d 7. c 8. d 9. a 10. b 11. c 12. b 13. d 14. a 15. c 16. d
17. b 18. b 19. a 20. c 21. d 22. c 23. b 24. a 25. d 26. b 27. b 28. a 29. d
30. d 31. b 32. c 33. a 34. c 35. d 36. b 37. d 38. a 39. c 40. b 41. c 42. b 43. d
44. c 45. d 46. c 47. a 48. b 49. b 50. a 51. c 52. d 53. d 54. c 55. a 56. b 57. a
58. c 59. b 60. d 61. b 62. a 63. c 64. b 65. d 66. a 67. b 68. d 69. b 70. a 71. c
72. d 73. c 74. b 75. c 76. c 77. a 78. b 79. d 80. d 81. a 82. b 83. c 84. a 85. d
86. b 87. b 88. c 89. c 90. a 91. d 92. c 93. c 94. a 95. c 96. a 97. b 98. b 99. d
100. c

INDEX